Thriving in the Care of *Many Mothers*

Rosemary Yvonne Borel

W0006253

Roselle
PUBLISHING

Book Design: Denise Borel Billups, Borel Graphics
Editor: Paula Stahel, Breath & Shadows Productions

ISBN 978-0-9968109-6-8
Library of Congress
Cataloging-in-Publication Data
2015951255

Cover and interior photographs courtesy of Rosemary Yvonne Borel family collections and permissions granted from others used in this publication.

Contents

$\mathcal{F}$OREWORD

$\mathcal{N}$ever in my wildest dreams did I think I would ever become the author of a book, printed and published for anyone to read if they cared to. The first glimmer of the idea of writing my memoir came from my son, Ainsley Julian Borel. Upon my retirement in 2006, he and his wife, Lois, presented me, as a Christmas gift, a leather-bound journal and ink pens. He said, "Now that you have retired, you have the time to write your story." Surprised, I replied, "I didn't think you'd be interested in all that old stuff." "I am," he answered, "And your grandchildren will be too. I know about the Trinidadian side of the family, but not so much about the Jamaican side."

Occasionally I would tell my children something from my past, but my feeling was that I should not dwell on what happened a long time ago, as the past was irreversible. Rather, I needed to concentrate on the present and try to plan for the future. Then I got to thinking that my life had been an interesting one, and that I had lived in a few different countries, so maybe I could write something down.

At first there were a few hiccups. I started writing in the leather-bound journal in longhand. Then I joined classes on life story writing at the University of South Florida's Osher Lifelong Learning Institute—OLLI, which offers educational programs for seniors in retirement. Unfortunately, after each course of perhaps eight weeks, my busy schedule took over and my writing stopped. Eventually a few of us budding authors met twice monthly in an informal setting at a convenient restaurant. We wrote our stories and offered constructive criticism of each other's work. It was at these meetings that I met Armin Wendt, who often chaired our informal sessions. He was one of my greatest encouragers since he felt I had a story to tell, and it is with deep regret that this book was not completed before he passed away.

The writing group fell apart after Armin completed and published his own memoir, but he was instrumental in introducing me to his editor at a Christmas party at his home. Paula Stahel was teaching a writing class at the Life Enrichment Center in Tampa, and joining her class was the best decision I ever made. Not only did Paula give me tips on how to improve my writing, she also was the ultimate motivator, offering constructive criticism but never to the extent that I felt crushed. After numerous classes and workshops with her, and having more than halfway completed my story, I gained confidence in my abilities and felt the urge to finish. This desire was further prompted by the Life Enrichment Center's publication of an anthology entitled *Pages of My Life,* which included two of my stories.

When the time came for editing, I wanted none other than Paula to do the job, and my thanks go to her for the excellent and professional way in which she accomplished this. The task of designing the layout and book cover fell to my daughter, Denise Billups, owner of Borel Graphics Inc., whose creativity and talents have helped bring the story to life. The whole adventure of publishing my memoirs brought my beloved husband, Charles Hull, on board. He has always been my greatest encourager, but from the time we thought of self-publishing he jumped on the bandwagon. He did all the research and work for the formation of a publishing company to produce and market this book. So the adventure and learning continues.

Now I no longer feel that the past should be left well alone, but that it has a place in helping me understand myself today.

This retrospection has allowed me to see many past events in a new light, and has helped color how I view myself now and how I hope to evolve in the future. Of course I realize that we do not control the future so we cannot worry unduly about what is to come.

Above all, I view this memoir as a legacy for my children and grandchildren, hoping that they learn more about me and about their forebears, and with God's help avoid some of the pitfalls we fell into.

Jamaica

Rosemary's mother, Frances Anderson, and herself as an infant.

*M*y life started off inauspiciously in the early 1940s in Jamaica. Unwanted and ignored by my biological father, my mother was determined to give me life and do everything within her power to provide for my material needs, my physical and spiritual development, and my education.

Although I did not know it at the time, my upbringing was unconventional. My mother worked in a hotel, starting in the catering department, next transferring to the office where she did secretarial work and bookkeeping, and finally became the manageress. This meant she had perforce to live-in on the job, and depended on relatives and friends to help raise me. I never felt a lack of love because I knew my mother loved me more than anything in this world. Still, as a young child I could not understand why I could not be with her all the time.

During my early years I boarded with different families while attending school. I like to think that having had different "mothers" who contributed in various ways to my development was a distinct advantage.

Home for me has never been about a particular place. Since I moved around so much as a child, I never got too attached to a special house or a particular building. So many of the homes where I spent my youth have been razed, victims of neighborhood development projects and commercialization, and now only live in my memory. Here or there exist a couple of photographs. Then, it never occurred to me to take pictures of houses, but rather of people. Home, therefore, was more about the people whom I loved and who gave me love, safety, and security. If I was with them, I was home; it did not matter where we lived.

Through it all, my aunt and uncle provided the stable and loving environment that every child needs, and I always went home to them during school vacations. When I was about fourteen, I remember my aunt telling me emphatically, "You have a home here with us! This is your home and will always be your home!"

Boarding school during my teen years, and later the move to Leeds, England to attend university, did not prove too daunting, as I had already got over the separation syndrome. Coming from a small island in the Caribbean, our people have always been outward looking. We learn about bigger countries such as the United States and England, and we jump at the chance to go there. I was therefore motivated to travel, visit other countries, and discover other cultures.

In my life there were periods of joy, particularly during my marriages, but also there were periods of sorrow and great challenge. Was I up to the challenges? Having been given the opportunity to live, could it be said that I made a success of my life?

CHAPTER ONE | $\mathcal{R}$ichmond

Rosemary Yvonne in her toddler years

$\mathcal{I}$t is 1942 in Jamaica. I am between two and three years old, and am traveling on a very crowded train with Mrs. Edna Palmer, "Aunty" to me. I do not know Aunty very well. I have just left the comfort and security of No. 45 Molynes Road, where Mama Jen and Poppa Fred, housemates but also acting as my surrogate grandparents, spoil me rotten. Mama Jen is Aunty's mother. The train is so crowded there is not enough seating for everyone. However, Aunty manages to secure a seat, probably because her husband, Mr. Albert Palmer—whom I call Uncle Bert, is a well-known and popular stationmaster with the Jamaica Government Railway. Aunty holds me tightly as I stand leaning against her knees. I believe this is just a little jaunt, and that I will go back to No. 45 Molynes Road that evening to sleep in my own bed.

The train departs the bustling terminus in Kingston, chugging along slowly and making long stops at the stations on the way. Then it leaves the lowlands and begins climbing the hills that make up the spine of the island. I see lush green countryside as we leave the dry southern plain. The train begins to labor as the slope steepens. We enter a series of tunnels and, frightened by the darkness, I cry and clutch Aunty more tightly. Then we emerge from the tunnels and all is well again. We pass one or two towns but the majority of the settlements are scattered villages and hamlets with houses composed of mud walls and thatched roofs. In places there are cultivated patches of land, including yam hills—rows of small mounds going lengthwise down the hillsides, each mound with a ten-foot stake planted in the middle, around which the yam vine is intertwined.

The railway line is one of the great engineering feats of the British colonial government. We travel through the great limestone gorge at Bog Walk, rising perpendicularly for hundreds of feet, with the dark green waters of the Rio Cobre River at the bottom of the narrow gorge. There is only enough space alongside the river for a narrow, winding, two-way road and the railway line. At one point the road crosses the river by the Flat Bridge, built by the Spaniards who were the former colonial masters of Jamaica. The Flat Bridge can accommodate only one lane of traffic, so what happens when two vehicles coming from opposite directions meet in the middle of the bridge? One of them has to back down and reverse.

The journey takes the entire day and finally we arrive at Richmond, where Aunty and Uncle Bert live. No one has told me anything, and I do not yet know this trip heralds a major change in my life.

When I first arrived in Richmond, I missed Molynes Road terribly. Children were not told the reason for decisions affecting their lives, so I received no explanation for the move. I longed for the comfort of Mama Jen's gentle hugs as she enfolded me to her ample bosom, and Poppa Fred spoiling me with gifts of candy every evening when he alit from the city bus that brought him home from work. I missed Sonia, Peggy, and Baby Brother, who were Mama Jen's great-grand-children, and Dahlia, Poppa Fred's granddaughter. On my arrival in Richmond, no playmates were around. Aunty did not know how to relate to young children, how to talk with me, hug me, and visibly show me love. Above all, I missed my mother.

Now I would see Mum only once or twice a year for a week or two, when she had vacation from her live-in job as head of catering at the Melrose Hotel in Kingston. While living at Molynes Road I had seen her much more frequently, at least once a week on her day off, and she unstintingly lavished on me all the love and attention I craved. I adored Mum, who was a tall, slim, pretty redhead with pale skin. She was considered a "Jamaican white" because, although she looked Caucasian, mixtures of African blood did flow in her veins. Her auburn hair was wavy and, unlike mine, did not require pressing with a hot iron comb. A quick wash and set before going under the hairdryer was all she needed. In Jamaica, hers was referred to as "good hair." For years I agonized because I was not blessed with "good hair" like hers. Up till when I was three years old, my hair could still drop-curl, Shirley Temple style, after it was washed. Later when my hair would not act according to my wishes, I cried and cried.

Mum was soft-spoken and loving and did fun things with me when she visited Richmond. She took me to fairs and the movies, and sang songs to me, "Oh My Darling Clementine" being my favorite. She always made me pretty dresses for my birthday and never failed to arrange a party, no matter how small, with cake and candles and ice cream. I was always heartbroken and bereft when she had to leave, and it was about that time that I started such negative habits as sucking my thumb and digging fingers into my navel. These habits afforded me some comfort, but the thumb sucking was responsible for my buck teeth, which eventually needed orthodontic treatment.

Aunty and Uncle Bert had no surviving children of their own. A daughter, Hyacinth, had lived to three years of age before succumbing to the dreaded typhoid fever. The loss of their child was a source of sorrow, and subsequently the Palmers took in and cared for a number of children while they attended school—Babs, Dahlia, and later Sybil. After my mother found out that I was on the way and my father refused to marry her, the Palmers came to the rescue and opened their home to me. Much later I surmised that my stay at Mama Jen's and Poppa Fred's had always been intended as a temporary measure. Was it because Molynes Road was already a full house occupied by two families? Aunty and Uncle Bert had the means to help out my mother and they did so admirably.

Richmond in the 1940s was a sleepy little village about thirty miles from Kingston, in a malaria-ridden valley in the hills of the parish of St. Mary, in the northeastern part of Jamaica. A parish is a local government subdivision of a county. As Richmond lay on the windward side of the island, it faced the prevailing rain-bearing trade winds, which were responsible for the verdant landscape. In the small town there was a post office, a drug store and a few other shops, an elementary school, an Anglican church, a police station, and the railway station. However, Richmond's main claim to fame was the Richmond Farm Prison, where white-collar criminals were confined while serving sentences of hard manual labor in the fields.

As stationmaster, Uncle Bert was provided with a house, which sat atop a hill on the opposite side of the track from the station. Constructed of wood, it boasted four bedrooms, a dining room, and a drawing room where there were rockers and chairs of dark mahogany wood, a gramophone, and a piano. A rather spacious hallway with a few chairs opened out near the front entrance just behind the veranda, which spanned the width of the house. In a small niche in the hallway, a huge black dial-up telephone hung on the wall. Uncle Bert used this on his job as stationmaster. The kitchen and latrine were located in separate buildings, to the back of the property. Later the back bedroom was converted into a bathroom with a toilet whose tank hung aloft, so the force of gravity released the flow of water to flush the bowl. This was a huge improvement, because when I first got to Richmond, every evening was a time when I was in the doghouse. I was too busy during the daytime to go to the bathroom. By evening when I was ready, there was great objection to my putting down a load into the "potty," the chamber pot that resided beneath the bed. By then it was far too dark to dispose of the contents in the latrine at the back of the house. I was reprimanded by Aunty every single evening until I got the message.

Aunty was the disciplinarian in the household. "Don't ever go near that mirror!" she would warn me, referring to the full-length mirror on the door of her wardrobe. Whenever I forgot and wandered there to view my image and, in the process, smeared the glass with grimy little hands, I was slapped immediately. Aunty also gave me small tasks, like dusting the mahogany furniture, and she paid particular attention to how I performed those duties. She carefully examined the lower pins between the chair legs and the rocking chair runners, and if these details were overlooked in the dusting process, I was ordered to do the job again. Any infraction on my part was rewarded with a slap.

When she wanted me out of the house she would say, "Baby, go outside and play." It was not much fun playing by myself but I had no choice. I would pretend I was a teacher and use a stick to mercilessly beat the small shrubs and plants, which were my pupils. One of my few toys was a ball that escaped and rolled down the hill, disappearing forever into a sinkhole. I lost a number of balls in this manner. If I scratched or bruised myself, I kept quiet and tied to hide it; the remedy would be iodine, which smarted so much that I screamed with pain. Iodine and Milton—the brand name for hydrogen peroxide, were Aunty's favorite remedies for all ills. I never escaped because it seemed that Aunty had eyes in the back of her head. Even though I thought she could not see me, she always knew when I got even the smallest scratch.

In the cooler months of the year, October through February, I would be awakened early, taken out from under the mosquito net, washed with water from an ewer and basin on a nearby washstand, and dressed in a little cotton frock that was covered with my warm red woolen sweater. Then I would be placed on the front veranda facing the morning sun to shell pigeon peas. This was a job I hated with a passion because many of the fat peas were infested with worms. The wriggling masses of green or white worms put a mortal fear in me but there was no getting out of the job. If the exterior of the pod gave even a suggestion of an infestation, I immediately dumped it in the trash.

Aunty was an accomplished pianist who even gave lessons to a few neighboring children. Every afternoon I was forced to take a nap, but my reluctance to sleep would be overcome by the dulcet strains of Aunty playing pieces such as Lange's "Flower Song" and Schumann's "Traumerei."

After my nap, Aunty would take me for a short walk in the village, visiting her friends at the post office and the drug store. I especially looked forward to visiting old Mrs. Nelson, who always served us crackers with homemade guava jelly. On these walks I was constantly on the lookout for dogs, which were never restrained by leashes and of which I was deathly afraid. On one memorable occasion a snarling dog confronted us. In an instant I climbed Aunty's five-foot frame as if it were a tree and clung to her for dear life. She had a hard time getting me off.

Another time I tugged at Aunty's hand, trying to persuade her to enter a little hole-in-the-wall shop. "Uncle Bert goes in there to buy me candy," I insisted. Horrified when she viewed the highly unsanitary condition of the shop, with flies pitching over the candies, Aunty absolutely refused to grant my wish.

Returning from our walks, Aunty always had difficulty climbing the hill back to the house. She was overweight, and malaria had weakened her system considerably. I recall many occasions when I pushed Aunty from behind to propel her up the hill.

One day Aunty was having a bad day and told me, "Baby, run outside and play. Aunty does not want to talk to anyone now." A little later, one of Aunty's friends knocked at the front door. When I answered, she asked to see Mrs. Palmer. I responded politely, "Aunty doesn't want to talk to anybody now." That lady never spoke to Aunty again and a friend was lost. She could not believe that a child so young would tell anything but the truth, nor realize that I could not understand the nuance of Aunty's statement.

Uncle Bert was completely the opposite of Aunty in personality. Tall, handsome, affable Uncle Bert loved people, especially children. His hearty laugh rang out throughout the house; his friends observed that they always knew when he was approaching because his laugh preceded him. He must have been barely eighteen years old when he enlisted to serve in World War I but he never talked about his war experiences. We heard later he had served in Egypt. It was our understanding that recruits from the colonies were not allowed to fight during the war and instead were relegated to menial jobs like cleaning the latrines. Maybe this was the reason he was silent about his experiences. Or was it because he bore the scars and ravages that war wreaks on mankind?

A very intelligent man, Uncle Bert listened eagerly on the radio to the BBC news and to cricket matches held in various parts of the far-flung British Empire. He also was very focused on educating young children. Once, he took me to his office at the railway station, pointed out the telegraph machine, and explained how it worked by using a series of dots and dashes to spell out words. His love of books spilled over to me. In my pre-teen years, when I became a voracious reader, he advised me to make a note of the title and author of any book I read. He taught me, at age twelve, to play bridge, and I would play with the grownups, sometimes beating them.

Uncle Bert was my knight in armor, my savior from Aunty the disciplinarian. There were certain foods I adamantly refused to eat, one being spinach, which the indifferent cook would dry up and burn on the stovetop, giving it a bitter taste. When it was served, my mouth clamped shut and no amount of coaxing convinced me to open it. After what seemed like an interminable standoff period, Uncle Bert would come home and swallow the offending spinach in one fell swoop, ending the argument and tears. Once, he even swallowed a dose of nasty-tasting castor oil intended to purge my system.

Uncle Bert took me on longer walks than Aunty did. He was always at least three feet ahead of me, with my short legs trying in vain to keep up with his long strides. Once, he took me on a five-mile walk to the next railway station at Troja. We returned to Richmond by a rail trolley, which, as stationmaster, he knew would be coming through. I loved accompanying Uncle Bert on his jaunts because, unlike Aunty, he bought me candy from dirty little fly-ridden shops.

The passenger train from Kingston stopped at Richmond each afternoon, with Port Antonio as its destination, and returned to Kingston in the morning. In addition, freight trains roared through, usually at night. It took me a while after I first arrived to get used to the rhythmic clatter of the trains passing over the wooden railroad ties, but eventually the hypnotizing sound of a passing train would lull me to sleep. I even learned to tune out the blare of their horns.

About six weeks after I came to Richmond, my solitude was broken by Babs' arrival. Later I realized that Babs, ten years my senior, had been with the Palmers long before I got there. Maybe she had been away visiting her father's family. Babs was a beautiful half-Chinese girl with straight black hair so long it reached her bottom. I was fascinated with and envious of her hair. Babs treated me like a little sister and helped Aunty by washing my feet at night before bedtime.

One evening while Babs was attempting to do her school homework, I tried to get her attention. "Miss Babs, Miss Babs! *Miss Babs*!" I kept repeating, as she tried desperately to concentrate and gave no reply.

The next minute, there was a huge outcry from Babs. "Aunty! What a naughty child Yvonne is! She's completely ruined my homework!"

Yvonne, my middle name, was used by my closest family. Indeed, I had. I had grabbed hold of a pen and struck angry lines across the page. By the time Aunty arrived I was hiding under the bed, trying to avoid the inevitable punishment.

Later Dahlia joined the household, also to go to school. Dahlia's home was with Poppa Fred and Mama Jen in

Kingston, but she stayed with the Palmers while attending a private school in Richmond. Five years my senior, Dahlia and I had been together at Molynes Road, so I was overjoyed to have familiar company. Dahlia and Babs teased me mercilessly, tickling me while I giggled uncontrollably until I reached exhaustion. Eventually I learned to steel myself until tickling no longer had any effect. When I was naughty, the girls would threaten, "The policeman is coming to get you!" in the same manner as one would say, "The bogey man is coming for you!" The police station was right next door to the stationmaster's house and for a very long time I had a morbid fear of policemen.

From time to time, friends would visit the Palmers for a week or two. These included Miss Cass, Babs' mother, and Miss Spence, a genteel spinster who always spoke in a stage whisper. Both ladies were postmistresses, holding one of the few jobs available to middle-class women in those days. Also, Mr. Laing, a childhood friend of Aunty's, visited once a year. He worked for the Jamaica Public Service, the electric company in Kingston. A confirmed bachelor, he was an exercise enthusiast, with dancing and swimming among his favorite activities—it was he who taught me to swim.

When Mr. Laing visited during the New Year holiday, the grown-ups would go out dancing. Aunty would don her long evening dress, a babysitter would come, and we would go to bed, not seeing Aunty or Uncle Bert till the following morning. One New Year's Eve a young lad named Alvin came to babysit Dahlia and me. Contrary to the usual instructions, Aunty advised, "Don't go to sleep! Stay up until we return." All three of us sat in the rocking chairs in the hallway, trying desperately to keep awake. Finally sleep overpowered us, and when the adults returned, they found us all, including Alvin, curled up in the chairs sound asleep.

One day when I was about four years old, a lady visiting Aunty said to me, "Hello! Do you want to come and spend some time with me on my farm?"

I was surprised to be noticed, because children were largely ignored by the grown-ups who came around. Normally I would have promptly replied, "No thank you." This time I wondered what would happen if I accepted. So I shyly said, "Yes." I then forgot about it. A couple of weeks later, a man on a horse came to take me to Good Hope Farm. I was a little fearful but the die was cast and I had to go.

The ride was rather bumpy but otherwise uneventful. On arrival at the farm, I was startled to find that my aunt's friend had a very large family, with about ten children. We played all day. As evening approached and the shadows lengthened I wished I could go home. Instead, I was put to sleep on a small cot.

During the night one of the sons, who was about ten years old, came to my bed and woke me. "Shhhh," he said. "Keep quiet and you'll be all right." He crept into my bed and took my pants down. Then he put his member into that private part of me "between my legs," as Aunty described that part of my anatomy. I believe he was experimenting or possibly was interrupted because he did not stay long. Before leaving he cautioned, "Don't say anything to anyone!" I was so used to obeying anyone older than myself that I did as I was told. But the next day I begged to go home. I did not feel comfortable telling Aunty about this incident because she was not an easy person for a little child to talk to, so I kept quiet and basically put the incident in the back of my mind.

A few weeks later I started running a fever, eczemas broke out on my legs, and the glands in my groins grew swollen. I remained in bed for weeks. Then one morning Aunty entered my room and said, "Yvonne, you can get out of bed and get dressed." As soon as I slid out of bed I fell flat on the floor. My legs, which had not been used for weeks, collapsed under me. It was as if I had to re-learn how to walk. Aunty helped me up and got me dressed. We caught the diesel train to Kingston where I was met by my mother, who had arranged a doctor's appointment for me.

It was much later, when I was about twelve, that my mother told me more. I had contracted gonorrhea but it was quickly cleared up by the prescribed medication. No one had any idea how I had caught this disease; they surmised the housemaid had somehow infected me and she was fired. During the early 1940s, knowledge of sexually transmitted diseases was still rudimentary and many people honestly believed it possible to contract the diseases from surfaces such as toilet seats.

To this day, no one was aware of the real reason, as I never said anything. Because of my upbringing, I was very shy about talking about sexual matters. People did not talk to children about such things and my aunt certainly did not. When I was approaching the age for my periods to begin, my mother told me what to expect and the physical preparations to make. She never told me that if I engaged in sexual activities as a young lady a baby could result. Knowing I was a bookworm, she did give me a book to read on the subject and left it at that.

It was perhaps around this time of my life that I connected that what the ten-year-old boy had done when I was four was responsible for my contracting the terrible disease. I do not remember being angry or upset. After all, it was in the distant past and I had long been cured. Perhaps there was a certain degree of shame but I did not see the point of telling my mother. I do not believe I was scarred for life by this experience. At age four, I did not fully understand what happened, only that it did not feel right and I was uncomfortable about staying at that farm any longer. Later this was not something I thought about or obsessed over; otherwise I do not believe I would have achieved successful relationships in my adult life. At this stage of my life I have no hard feelings against that boy because I believe he himself had been a victim, or he would not have known how to perpetuate this act on a smaller child.

The lesson I learned was the need, as a parent or guardian, to watch over my children carefully during their vulnerable years, because no one knows who might interfere with them, even curious ten-year-olds. It is ironic that the adults must have been trying to protect Dahlia and me from such an abuse when, on that New Year's Eve in the early 1940s, we and Alvin, our teen-aged babysitter, were advised not to go to sleep.

When I attained my fifth birthday, my mother made arrangements for me to live with the Smith family in Kingston while attending my first school there. I did not know what to expect, but I do not remember being fazed by this news, although I was being uprooted from a life with Aunty and Uncle Bert where I had become quite comfortable. The assurance that my home was with them, and that I would be returning home to Richmond during the vacation was enough to satisfy me.

The Smith family resided at No. 16 Upper Camp Road, immediately opposite the British military camp at Up Park. In fact, every morning at six, bugle reveille woke not only the intended targets but also the residents of nearby houses. Although my purpose was to attend school, my return to Kingston gave me great contentment, as I again was able to see my mother on her weekly day off, and speak to her every afternoon on the telephone.

Growing up in Kingston, Jamaica

Mrs. Emma Smith, whom I was told to call Mother, was a brown-skinned lady about sixty years old, of medium height and build, with a kindly face and long gray hair she usually wore in one fat braid wound around the crown of her head. A perfect mother figure, she showed me love and affection but also meted out discipline when necessary. A great raconteur, Mother Smith told me Bible stories every evening before bedtime. This was when I first heard stories such as Adam and Eve in the Garden of Eden, Noah's Ark, Daniel in the Lion's Den, Samson and Delilah, and Jonah and the Whale.

Mother Smith's three grown daughters lived with her. Aunt Madge, the eldest, worked in the Jamaican Civil Service as secretary to the financial secretary. The youngest sister, quiet and reserved Aunt Carmen, was also a civil servant. The middle sister, Aunt Millie, did not go out to work. She took an interest in me but I was a little wary of her. Aunt Madge was my favorite. Vivacious and pretty, she talked quickly and laughed a lot. She loved life and was always entertaining, hosting tea parties and welcoming friends who dropped in continually. Aunt Madge adored children and paid me a great deal of attention. She took pride in showing me off to her friends. I would be asked to sing songs or recite poems I had learned in school. In my babyish voice, I would sing:

> *"Jingle the bells for Charley,*
> *Send him to school quite early.*
> *Jingle the bells, jingle the bells,*
> *Jingle o' jingle o' jingle the bells."*

I had difficulty pronouncing the word "quite"—it came out of my mouth sounding like "qurite," which the adults found adorable.

Another little girl, from Haiti and named Jeannine, started boarding at the Smiths to attend school. One day Jeannine and I, while interfering with Aunt Millie's things, found a small tin filled with farthings. A farthing was the lowliest of British coins, worth a quarter of a penny. "Look," I exclaimed, "Aunt Millie is saving farthings! She's so miserly!"

"Let's take some," Jeannine said. "They're not worth much anyway, and she'll never miss them."

So we took some and thought Aunt Millie would never notice the loss. However, she did. She summoned us to her room and lectured us soundly on the sin of stealing. We had to return the farthings and never took anything from Aunt

Millie again, but we still considered her to be parsimonious.

The house at No. 16 Upper Camp Road was extensive, with many large rooms—a huge living room, a dining room, and tiled front and back verandas. Occupying a corner lot, the spacious yard included a front lawn and garden bordered by a grilled iron fence and grilled double gate. The yard was dotted with many fruit trees, including a huge Bombay mango tree, the king of all mangoes. More rounded than elongated, this mango does not develop any strings in the delicious, delicately flavored fruit, and therefore was ideal as a table mango, often served to guests in the hotels. The fruit was usually cut horizontally around the middle, revealing its large stone, which was easily removed from both halves. Since the succulent flesh had the consistency of a cantaloupe, it could be consumed elegantly with a teaspoon.

Another favorite of mine was a cherry tree that grew next to a side patio, where an easily climbed lattice wall afforded access to the coveted fruit. The exterior of this Caribbean fruit resembles the northern cherry, and the color of the small berries graduates from scarlet red when mature to dark ruby when fully ripe. However, on biting into the fruit, one does not encounter a hard stone in the center. Instead, a soft seed the consistency of cartilage meets the tongue, and can be chewed easily and spat out.

The back veranda gave access to two bedrooms. One was occupied by a sister of Mother Smith, the other by two elderly spinster sisters, Tan Tan and Gigi. I never figured out if they were related to the Smith family or if they were very good friends. Tan Tan was the taller and more robust of the two. To my five-year-old eyes the ladies seemed very, very old, so it took me by surprise one day to see Tan Tan get down on her knees to search for something that had fallen under the bed. I never thought she could do that!

Each morning I would rise early and, guided by the pungent aroma of freshly brewed Blue Mountain coffee, go to Tan Tan and Gigi's room, where they offered me coffee sweetened with condensed milk. They served it to me in a saucer so it cooled quickly and did not burn my tongue. How I loved that coffee, the smooth creamy liquid trickling down my throat and exciting my taste buds! The only trigger to my awareness that perhaps something was not quite right was the warning from the old ladies that I should keep my coffee drinking a secret.

Gigi was small and wizened and bent forward considerably, which seemed to testify to her great age. To her fell the tasks of darning the family's socks and combing the children's hair, at which she showed considerable talent. As I sat on a small stool in front of her knees, she meticulously greased my hair with cocoa butter until it shone and highlighted the waves in it. The cocoa butter was in the form of a small, hard white ball, rather like a round specialty soap bar. Then it was easy to comb out the knots in my hair and and plait it into two or three thick braids.

On Sundays we all attended St. Paul's Presbyterian Church, which was close to the Melrose Hotel where Mum worked. After the service, I always walked over to pay her a visit. One Sunday on arriving at the hotel, Mum kissed me and then asked, "Why does your hair smell so funny?" I replied, "Gigi mistook a piece of cheese for cocoa butter and put cheese in my hair." This cheese was particularly pungent because after the mistake was discovered, no amount of washing removed the terrible odor, which lingered for several hours. Needless to say my mother laughed her head off, and to my great embarrassment repeated the story to friends and family.

My school was Rushbrook Preparatory School, three blocks away on the same side of Upper Camp Road as the Smith's home. On the first day, Mother Smith's domestic helper walked me to school, teaching me to cross the side streets. The second day I was on my own. Those were simpler times, when no one worried about little girls walking alone on the road. Mother Smith had instilled in me the rules of crossing streets safely. Look left, then right, then left again, and then walk—do not dart, across the street. In Jamaica, as in Britain, all vehicles drove on the left, so the instructions were the opposite of those in the USA.

Rushbrook, managed by Miss Annie Wood, was a typical dame school. Dame schools were private schools run by female teachers, who required no special license, training, or credentials. The quality of the education varied, some basically functioning as day care facilities overseen by unqualified women, with others providing students a good basic education.

The school occupied a big old house with several large rooms, but the kindergarten class was in a converted garage to the rear of the main building. The young assistant teacher bonded with us, her small pupils, and we had great fun singing songs, playing games, and forming different shapes with plastocene, which we know today as Play-Doh®. We were taught our A-B-Cs, to read simple words, and rudimentary addition and subtraction.

In the class at the next level, I progressed to reading more difficult words, reciting poetry, and learning multiplication and division. Learning by rote was accepted practice then, so we memorized our times tables as well as other tables of measurement. We also were given sewing classes, where we learned basic stitches such as the hemstitch and blanket stitch, and went on to learn embroidery. Some of the girls were extremely talented, producing beautiful pieces of sewn art, with bright flowers and green leaves filled in with satin stitches. Unfortunately, I was not gifted at sewing skills. Classes in drawing were far more satisfactory. It was my pride and joy to receive a certificate for drawing in an exam set in London, England for the colonies of the British Empire.

At Rushbrook, I started my first piano lessons, an extra-curricular activity for which my mother paid an additional fee. My music teacher taught me the name of each white note by writing the appropriate letter on each key in pencil. In this way I learned the C major scale—C, D, E, F, G, A, B, C. I must have been an apt pupil because I soon started taking lessons from a certified piano teacher at a nearby studio.

At the end of the school year was an annual prize-giving. My first prize-giving was an exciting affair. I was decked out in a new appliquéd white dress, with a huge sash and a bow at the back, sewn by my talented mother. Also, I patronized my first hairdresser, who "lightened" my thick mane with a hot-iron comb. Drop curls circled my head in the coveted Shirley Temple style and I was thrilled to bits. The Smith family, as well as my mother, attended the celebration, where I joined with the other six-year-olds to sing:

> "Oh good evening, how do you do?
> We are babies come to sing to you.
> Eyes like saucers, hair all in a curl,
> How'd you like to be a baby girl?"

But that was not all. I also played in the school band, my percussion instrument being the triangle, and was chosen to conduct the orchestra in two of the pieces. With my back to the audience, I waved my hand in four-four time in one piece, and three-quarter time in the waltz. It had not occurred to me to tell any of the adults about this, so Mum, completely taken by surprise, was bursting with pride when she saw my conducting skills.

My time as a boarder with the Smiths came to an end when my mother decided I was not learning enough at Rushbrook Preparatory because, even though I excelled in the arts, my math was sub-standard. I was happy at the Smiths, where they treated me like family and encouraged me to shine. I do not remember being shy while living with them, and I relished the opportunity to see Mum frequently. However, my intelligent, ambitious mother knew the road to upward mobility was through a good education. Her greatest desire was to see me excel academically as well as develop in character. Now I was to board with her old schoolteacher and his family, the Robinsons, in Thompson Town, a little village in the hills in the center of the island, some thirty to forty miles away from Kingston.

CHAPTER THREE | Thompson Town

When I was six years old, Uncle Bert picked me up from the Smith's to embark on the long journey to Thompson Town. I had gone on many joyful adventures with him before, but they were relatively short. It was a bright sunny day and Uncle Bert took me and my packed suitcase to Parade in downtown Kingston, where the journey began.

Parade, a huge open paved area, was formerly the parade ground for British soldiers. This place, bustling with activity, was the hub for all the city buses, trams, and country buses. Hordes of people dressed in colorful clothing filled Parade at all times. Vendors hawking their wares positioned themselves at strategic spots. In contrast, Victoria Park was situated in relative serenity to the north of Parade, with a huge statue of Queen Victoria at its entrance. Geometric beds of Canna lilies—some red, some yellow, and some orange, beautified the gardens of the park. From Parade the city streets fanned out toward the waterfront of Kingston Harbour, about one mile away. Department stores, most owned by Lebanese and Syrians, fringed Parade and lined King Street, the main street that ran to the harbor. Uncle Bert searched the lines of colorful country buses, painted in bright red, yellow, and green, for the correct one for us to board. We paid our fare, got in, and settled down.

"Lemme pass," said a fat market woman as she moved toward the rear of the bus with a huge basket of produce. "Just dress down a likkle so ah can sit," she ordered a younger woman. When the storage area in the rear was filled to capacity, extra baskets, boxes, and suitcases were loaded on the roof. As the bus slowly filled there was loud talk and cheerful banter among the passengers. Although the bus was licensed to accommodate forty-five people, it seemed that double the amount squeezed in. Considering there were only two daily buses going to our destination, the driver and the conductor did not wish to leave anyone behind. Finally, with passengers packed like sardines in a tin, we set off, flying down crowded Spanish Town Road, the main trunk road leading toward the central part of the island.

As we reached the outskirts of Kingston, the buildings started to thin out. We went west along the dry southern plain, passing large estates planted with sugarcane, their frilly white fronds waving gaily in the breeze. Irrigation canals, the main life source for the canes, ran parallel to the rows. Some fields were lined with tall coconut trees that acted as a windbreak for the crop. We passed tobacco fields and rice paddies and then, as we approached the foothills of the island's central spine, banana plantations came into view.

At the big market towns the bus stopped, sometimes for up to half an hour, to let off and take on passengers. At one of these stops Uncle Bert said with satisfaction, "This is Chapelton!" It looked like an ordinary town to me, with houses that had big yards and grilled iron fences and gates, stores and rum shops, an Anglican church, and a clock tower standing proudly in the middle of the town square. Later I realized that Chapelton must have brought back fond memories for Uncle Bert, as this was Aunty's hometown, where he must have spent happy hours courting her.

After leaving Chapelton, the bus climbed the island's hilly interior along a narrow, unpaved road. There were numerous hairpin curves winding around the contours of the mountains, often with a steep rock wall on one side and a precipitous drop on the other. The bus conductor, also known as the "side man," had the job of warning the driver if he was too close to the rock wall or about to plunge into the precipice. Sometimes the bus labored up the hills and, considering how packed it was, I wondered if we would make it. In most places the road was too narrow for two large vehicles to pass. Every time we approached a blind corner, the driver blared his horn repeatedly and literally raised himself out of his seat, trying to get a premonition of whether a vehicle was approaching from the opposite direction. Once we heard a responding horn. It was the afternoon bus heading towards Kingston. Our driver had to reverse down the slope until he reached a bend where the road widened a little and the two buses slowly inched their way past each other.

Finally we reached our destination, Thompson Town. We alighted from the bus and extricated my suitcase from the mountain of luggage on its roof. Looking around in the waning daylight, I saw a gravel road rising abruptly up a hill covered in red clay. This was the road we were to follow. Out of breath from walking up the steep ascent, I was glad for a respite when the road leveled off somewhat. At this point we turned left onto a side road that followed the contour of the hill. It led to a rather large plateau-like area, which accommodated Thompson Town Elementary School. Adjacent to the school was the cottage where the headmaster, Alan Robinson, and his family resided.

Uncle Bert hastily introduced me to the Robinsons, and left immediately to catch the return bus to Kingston. Again a feeling of abandonment. I was once more taken from a life I knew and plunged among strangers. I felt as gloomy as the night that was fast approaching. Mrs. Robinson, who was also a teacher and the mother of four, took me under her wing and allowed me to sleep in her room with her youngest daughter, Bebe. (Teacher Rob, as everyone called him, had his own bedroom on the opposite side of the house.) She invited me to call her "Mother" just like Bebe did. Bebe's given name was Greta Faye but everyone called her by her nickname. She was about eighteen months my junior and several years younger than her three siblings. Mother Rob liked to say, in the Jamaican dialect, that she had three children and Bebe was the "brawtah." This was the equivalent of the thirteenth in a baker's dozen or lagniappe in the French tradition.

My mother was a former pupil of Teacher Rob's, and had kept in touch with the family over the years. Desperate to give me a good educational foundation, she begged the Robinsons to allow me to board with them and receive coaching in all subjects, especially in arithmetic and English. What my mother paid the Robinsons in monetary remuneration would never fully repay what they did for me. In those days in Jamaica, secondary education was not universal or free. Those who could not afford to pay vied for scholarships to attend secondary school. Only two scholarships were awarded annually in each of the island's fourteen parishes. Of course, teachers' children held an edge since they were coached both at home and at school. The Robinsons' three older children had won scholarships to prominent secondary boarding schools and returned home only during vacations. I was now being given the advantage of extra coaching in the hope of someday winning a scholarship myself.

Although the Robinsons were not effusive, they treated me no differently than their own flesh and blood. If we mis- behaved, both Bebe and I "got licks" since corporal punishment was a popular form of discipline then. We both were given the same food, even the same vitamins.

I did not see it at the time, but had it not been for Bebe

I probably would not have made such rapid progress in my education. Bebe was very smart and quick, and these attributes spurred great competition between us. After all, since I was older I could not allow her to outshine me. The only area where I could not compete was in handicraft. I am convinced I was born with two left hands. When Mother Rob taught us to crochet, Bebe caught on quickly, even completing a small skullcap while I was still struggling with a bedraggled couple of rows of crocheted stitches. Despite the competition between us, Bebe was a great playmate and we enjoyed such games in the backyard as hopscotch, jacks, and donkey. In playing donkey, we tossed a ball to each other. When one of us failed to catch it, a letter was acquired, starting with "D," the first letter in the word "donkey." Whoever reached "Y" first became the donkey.

There was a huge tangerine tree in the back, heavily laden with luscious orange-colored fruit. Each tangerine must have weighed a half-pound. Peeled, they revealed sweet juicy pegs, a food fit for the gods. This was the first time I experienced being able to pick unlimited fruit at will, and satiated myself with its sweet nectar. During mango season, we children ate that too until it seemed our bellies would burst.

In Thompson Town during the months of December through March, the evening temperatures dropped drastically and I needed my warm red cardigan to cover my thin cotton frock as protection against the chilly land breezes. Mother Rob often remarked, "Just a little breeze has to blow on you and you get sick!" Indeed, I caught colds easily and was dosed daily with a spoonful of nasty-tasting cod liver oil—the liquid, not the more palatable capsule.

On the day that I turned seven, I rose from bed excitedly. When I put on the new dress Mum had sent me, Mother Rob viewed me with surprise. "Why are you wearing your new dress?"

"Because it's my birthday! I always wear a new dress on my birthday."

"Just take it off immediately!"

"Aren't we going to have a party?"

"Not at all. Go and take off that dress!"

With tears in my eyes I obeyed and thought longingly of my mother. Mum always made me a new dress for my birthday, and even if we had only two people around, there was always a cake with candles and ice cream. Welcome to the real world!

Nevertheless, Mother Rob was consistent. Bebe's birthday was not celebrated either. For the first time I realized that not every family took special note of each birthday, and that not everyone considered life as a series of celebrations. The Smiths had paid special attention to me and encouraged me to shine and acquire all the social graces. Now, from the Robinsons I was finding out the world did not revolve around me.

It took me some time to get used to life in Thompson Town, a small village situated in the Mocho Mountains in the center of the island. The area was so rural that anyone who admitted to coming from Mocho was considered a country bumpkin. There was no electricity, no running water, and no paved roads. Because of the hilly nature of the terrain, the buildings were scattered around a couple of nodes. Clustered together in a rather flat stretch were the Chinese shop (the grocer), pharmacy, gas station, and the terminus of the local-based "Herolin" country bus. (Country buses all had names, reminiscent of the names of boats and other watercraft.) About half a mile away were the post office and the Baptist church, with its nearby manse where the parson, an Englishman, resided. Another half-mile down the hill were located the elementary school and the teacher's cottage, where we lived. Further down in the hollow, called Wesleyan Gully, sat the Wesleyan church, also known as the Methodist church.

Thompson Town was covered with a red clay, good for making pottery but hard to dig for planting. The Jamaican red dirt was considered highly undesirable until the discovery in the 1950s that it was rich in bauxite, the ore from which aluminum is derived. After that, for about three decades Jamaica prospered greatly from bauxite mining and processing of alumina. Every evening we kids were covered with a red dust after playing, and had to wash our legs and hands thoroughly before being allowed to slip between the white bed sheets. Colored or patterned sheets were unknown in those days. Over time the sheets gradually turned pale pink, an undesirable color which people tried to remove by bleaching. Out in the backyard a big wire stand had been specially constructed for accommodating the laundry, which was lathered with a hard blue soap and laid out in the sun to bleach. The use of blue soap, or sometimes a blue powder diluted in the rinse water, and the occasional boiling of sheets in soapy water in a huge drum on an outside coal fire were attempts to remove the unwanted pink, but never completely eliminated it.

As there was no running water in Thompson Town, people had to trek to the nearby spring to catch water. The pictures of young girls of Africa carrying drums of water on their heads that one often sees was certainly true of Jamaica in the 1940s and 1950s. A long piece of cotton cloth was twisted and then coiled around and around until it made a sort of a small mat called a cotta, which was placed on the head. The load then was balanced on the cotta. It was amazing how people, including young girls, could balance the water drums unaided by their hands, and trudge up and down the hills without spilling a drop. We kids would try to do the same and failed miserably.

Sometime later, Mrs. Rob took into the household a fifteen-year-old local girl, Evelyn, to help with the chores. She was fed, given a room, and provided school uniforms and books. In return Evelyn fetched water, went to the market, cooked, and cleaned. When her work was done, we often played together in the evenings by lamplight. We played board games such as snakes and ladders, or Chinese checkers, dominoes, and cards. She also related "duppy" stories—ghost stories, which frightened the daylights out of us.

Being still quite young, Evelyn needed supervision. Mrs. Rob would give Evelyn money to purchase staples such as flour, rice, sugar, and oil from the Chinese shop once a month, and to buy meats and produce twice a month from the local market. However, Evelyn did not know how to ration the food to last through the month. Often it was "feast today and famine tomorrow," as Mother Rob would say. One day we had only sweet potatoes dug from the garden and roasted for our meal. This was the one food that I absolutely abhorred. Believe me, even though I disliked sweet potatoes, I ate them. Otherwise I would have gone to bed hungry. Although I have never been a picky eater, after this experience I learned to eat whatever was put before me, even if I did not care for that particular food. At least I did not starve. What about those children who had absolutely nothing to eat and were perpetually hungry?

Even though Thompson Town was "back o' wall," so remote that many were reluctant to acknowledge any association with the place, I learned valuable lessons during the four years of living there during my childhood. I learned to appreciate simple country people. I learned to respect all people regardless of their stations in life. You never passed anyone on the road without saying good morning, whether you knew them or not.

Miss Fanny, an elderly woman, was our nearest neighbor. Her small house, halfway down the hillside, was always sparkling clean. She would go down on hands and knees to scrub the wooden floor with a coconut brush, and then apply a red wax to polish the floor until it shone. Every morning she made a strong brew of coffee in an old tin can. I am sure the fresh coffee beans came from the trees that flourished in the area. The pungent aroma would reach us as we neared Miss Fanny's hut. "Morning, Miss Fanny," we would call out. "Morning," she would reply. "You is so mannersable, real mannersable." She had coined a new word to describe how well mannered she found us to be.

Shortly after I arrived in Thompson Town, Teacher Rob, having reached sixty, the mandatory retirement age, bought a beautiful property in the lowlands near Chapelton, about fifteen miles away, and settled down as a gentleman farmer. We stayed with Mrs. Rob at Thompson Town, commuting on weekends to Scott's Pen, where Teacher Rob had taken up residence. In Thompson Town, we had to move out of the teacher's cottage to make way for the new headmaster. There was a long waiting period for a new cottage to be built for us to live in. In the meantime, we rented a room from Mr. DaCosta, who lived further down the road.

Mr. D, as everyone called him, was a brown-skinned man of medium build with salt-and-pepper hair. Judging from his name he was probably part Portuguese, but in Jamaica no one bothered to find out lineage because we are all so racially mixed. Mr. D was a well-traveled man, having lived in Costa Rica and where he had apparently made some money, presumably in the banana industry. Many Jamaicans had done this during the early part of the twentieth century and remained in Costa Rica. Mr. D, however, came back home to his roots, built his house, and had a small farm growing subsistence crops. One daughter, who lived with him, had a baby while we were there. Then another grown daughter appeared on the scene later. We did not think anything of it, even though Mr. D was a respected deacon in the local Baptist church. Mr. D loved children and we adored him. He often related folklore and other stories to us. Every evening before bedtime everyone in the household met in the living room for evening prayers. Mr. D would read a Psalm—he loved the Psalms—and then offer a long prayer until tears rolled down from his eyes while we all knelt obediently on the floor beside our chairs.

At night Mother Rob, Bebe, and I shared a full-sized bed jammed against the wall in our rented room. We girls slept all over the bed and poor Mother Rob must have endured many kicks from two sleep-drugged children.

One night she woke us to observe the eclipse of the moon, which we spent a long time viewing through smoked glass. Then we returned to bed. The next morning Mother Rob asked how we liked the eclipse, to which I replied, "Oh, why didn't you wake me up to see it?"

She remonstrated, "But I did! You oohed and ahhed and even said 'Oh, how beautiful!'"

"I don't remember that," I replied. With a jolt I realized I must have been sleep walking through the whole eclipse episode.

Another time our room was overrun by huge red ants, some about three-quarters of an inch long. It was the rainy season and their nest must have become flooded. The ants squeezed through the gaps of the door and covered the entire wooden floor. We stomped on them, trying in vain to squash their bodies. I had heard of the insecticide DDT, but we had none so we were fighting a losing battle. Beating a retreat, we got into bed and thought we were safe, only to find them climbing up the bedposts. Like an army, they spread out over the white sheet, covering every inch until the sheet was a seething mass of brownish-red life. The ants were winning as we tried in vain to knock them off the sheets. Realizing the uselessness of our efforts, we ducked under the cover sheet, leaving just our noses exposed, in an attempt to shield ourselves from the ants. Even so, one mean old ant bit me on my nose. A painful and horrific experience!

Running barefoot in the yard, we constantly got chiggers in our toes. These are the larvae of small mites living in the ground in tropical areas. The chiggers are enclosed in a sac that buries itself in the skin, producing intense itching. We sterilized a needle by passing it through an open flame and then used it to carefully remove the sac. If the sac burst, forget it, the infestation continued. Another parasite I once acquired, from one of the children in school, was lice. As I had a thick head of hair, it took ages to eradicate the lice.

Mosquitoes and flies abounded in the hot, damp climate, with the flies especially taking up residence in the outdoor latrine. The latrine was not a favorite place of mine to visit. This small building not only reeked of offensive odors but also harbored lizards, of which I was deathly afraid. On entering, I searched anxiously around to see if any lizards were staring at me. I disliked them all. The big green iguanas with huge ugly combs on their backs. The small brown polly lizards moving in snake-like, wriggling motions along the wooden panels of the latrine. The pale, croaking lizards that attached themselves to the rafters. I had horrible visions of these creatures falling on me. Little did I know then that their feet operated like suction cups, so there was hardly any danger of such an occurrence.

It was quite an education to discover how the latrine system worked. While we were at Mr. D's, the latrine filled up. A team of neighboring men came and in one day dug a new pit, transferred the little house to the new location, and covered up the old hole with dirt. This was how the villagers cooperated to complete projects. If someone needed to build a house, all the able-bodied men in the village helped and the women cooked enormous pots of food to sustain the workers. Next time it would be another villager's turn to receive assistance. The cooperative effort was like a huge celebration.

Finally the new cottage, built for us next to the teacher's cottage, was completed and we moved out of Mr. DaCosta's house.

On weekends Mrs. Rob, Bebe, and I traveled to Scott's Pen to visit Teacher Rob. Sometimes Bebe and I went alone on the bus, as by then we were nine or ten years old. We knew the way, the bus driver knew us, and in those days nobody interfered with children.

It was a pleasure to visit Scott's Pen. The house sat on top of an isolated hill, the highest point in the area, and commanded a bird's eye view of the surrounding plain. I believe the original owner was an expatriate, probably an Englishman, because the house had only two large bedrooms, suitable for a bachelor who might have a guest or a couple with one or two children. A large entertainment area included a drawing room that jutted from the front of the house and was wrapped on three sides by a veranda. A long driveway wound its way up to the house from the gate at the road. The property was dotted with several fruit trees, brought originally from the Far East. I can hardly think of any tropical fruit tree that was not found at Scott's Pen—breadfruit, avocado, guava, citrus of every kind, mangoes of every variety, and tall coconut palms. In addition there were more unusual fruit trees, such as naseberry, soursop, sapodilla, cashew, custard apple, and jackfruit. We children roamed the property all day, playing, climbing trees, and eating so much fruit that we filled ourselves to capacity.

Whenever we spent the weekend at Scott's Pen, Bebe and I missed our Baptist church in Thompson Town. The Anglican church in Chapelton was about six miles away, too far for us to walk. One day when Bebe and I alighted from the Herolin country bus on the main road, we noticed a little church just opposite the side road we took to the house at Scott's Pen. I exclaimed, "Look Bebe, there's a church. The sign says Baptist Church of God."

"Could it be the same as our Baptist church in Thompson Town?" she wondered.

"We could try it out and see if we like it," I replied. So on Sunday morning, bright and early, we walked the half-mile to the little church, entered, and sat near the back. A woman sitting in the same pew greeted us warmly. So far so good.

A black woman of about forty years, in a long-sleeved white dress, appeared at the podium to conduct the service. She read a passage from St. Paul's Epistle to Timothy, with interjections of "Hallelujah!" or "Amen!" after every phrase. We found it strange that her "Hallelujah" punctuated even a reference to Satan in that passage. Bebe and I exchanged shocked glances. Neither of us was accustomed to this form of service. Then the woman proceeded to preach vociferously. It seemed she was ranting and raving as she preached while walking up and down the center aisle. At one point, she accidentally knocked off a woman's hat without even realizing it and, of course, without an apology. By this time Bebe and I were edgy and wondering how we could leave without being noticed. This church was not what we expected. Eventually it was time to pray, and each congregant prayed loudly and simultaneously. The church was a veritable Tower of Babel. In fact, some seemed to be speaking in tongues. They were so self-absorbed in their supplications that Bebe and I saw our opportunity. As if on cue, we crept out stealthily. No one seemed to notice our departure.

At a safe distance, we breathed a sigh of relief. "Whew! What was that?" Bebe queried.

"It was pandemonium!" I exclaimed. "I can't believe that was a church service." Needless to say, we never went back.

One weekend in 1950, Mrs. Rob quite inexplicably brought me to Kingston on a brief trip. On the way, she matter-of-factly informed me that my mother was in the hospital and that we were paying her a visit. I remember seeing Mum in the Kingston Public Hospital, her face ashen and her body wracked with pain. I was not allowed to stay very long. Several years later, I heard Mum recount what had happened. Surgery had been performed to remove a stomach ulcer, and an infection had developed. The wound had become septic and Mum ran a continuous low-grade fever. The doctor was not inclined to do anything, but a very conscientious and pushy nurse pressured him to go back to the site and drain the wound, thus saving her life. At the time I had no idea that my mum was so sick. It was only later that I realized that at age ten I could have lost my mother, my chief source of love and support. One of Mum's favorite quotes was "Children don't owe their parents anything, but we as parents owe our children everything, because we chose to bring them into the world."

On my arrival at Thompson Town elementary school I entered Standard One, in a class of about seventy pupils controlled by one teacher. Although I was lucky enough to have shoes, many of the children were barefoot, some of whom walked many miles to school. Attendance was lower on Fridays and during the harvesting season, when all children were expected to help their parents in the fields. Because of the many morning chores children had to perform, the school session did not begin until nine a.m. We sat on long wooden benches fronted with desks of the same size. The teacher stood before the class and instructed us orally with the aid of a blackboard.

Learning by rote was popular, so we had to memorize all the tables of measurement printed on the back cover of our exercise books. After lunch, we children would chant aloud the multiplication tables in a singsong tone. The educational thinking of the time was that we would automatically learn and remember what was instilled in our brains and that we would have these computations at our fingertips. We had single-line and double-line exercise books, the latter used for penmanship. We learned to form the cursive lowercase letters between the double lines. Capital letters, with flourishes almost as intricate as those made by medieval monks, rose to the line above.

Because of the size of the class, discipline was strictly enforced. Any misconduct, failure to learn our lessons, or neglected homework was "rewarded" with a flogging with a leather strap. I got a taste of the strap once for not knowing the correct answer to the teacher's question. Since it was not a happy experience, there was every incentive to learn my lessons thoroughly.

There were two recesses, one in the morning and another in the afternoon, and the school closed for one hour at lunch. During recess we played games in the schoolyard. Two opposing teams competed in passing a "ball" to team members while attempting to keep it out of the hands of the opponents. The ball was usually an orange or grapefruit, not too ripe to easily squash or splatter. The older children also cut vines from the forest to make skipping ropes. Turned by a playmate at each end, these were long enough to accommodate six or seven of us jumping rope.

After school each day, Mother Rob tutored me on remedial work in arithmetic, my weakest subject. She provided me a slate and slate pencil, then gave me an addition sum to work out. After the sum was completed and corrected, she erased it and set me another one, and then another. Next she went on to subtraction and continued in the same manner. We got through these pretty quickly, as I already knew how to add and subtract. When it came to multiplication she had to coach me, and then I worked out the examples on the slate. Once I was competent in multiplication, we went on to division, first simple division and then long division. After she showed me the steps, it was practice, practice, practice. By the end of my four years in Thompson Town, I was utterly tired of slates and did not want to see another one. Mother Rob also taught me to do mental arithmetic, computing simple sums in my head without writing them down. This was a really difficult exercise for me, but it increased my brain's agility. Eventually I got the hang of it and became quite proficient in mental arithmetic.

From time to time, maybe once a year, the movies came to town. In the hours prior to show time, a car with a loudspeaker drove through the village blaring out its theme song, "Now Is the Hour (When We Must Say Goodbye)." We children jumped with excitement because we knew the movies would be shown in the schoolhouse that evening. The large, sturdy concrete building was divided into three sections. The Lower Division, accommodating the junior classes, was sandwiched between the

Middle and Upper Divisions. Those divisions were completely enclosed while the Lower Division was open at two sides, with huge overhanging eaves to prevent rain from blowing in too far. The movies were shown in the Lower Division, as it was the most spacious area in the school and enjoyed "natural air conditioning" from the free-flowing breezes through the open sides. Practically the whole village attended. A white sheet was draped against the wall adjoining the Upper Division. We had to wait till after dark for the action to start. First the BBC's black-and-white newsreel was shown, apprising us colonials of happenings in the British Empire. Many of the news stories were about the British royal family.

Then came the part we children looked forward to eagerly—the comedies. Charlie Chaplin's silent movies were our favorites. His miming was so clever and the comedy so slapstick that we roared with laughter. One hilarious episode stuck in my mind. In the movie *The Bank,* Charlie was a janitor trying to win the favor of beautiful Edna, who usually ignored him. This time she was receptive to his overtures and allowed him to kiss her and run his fingers through her curly hair. But it was all only a dream. To his horror, he awoke to find himself kissing and running his fingers through the strings of the wet mop he used to clean the floor. Indeed, he had fallen asleep holding his mop, after sitting down for a short rest on his job as a janitor. People were very vocal in their pithy comments as the show proceeded, with the whole "theater" often erupting in raucous laughter.

The Jamaican dialect in this part of the country was slightly different from the Kingstonian drawl. Most of the young children did not even know or speak Standard English. One day when a few kids stood at the gate to our cottage, Mrs. Rob called out to them, "Come here!" They just stood and stared at her. "Come here," she repeated and received the same reaction. Eventually Mrs. Rob said, "Unoo cum yah"—which means "you all come here"—and immediately the kids came running. As middle-class children, Bebe and I were actively discouraged from using the Jamaican dialect. Mrs. Rob, Aunty, Mum—in fact, all my "mothers"—constantly corrected my speech, encouraging me to use the King's English. They understood that how I spoke and proper pronunciation were a passport to upward social mobility.

The mispronunciation of my name was a source of great annoyance to me. Up to the end of elementary school I was called by my middle name, Yvonne. In Thompson Town the schoolchildren called me "Yvanne," with an open 'a,' which I hated with a passion. Many years later I visited County Cork in Ireland and heard the very same accent—"Bab" for Bob, "map" for mop. I realized then that many of the forebears of the people of Thompson Town must have originated in that part of Ireland.

Thanks to Mrs. Rob's coaching, I moved quickly through the grades at school, even skipping Standard Three and Standard Five. By the age of ten I had reached Standard Six, the highest grade in the elementary school. In this class we were taught by the headmaster, Teacher Gayle, an excitable man with a great capacity to enjoy life.

Fair in complexion, he was what Jamaicans would refer to as a "red man." People with his ruddy complexion were often found in the parish of St. Elizabeth, where Teacher Gayle had been born and raised. Germans who came to Jamaica in the eighteenth and nineteenth centuries settled in isolated pockets around the island, and established towns with names like Germantown and Seaforth Town. The settlers inter-married with the local population, and in parts of St. Elizabeth one still finds a population with light skin, blue eyes, and blond or red hair, although sometimes the texture is more African than Caucasian.

Teacher Gayle was proficient in all the subjects but he loved the arts, especially singing. He formed a school choir and had us singing such old English ballads as "The Lass with the Delicate Air." That year, the Thompson Town school choir entered an eisteddfod, a singing competition popular in Wales and brought to the island by the British. Several schools from the parish of Clarendon gathered in the town of Spalding, ten or fifteen miles away. Our choir sang beautifully, especially the *sotto voce* passages, but came in second instead of first as Teacher Gayle had expected. He was convinced that politics were involved and the reason we were not awarded first place.

Disappointed, we returned home in a hired truck fitted with several rows of benches to seat us. Night had fallen and some of the children nodded off. Suddenly everyone was awakened. We were careening wildly in the dark. The out-of-control truck was rushing down a steeply descending mountain road. The road twisted and turned and our hearts were in our mouths. Many of us screamed and screamed. We thought we were going to die. Gradually the truck driver, who was quite experienced, managed to gear down and eventually stopped by turning the wheels toward the bank.

We all scrambled out with alacrity. Someone called out, "Come and see this!" The truck had stopped just twelve inches short of the precipice!

It turned out the brakes had failed, and God alone knows how the driver brought the truck to a halt. An angel had to be watching over us. We breathed a collective sigh of relief and thanked God for such a close escape. We had to wait hours for a mechanic to come and install new brakes. In that area, where transportation was difficult, especially at night, there was no possibility of exchanging the vehicle for another. We did not arrive home until about four a.m. but were thankful to be safe and sound.

Students who reached Standard Six could sit Jamaica Local Exams. Candidates who passed the Third Jamaica Local Exam, usually by the age of sixteen or seventeen, were eligible to enter teacher training college, to teach in an elementary school. I sat the First Jamaica Local mainly for practice at ten years old. While there was no desire on my part to become an educator, this exam afforded me a useful practice session in sitting my first big test. The all-important Island Scholarship exam would come later. The First Jamaica Local Exam was easy and I felt adequately prepared.

Three months later, the results were sent by telegram to Teacher Gayle, who read out the names of the successful candidates at the school assembly. My name was not among them. It seemed unbelievable that I had failed my first major exam. I was considered a bright student and expectations for me had been high. There was a sinking feeling in my chest, and tears welled up in my eyes but I held them back. I dared not cry in front of the entire school.

After dismissal I walked home dejectedly. Gloomily we ate supper and went to bed. At about ten p.m. a loud banging on the front door awakened us all. This was unusual because country folk retired early, like the chickens, and rose at the crack of dawn to complete the morning chores in the cool of the day. Again came another urgent rap. Mrs. Rob rose and opened the door. There stood Noel, the headmaster's son. He presented us with a copy of the *Jamaican Gazette* and a note from Teacher Gayle. The note stated that indeed I had passed the exam. My name had not been included among the general body of successful candidates because I attained *two* distinctions and my name was listed in a section near the front of the *Gazette*. A great weight was lifted from me. I was not such a failure after all! Overwhelmed, tears of joy now filled my eyes. Time had stood still when I thought I had flunked the exam. My confidence was restored. Now I could move on with my life.

Not long after, I sat the all-important scholarship exam but did not win one of the coveted island scholarships to enter secondary school. I did receive a half-scholarship, which covered tuition at St. Hugh's High School in Kingston. Since Aunty and Uncle Bert had moved to Kingston, where they had bought a house, I would be able to live at home again and ride the bus to and from school each day.

During my time in Thompson Town, I had returned home during Easter and Christmas holidays, and for summer vacations, but now it was time to pack all my belongings and leave for the last time. I was ambivalent in my feelings. On the one hand, I was sorry to leave Bebe and Mother Rob, who indeed had been a mother to me. On the other hand, I looked forward to the prospect of living in "civilization" again, and where I could enjoy more frequent visits with my mother.

Mother Rob had been fair in her treatment of me. I never felt like a poor relation and she devoted invaluable time and attention to teaching me, not only in academics but also in the arts and other skills, such as playing the piano, science projects, sewing, and handicraft. She read constantly, ordering library books through the mail. Her love of books, like Uncle Bert's, spilled over to me. A voracious reader, I would secretly borrow her books, devouring their contents when she was not at home—I recall reading *The Robe* and *The Big Fisherman* by Lloyd C. Douglas, and books by Grace Livingston Hill. All had a Christian theme but still were not considered suitable for ten-year-olds, as they all included romances between fair-haired heroines and tall, dark, handsome men with hazel eyes. A devout Christian who instilled in us positive values, Mrs. Rob never stridently imposed her beliefs on others. Rather she led by example, and remains a model for me up to this day.

Mother Rob encouraged me to embroider a doily, which was to be my parting gift to her. Embroidery was the one craft that I could do reasonably well. She bought the material, imprinted a pattern on it, and even provided the thread. All I had to do was put in my effort. There were flowers and green leaves, which required the labor-intensive satin stitch. Patience was not a virtue with me, and when it came to embroidering I grew bored easily. It took me a long time to complete the project. In fact, it was still unfinished when I left Thompson Town. It was several months before I completed the doily and mailed it, with a letter of appreciation, to Mrs. Rob.

The part that the Robinsons played in determining the direction of my life cannot be over-estimated. Mother Rob was an exemplary role model. Her husband, Teacher Rob, made it possible for me to experience attending boarding school, which had an overwhelming influence on my development.

Uncle Bert and I on the front porch of home

During my boarding days with the Smiths and the Robinsons, I always went home to Aunty and Uncle Bert during the vacations. Aunty always fiercely reminded me, "*This* is your home. *Always* remember that!" She knew that every child needed the stability of a home, especially as I led a somewhat nomadic life. At first I returned to them in Richmond. After Uncle Bert was transferred to Highgate, that was where I went.

Highgate, situated in the hills facing the prevailing northeast trade winds, enjoyed a salubrious climate. Many an afternoon when forced to nap, I was lulled to sleep by the soft whistling of the wind through the bamboo stands and fanned by natural air conditioning of the cool, zephyr breezes blowing the curtains at the open window.

Unlike malaria-ridden Richmond, Highgate sat on a plateau in the healthy climate that had encouraged its settlement by people of European descent. These were upper-middle-class families who lived in beautiful homes with gardens. Some were even able to afford Delco plants that provided electricity—Highgate was not yet on the island's power grid. A thriving town, Highgate had a number of businesses, an Anglican church, two high schools, and a cinema, and attracted many solid professionals, such as Dr. Dryden, who provided us children with the obligatory worm medicine.

During each school vacation we were subjected to a three-day de-worming process. First we were given a huge capsule containing a liquid, rather like fish oil capsules. The next day we were dosed with castor oil, and on the third day Epsom salts was given for good measure. This purging process cleaned our digestive system of worms and any other strange objects. Purging was absolutely necessary in those days because children ate so much worm-infested fruit, such as mangoes and guavas, some with numerous small seeds that were also consumed. I was told these small seeds could get stuck in the appendix, causing acute appendicitis. Whether this fear was based on medical science or merely an old wives' tale is anybody's guess.

It was while Uncle Bert was stationed in Highgate that he and a few other maverick stationmasters were forced into early retirement for speaking out against certain deficiencies in the Jamaica Government Railway. We moved from government housing into a rented cottage, and Uncle Bert took a temporary job on contract at the Kingston station. It meant that he was away during the week, returning home only on weekends.

One night when Uncle Bert was in Kingston, Dahlia and I, who shared a bed in the back room, were startled awake from deep slumber by a rattling noise. Normally we were completely dead to the world all night, but this noise was nearby and insistent. Sleepy-eyed, we slowly became aware that the outside door, which opened into our room, was shaking vigorously. We froze. Mesmerized, we saw the metal draw latch moving up and down. The wooden door with its flimsy latch rattled and shook. Paralyzed with fear, we were too scared to even scream. Would the latch hold, or would the ferocious shaking break it open? This nightmare continued for what seemed like an eternity before it stopped. We heard footsteps outside as the would-be intruder moved from the side to the front of the house. Then he assaulted the front door, trying to break it down.

By then Aunty was up. Brave woman that she was, she brought out Uncle Bert's rifle. He had tried to teach her to shoot, but not much of the instruction stuck in her brain. The intruder did not know that, though. It was a moonlit night, and through the clear glass upper panes of the front door she could clearly see a man. The small kerosene lamp in the drawing room flickered, but its light could not compete with the brilliance of the full moon outside. Aunty raised the gun to her shoulder, pointed it at the intruder, cocked it, and shouted determinedly, "If you break in on us, I'll shoot!" In a jiffy, the man disappeared and we all breathed a sigh of relief. It was a good thing she did not have to carry out her threat. It turned out that if Aunty had fired, the way she had cocked the gun would have sent her sprawling backward.

I was a big coward and could not believe that Aunty, a short stocky lady, barely five foot tall, was so courageous. There were so many admirable qualities she displayed, which I hope I would emulate if faced with a similar situation. I do not know if I would pass the test.

One Christmas vacation when I was about seven, I was the only child in the house, as Dahlia had returned to Kingston to spend the holidays with her family. One day was bright and sunny, the blue sky dotted with small, puffy white clouds.

In the distance I heard the tom-tom of drums. Gradually the sound got louder—bonga ... bong bong, bonga ... bong bong. Bursting with excitement, I raced to the front fence. A John Canoe band was approaching! Now I also could hear the shrill sound of the fifes above the deep bass of the drums.

John Canoe—or Jonkonnu, has its roots in West African traditions that slaves brought to the New World. The chief performers are of African descent and the dance and music—especially the drumming, and masks point to its African origins. After emancipation of the slaves, there appears to have been an infusion of some English traditions of masking and mumming. The bands came out from Boxing Day—the day after Christmas, to New Year's Day. Sadly, the tradition of John Canoe is dying in Jamaica and probably only occurs in isolated areas of the countryside now.

I climbed the fence, trying to see better. The band members were dressed in colorful costumes. One depicted a large plumed bird in colors of red, yellow, and green. Another wore a cow's head, and yet another sported a horse's head. Most frightening of all was the Devil. Painted red, he had a long tail, two horns on top of his head, and a pitchfork in his hand. All held wooden cutlasses—machetes, aloft as they danced.

They approached me at the fence, begging for money. I recoiled but still stood my ground in the yard. When not given money, they raised their menacing cutlasses in a mock gesture of attack. I retreated still further. The front gate was securely latched and, even though the band occupied the entire road, there was no danger of them entering our property. Or so I thought. I spied one band member open our neighbor's gate and march right up to Mrs. Brown's front door. What horror! Not waiting to see any more, I sped into the house, into my room, and under the bed. If one of these creatures had the gall to enter Mrs. Brown's house, I knew we too were not immune to their incursions. It took Aunty a long time to pry my cowering little body from under the bed.

Aunty and Uncle Bert enjoyed a happy life in Highgate, with many good friends, chief of whom were the Yarids. Mr. Yarid, originally from Lebanon, owned a dry goods store in Annatto Bay, about ten miles away on the coast, and the family was relatively well to do. Mrs. Yarid, née Anderson, was my mother's distant cousin. A very generous lady, she often gave Aunty remnants from bolts of cloth to make dresses for Dahlia and me. The Yarids had two children, a boy whom they called "Son," and Dorothy, who was treated like a little princess, especially by her doting father. Mrs. Yarid's niece, Sybil, lived with them for a while, and later also spent some time living with us, while I attended high school. Sybil was five or six years older than I and, at fifteen, considered herself quite grown up. I was the "little sister" who tagged along and got in the way.

When I was either eight or nine years old my mother decided I should become acquainted with her family roots. That summer we traveled by taxi from Kingston to the dark green hills in the mountainous spine at the center of the island. The car laboriously climbed the narrow winding road cut into the contours of the hillsides, with a steep rock face on one side and a precipitous basin dropping off on the other. Mum told me that this hazardous road, with multiple hairpin turns, was known as The Devil's Racecourse. We arrived at Guy's Hill, the largest town in the area and the meeting point of three parishes—St. Catherine, St. Ann, and St. Mary. We took a room for the weekend at the only guesthouse in town.

The following day we ventured up to the little village of Blackstonedge, situated about three thousand feet above sea level in the parish of St. Ann, where my mother was born and raised. On the way we were greeted heartily by a number of villagers who had known her as a child. We visited Miss Fran, my mother's elderly cousin. Miss Fran was a tall, white, thin, almost skeletal figure, whom Mum would eerily resemble in her declining years. Miss Fran's son, Lucian Hayes, was about my mother's age. Unfortunately I did not get to meet him. Mum told me that in their youth he had taught her to drive, and gotten them involved in many hair-raising adventures. She told me tales of Lucian driving at such high speeds that their heads hit the roof as the car bounced over the country roads.

Next we made our way along the rocky, unpaved road to the end of Greywood, a section of Blackstonedge, where stood a ramshackle old house that had seen better days. There we met Miss Mag, the wife of one of Mum's uncles. I was frightened of Miss Mag, an old white woman with an enormous goiter. I later met her three daughters, Mum's first cousins, in Kingston. They were all fair and I remember the youngest, Tilly, was blonde with blue eyes.

We passed Tyndale, Mum's childhood home. The house and land, with bananas and other cash crops, had been inherited by Mum's father, Urquhart Anderson, from his forebears. People called my grandfather "Mas'" because he was descended from one of the old landowning families in Jamaica. Mum related to me that her grandfather had twelve sons, and the land was subdivided amongst them. Miss Mag's property at Greywood and Mas' Urquhart's house and land at Tyndale were two parcels of the subdivided inheritance.

Mas' Urquhart and his wife, Miss Angie, were childless and, to prove a point, he went outside the marriage to a widow in the village, begetting a child he brought back to be raised in his home. Miss Angie, cold and resentful, showed no love for this child—who was my mother, although she did provide for all her physical needs. A promising student, Mum was

sent to Kingston to attend Alpha Academy, where she passed
the Junior Cambridge Exam set by Cambridge University in
England. Before she could sit the Senior Cambridge exam,
she was pulled from school at age fourteen to care for her
stepmother, who had fallen ill. After his wife's death Mas'
Urquhart went to pieces. He took to drink and lost the house,
land, and all his worldly possessions. Maybe because of his
Scottish roots—he was an Anderson after all—he was partial
to his "waters," referring not to Scotch whiskey but to the local
rum. Mum told me that when she was growing up her father
never suffered from a cold or the flu: the large quantities of
rum he imbibed insulated him from all such illnesses.

Wending our way along the rocky dirt road, we reached
the house where my grandfather now lived. He was an old
man, tall and rather gaunt, with white skin and grey hair.
Mum told me that she had never known him with anything
but grey hair; she had once asked him what color his hair had
been, to which he replied it had been brown. On the day I
saw him, my grandfather had large sores on his shins. He had
fallen on the rocky road, maybe from weakness or a state of
inebriation. I was absolutely afraid of him, and he completely
ignored me. He talked to Mum as if I did not even exist.

I did not really know my grandfather. I met him only that
one time, and what little I knew about him was recounted by
my mother. Not long after our trip, Mum visited him on his
deathbed. She told me later that he showed deep remorse for
having wasted his patrimony and having nothing to leave to
her, his only child.

It was in 1950, while I was boarding with the Robinsons, that
Aunty and Uncle Bert Palmer bought a home at No. 17 Kew

Road, in a respectable middle-class neighborhood of Kingston. The three-bedroom stucco house occupied a corner lot, with the front gate on Kew Road and a large back gate on Crescent Road, where vehicles entered the yard. This gate also offered access to a stand-alone garage that was later converted into a two-bedroom rental bungalow. In the main house, the polished wooden floors contrasted with the step-down tiled areas of the front porch, kitchen, dining room, and bathroom to the back. Soon after the Palmers moved in, they added a veranda to the side of the front bedroom. This was often the coolest part of the house, as it was shaded on one side by a large East Indian mango tree and by a tall black mango tree on another side. Two squat, wide Julie mango trees stood on the lawn on either side of the front walkway. When the veranda was completed, everyone celebrated with a drink of rum and ginger ale, including a small one for eleven-year-old me. While it was not common practice to provide children with liquor, this was considered a special occasion, so I was included.

The move to Kew Road pleased me enormously. Not only was I back in "civilization" again, but there were more opportunities to see my mother. Mum came home to Kew Road on her one day off each week. At the Melrose Hotel downtown, she had graduated from the catering department to the front office, where she used the typing and bookkeeping skills she'd acquired at commercial school. Mum often did fun things with me on her day off, such as taking me to the movies and to the beach.

Most of all, I looked forward to our attending the annual Christmas pantomime produced at the Ward Theatre downtown. This was a musical comedy stage-production for family entertainment. It started off as a typically British production loosely based on fairy tales like *Cinderella*, or stories such as *Dick Whittington and His Cat* or *Jack and the Beanstalk*. The cast always included an actor who cross-dressed to play the part of a woman. Also included were small skits poking fun at current events in Jamaican society. These skits, spoken in the local dialect and performed by local comedy teams, such as Bim and Bam or by Jamaican folklorist and radio personality Louise Bennett, produced the greatest applause. Over the years, local teams began writing scripts for the pantomime, which gave them a distinctly Jamaican flavor. There were pantomimes on B'rer Anancy, a smart spider from Afro-Caribbean folklore. Eventually the local pantomimes no longer even faintly resembled their English counterparts, simply becoming local plays with long runs extending way past the Christmas holiday season, one year even continuing until Easter. Mum never missed taking me to the pantomime, except for the year Uncle Bert gathered friends' children and fourteen of us congregated in the gallery to watch the performance. As one of the older kids by then, I was responsible for helping Uncle Bert keep the younger ones in line.

It was at Kew Road that I experienced my first major hurricane. On August 17, 1951, Hurricane Charlie dealt a serious blow to the island. In previous years hurricanes had been given only female names, and although they threatened, they never hit us. Ironically, Charlie brought widespread devastation. Did that mean most women talk but do not act out their threats, whereas men mean business?

In 1951, we had no television so we depended on radio forecasts, which declared that for sure Hurricane Charlie was headed directly toward our island. Mum was home because of the impending storm. We did all we could to prepare for the coming onslaught. Uncle Bert obtained plywood to batten down all the windows. We stocked up on canned food, candles, and lanterns. Water was stored in the bathtub and any other containers we could get our hands on. Then we waited.

As a child about to experience her first hurricane, Charlie could not arrive soon enough for me. I listened excitedly to the weather forecasts, and darted about as my mother calmly whirred the sewing machine while mending articles of clothing. I could not understand how she could be so serene, because Mum was not naturally such a calm person. Looking back now, I believe she was praying silently. At eight p.m. I cried out, "Why is the hurricane not here yet? The radio said the winds would start at eight o'clock." At eight-thirty I continued in the same vein, and again at nine o'clock. Eventually, around ten, wind speeds started picking up, with gusts blowing ferociously.

As the wind howled and the deafening noise of falling trees and roofs ripping off grew in magnitude, I became scared. It was only because the adults remained calm that I did not lose my cool, at least on the surface. Privately I was really frightened. Despite our precautions, water penetrated through the cracks of the enclosed tiled front porch and the dining room and kitchen to the back, which became completely flooded. Luckily those areas were a step down from the rest of the house. Two of the bedrooms got wet, the only dry room being Uncle Bert's on the leeward side of the house. We all bundled in there while the wind roared. Looking through the window, I saw, with fear and trembling, a tall coconut tree in the neighbor's yard swaying in the howling wind, its fronds touching the ground as the wind whipped it from one side to the other. Surely that tree would not be standing in the morning! With horror I realized that the tree was so close, if it fell on our side it could easily demolish our house. Finally and mercifully I fell asleep.

On waking in the morning, the day was calm, bright, and sunny. The first thing I did was run to the window to see if that coconut tree was still standing. Miracle of miracles, it stood triumphantly!

Later in the day one of the family from Molynes Road, by picking his way around obstacles of debris, arrived by bicycle to check on us. He told us that Mama Jen's and Poppa Fred's old house there had survived the destruction of the majestic eucalyptus tree that, miraculously, fell along the length of the fence. If it had fallen to either side, a house would have been completely annihilated. We ventured out into the neighborhood to view the damage wrought by the hurricane. So many trees were toppled that we could see for miles in several directions. Telephone and electricity poles lay prone on the ground, their wires dangling. Roofs were ripped off. Galvanized zinc sheets, the popular roofing material in those days, were scattered far and wide after a night of sailing through the air. Some houses were utterly destroyed. Oddly enough, the newly constructed concrete houses suffered the greatest damage, while Kew House, a large old two-story building that was the former Great House of the area, still stood. Something has to be said about the materials and workmanship of the older buildings, in contrast to more modern construction techniques. I was flabbergasted by the devastation and it was only then that I knew a hurricane was something to be taken seriously, a force that could wreak terrible damage on lives and property. I could only thank God that my family and I survived without serious loss.

Soon after the hurricane passed through, Mama Jen, who had been suffering from eye trouble, went blind and could no longer manage her household at Molynes Road. She came to live at Kew Road where she was tenderly and lovingly cared for by Aunty, her only surviving daughter.

Although Mama Jen was not my blood relative, she was a grandmother to me. Despite her physical infirmities, I never once heard Mama Jen complain or rail against God. Her unflinching faith and calm demeanor were qualities to be emulated. Always looking on the bright side, Mama Jen had a stock of jokes she would tell and retell on demand. Because she was such a good storyteller, we always laughed, even though the jokes were all too familiar. Mama Jen spent most of her days sitting in her rocking chair in the hall, yet she still was able to perform a useful function. The young couple who rented the bungalow in the back would bring their infant son to rest on Mama Jen's ample bosom. Humming, she rocked the fretful child, who in a few seconds would settle down and fall asleep peacefully.

Mama Jen had been an avid reader all her life, with romance novels being her favorite literature. When she went blind, I read to her books either acquired or borrowed from the library. One summer we ran out of reading material and I decided to write my own novel to read to her. This was my first attempt to write anything other than school essays. I thought it was pretty good and Mama Jen was complimentary. I have no idea what became of the manuscript—it probably got thrown out when I moved from Kew Road.

In 1952, I started as a day student at St. Hugh's High School, where I had won the half-scholarship. I lived permanently at home and either took the city bus or walked the two and a half miles through the city to and from school. One day while walking home, a brown-skinned lady in a housedress called out to me from the veranda of a house I was passing and invited me into the yard. Being obedient of my elders, I did as she requested. She did not give me her name, but examined me carefully from the veranda where she was standing. Then she called to an old lady inside, to come take a look at me. Finally she said I could go. I was really puzzled by this behavior and, on reaching home, told my aunt. Aunty listened very solemnly, then announced that the women were my father's wife and mother. This was the first I knew that my father was alive, that he had a wife, or that they lived on our street. I always thought my father was dead, because that is what my mother had told me when I was five or six years old. I guess she was right in a way, because he was dead to us both.

Some time elapsed before, while attending Sunday school at St. Clement's in the neighborhood, I saw three smaller children there who shared my last name—Smellie. As this was an unusual name, I suspected they were my half-siblings. We did not speak to each other and I did not know what they knew. To my relief, the family moved shortly after that.

Now that the cat was out of the bag, my mother admitted that a mutual friend was trying to get her to allow my father to meet me. Still very bitter, Mum adamantly refused. She confided to me that my father had not wanted me, had refused to marry her when I was on the way, that he'd suggested she have an abortion, and gave no support when I was born. She was particularly hurt that when she needed money to buy milk he had refused to give it. I do not remember having any particular feelings about my father at this revelation. I had no real curiosity about him. He was not a part of my life and I would just as soon not have had anything to do with him and his family. I was perfectly happy with my life with Aunty and Uncle Bert, and with the opportunity to see my mother once a week.

At St. Hugh's High School

On January 1952 I entered St. Hugh's High School, an all-girls Anglican school of about four hundred students, situated at the end of a cul-de-sac on Leinster Road in Kingston. The grounds were extensive, accommodating the preparatory school as well as the high school. A big old house served as the main administrative building, while classrooms and a pavilion for assembly occupied several outlying buildings. There also was ample room on the grounds for netball fields and tennis courts.

The headmistress, Mrs. Rita Landale, often displayed certain affectations in her speech and manners, rather reminiscent of ladies in Jane Austen's novels. Quite the lady, she maintained discipline in a quiet manner, while depending heavily on the assistant headmistress, as well as on the prefect system, to enforce the school's rules. The prefects were seventeen- and eighteen-year-old senior girls in the Sixth Form who were assigned to keep order among the younger students. In our school system, each grade was referred to as a form, for example Form 3B, or Form 4A. Every morning each class, led by its prefect, marched single file down to the pavilion hall where we lined up for assembly. The hall had no seats, only standing room for the student body. We stood in neat rows, form by form, and although packed in tightly the heat was somewhat relieved by the building's open sides with wide, overhanging eaves.

With all the teachers seated on the stage overlooking us, Mrs. Landale conducted morning prayers. We started off with a hymn, accompanied by a pianist positioned in a corner of the stage. As a music student, I was coerced by the Head Girl, who assisted the headmistress and staff in student matters, to play the hymn. Being in the spotlight was something I never enjoyed, and playing the piano for the school prayers was not my cup of tea. I demurred for a long time with the excuse that I did not know a march, which had to be played for the student body to exit the hall at the end of assembly. The Head Girl offered to play the march and continued to do so for a while. One day she was absent and I had to provide the march too; luckily, I had been practicing one.

After prayers the headmistress announced the names of all the pupils who had earned stars, as well as those who had received detentions resulting from refused lessons because of poor work, or order marks due to bad conduct. Because of the small size of the school, Mrs. Landale and the teachers knew every single one of us personally, so it was very difficult to remain in anonymity. Usually she ended with a homily about behavior or how the school uniform should be worn. Once Mrs. Landale brought the attention of the whole school to an unfortunate girl by saying, "Dear, a little bit of skin is showing in front." There were gaping spaces between the buttons of a rather tight blouse, and the poor girl was severely embarrassed.

Our uniform consisted basically of three pieces—a blouse, a pleated skirt buttoned all the way down the front, and a bloomer worn beneath the skirt and which had a waistband and elastic on the legs. The bloomer made the use of a petticoat unnecessary, and when we took part in sports we simply took off our skirts and played in the blouse and bloomer. The uniform was not too bad except that it was a green color most of us abhorred. In fact, children from other schools teased us, calling us "Green Lizards." To complement the uniform was a broad-brimmed, 1920s-style jippi-jappa straw hat, which caused a continual struggle between the staff and students. We girls found the hats extremely old-fashioned and often neglected to wear them. The teachers, however, insisted hats be worn whenever we were on the streets, since the hatband was embossed with a picture of a white swan, the symbol of our patron saint—St. Hugh of Lincoln, set above the school motto, *Fidelitas*.

There was one occasion when we were glad to have our unfashionable broad-brimmed jippi-jappa straw hats. During my second year, in November 1953, we were excited to hear that the newly crowned Queen Elizabeth II was visiting Jamaica. Schoolchildren from all over the island gathered to welcome Her Majesty at Sabina Park in Kingston, a venue for important cricket matches on the island. In our hats and school uniforms, we stood for hours in the broiling sun, waved our tiny Union Jack flags enthusiastically, and sang "God Save the Queen." In those days no one knew anything about sunscreen and the importance of bottled water. Instead, we were advised to drink plenty of water before getting there, and to keep a bar of chocolate candy—yesteryear's energy bar, in our pocket in case we felt faint from hunger. I was most surprised that the teachers would advise us to eat a chocolate bar because sweets, considered the prime source of tooth cavities, were not encouraged by adults. The Queen, accompanied by her handsome consort Prince Philip, looked young and radiant, although her pink cheeks were probably caused by the heat. There was no outward sign that she was grieving the death of her father, King George

VI, who had passed away the previous year. As teenagers, we were more tickled to see Prince Philip than the Queen herself. At the end of the day, I was horrified to find that my skirt pocket was a sticky mess. The unused chocolate bar had melted in the broiling heat of the midday sun.

During my first year I became quite friendly with Brenda Shim, a quiet Chinese girl who sat near me. Once she invited me to her home, where I met her parents and siblings. What surprised me was that her father did the cooking for the household. Jamaican men typically took no interest in domestic affairs, leaving those and child-rearing duties to their wives. I remember Brenda's father prepared a huge bowl of soup that was placed in the center of the dining table and each person took from it. That was a novel experience for me, as at home food was plated before it was served.

My first year in high school was a breeze. Except for Algebra and French, which I was beginning for the first time, I was well versed in the other subjects, as we had studied them in depth for the scholarship program in elementary school. To my great surprise, I came first in class, earning distinctions in all subjects. In our schools, students were placed according to exam results from first to last, and then streamed according to performance. The girls vied keenly to reach the top of the class, and I was under pressure to maintain the highest marks throughout my school career.

After completing my first year at St. Hugh's, Teacher Rob still felt I should have won a full scholarship, including tuition, books, and board. He offered to have me spend the summer at his home at Scott's Pen, and receive coaching to sit the scholarship exam a second time. It was with some trepidation that I took up the offer, because Teacher Rob was known to be a hard taskmaster. His older children were deathly afraid of him. I once heard that his eldest daughter actually turned green with fright when he was preparing to whip her for not knowing her lessons. However, Teacher Rob was surprisingly patient with me. He provided me with an exercise book in which he wrote down, in indelible pencil, the answers to questions I could not answer. Each day he would ask the same questions in math, English, and general knowledge; whenever I could not remember the answer, he wrote it down. Eventually I was able to quickly answer all the questions posed. I re-sat the scholarship exam, and this time won one of the two coveted scholarships for the parish of Clarendon. With a full scholarship I could have transferred to another school with greater name recognition, but as I had already started at St. Hugh's and had made some friends, I elected to stay there and board at the school hostel.

After coming first again in my second year, this distinction of honor was wrested away from me by Diana Lindo, who had entered the school a year after me. Diana cultivated my friendship and at that stage I considered her my best friend. Thereafter, as we progressed through school, Diana and I always took top honors, sometimes with me taking first place and at other times vice versa. As "birds of a feather flock together," we—the two brightest students in the class, stuck together and Brenda Shim was edged out. However, Brenda remained loyal to me throughout our school years. We lost touch when she left school to help in her father's store, after sitting the Senior Cambridge Exam in Form 5. It was only in 2004 that we reconnected, after forty-eight years.

Diana and I were in the A stream throughout, which meant we studied Latin instead of Home Economics and attended Mrs. Kensett's math class instead of Miss Thomas' class for the slower math students. Mrs. Kensett was a brilliant mathematician who, unfortunately, did not know how to impart her knowledge. She would give us some notes on each new concept, which we did not really understand. Then she taught mainly by giving examples, solving different types of problems on the blackboard. When we were given our own problems to solve, she migrated around the room, stopping at each desk to see how we were doing. If we seemed stuck, she filled in the next line for us. Winsome, one of the girls in our class, was bright but rather indolent. Mrs. Kensett would come to Winsome's desk and fill in a line. The second time around, Mrs. Kensett would fill in the next line, and this continued until Mrs. Kensett had completed the problem without Winsome lifting a finger. It was only afterwards that the teacher realized how she had been used.

Mrs. Saunders, our math teacher in the junior forms, got really frustrated with Winsome. One day when the annual prize-giving day was approaching, she made a sarcastic remark in her singsong voice, "Winsome, at prize-giving we ought to have a category for the laziest girl in school. In which case, *you* would get it!"

The most intimidating of the teachers was Miss Kingdon, a tall, big-boned, masculine looking figure with thinning hair. In all the years that St. Hugh's girls knew Miss Kingdon, she looked the same, not a day older and not a day younger. She occupied a small apartment upstairs in the main building and assumed the role of warden or watchman over the school grounds. She especially undertook to be guardian over the luxuriant grapevine that grew on the outer edge of the main building's veranda, entwining itself in the latticework of the wooden rails. Students were strictly forbidden from touching the clusters of luscious green fruit, which were carefully wrapped in cheesecloth on the vine, and woe betide any girl Miss Kingdon caught stealing them.

A history teacher as well as a teacher of religious knowledge, Miss Kingdom was a product of the Calvinist tradition.

She was excessively biased in portraying historical figures, although we did not realize it at the time. Oliver Cromwell was her hero. She had no use for English kings who showed Roman Catholic sympathies, such as Charles I and Charles II, and she referred to James I as "the greatest fool in Christendom." She was particularly hard on those students who happened to be Catholic, giving them poorer marks for assignments. Even though we were not very experienced with life, we did have the sense that it was not fair for Miss Kingdon to inflict her biases on us. If we regurgitated all that she rammed down our throats and produced that material in the tests, she gave glowing marks, but now I know this was not the best way to educate young, impressionable minds. We were not allowed to look at material and decide for ourselves what we wanted to believe.

She also had her pets. By the time we reached Sixth Form, we realized she showed favoritism toward Diana Lindo in the use of the reference books in the library. Miss Kingdon also was school librarian, acting like the proprietor of her domain, so much so that we girls always referred to the library as "Miss Kingdon's library." With no more than two copies of a particular reference book, the girls scrambled to get them whenever we were given assignments. Miss Kingdon, however, always set aside a copy for Diana before anyone else got a chance to do research on an assigned book. Her actions probably stemmed from the belief that Diana was her best student, with the potential to gain the prestigious Jamaica Scholarship for Girls. Cambridge University in England set the Higher Schools Examination for all overseas students in the British Commonwealth, and what better way of enhancing the reputation of a school than to have one of its students come first in the island in this exam, thus gaining a scholarship for entry to a British university.

Granted that Diana and I were academic rivals throughout our school years, my attitude towards her might have involved some jealousy on my part. We still remained "friends" but in the back of my mind I remembered that she cultivated friendship with me in Form 4B when she wished to find out more about her competitor. In Sixth Form, when we did not choose to study the same subjects, except for history, we were not as close. Although I was a little upset by Miss Kingdon's overt favoritism, I did not grumble outwardly. All the other girls, especially those who entered the school later and therefore did not progress through all the grades with Diana, resented the preferential treatment given her by Miss Kingdon. They really disliked her intensely but my attitude was more ambivalent. I remember that she once invited me to her home where I met her parents, her brother, and her younger sister. She even told me how she played a trick on her brother. A couple of Venezuelan girls who had come to Jamaica to learn English were living in the house next door. Her brother, who spoke no Spanish because he had studied French in school, asked Diana, who did speak the language, to tell him how to say, "You are beautiful." Instead, she taught him the Spanish for "You are ugly," which he immediately tried on the pretty girls next door. Of course he was unsuccessful in getting a date with either of them.

The curriculum at St. Hugh's was heavily weighted toward the liberal arts. Classes in physical education, music appreciation, and art were offered on a weekly basis but I was not very good in those subjects. In my day, very little science was included in the curriculum. In the lower forms we studied general science, while botany and biology were offered at higher levels. Any girl who wanted to study medicine had to take afternoon lessons in physics and chemistry at St. George's College for Boys in Kingston.

Miss Baxter, the science teacher, was highly qualified but rather ineffective in keeping discipline in the lab. One day I happened to be at the same table with two or three girls, including Winsome, "the laziest girl in school." While Miss Baxter was trying to teach, Winsome kept up a running commentary. "What is the plural for bwoy (boy)?" she whispered.

We were puzzled. Finally we responded "Bwoys!"

"No," she corrected. "It's de bwoy dem."

We all laughed because in the Jamaican dialect "de bwoy dem" was perfectly right. We just were not as well versed as Winsome in the dialect. I could not understand how Miss Baxter did not pick up on our inattention and our disruptive behavior. I made a mental note to avoid being at the same table with Winsome from then on, because I had every intention of keeping my grades up.

When I reached Sixth Form, I joined the Alliance Française, an extracurricular outreach organization from the French Embassy, which students studying French were encouraged to do. As members, we were invited a couple of times to view movies aboard French ships visiting our island. Once we attended a cocktail party at the embassy in honor of French naval officers whose battleship was visiting the port of Kingston. I was about seventeen at the time and thrilled to meet and converse with handsome French officers. Looking back now, they must have been terribly bored to have to talk with gauche schoolgirls who had seen nothing of life yet.

Extracurricular activities were few and far between. The school's annual sports day brought out the girls who displayed great athleticism. The boys from our Anglican brother school, the all-boys Kingston College, had great fun girl-watching, with many of their remarks not being very complimentary. Once, St. Hugh's produced an operetta in which I participated as the rejected suitor of the Japanese princess in the Chrysanthemum court. A couple of times the school organized a fair, with stalls offering games and food, a merry-go-round, and a dance party on the tennis courts near the edge of the school grounds. This was in the mid-1950s, when The Platters and the Everly Brothers were at the height of their popularity, so we were very happy to join in the dancing.

Of the extracurricular activities available to us, the highlight was the biennial Schools Drama Festival in which St. Hugh's always participated. It was the practice of the secondary schools in Jamaica to hire English teachers on two- or three-year contracts to teach English Language and English Literature. One such teacher, Miss Mather, wrote a Jamaican play entitled *Market Women,* which was our school's entry to the competition in 1956. Our play was a deviation from the norm, because most schools performed scenes from Shakespeare or other foreign plays. Since we played the roles of market women, we had to speak in the dialect, which was difficult for Miss Mather to get right. Our lead actress, Barbara Straughn, who was extremely talented, not only changed the syntax so the dialog sounded authentic, but also threw herself into all the passion and pathos of her role. Proud to be portraying a local scene, we spent many hours practicing our Jamaican dialects, something that did not come naturally to us since we all were constantly admonished by our elders to speak proper English. At the school hostel dinner table, we practiced with our schoolmates:

"Pass de salt fi me." (Pass me the salt.)

"Me no like dis food. It have no taste." (I don't like this food. It's tasteless.)

"Is only 'cause me 'ungry why me even nyam off dis food." (It's only because I'm hungry that I even eat this food.)

Finally the big night arrived. We were filled with anticipation and our nerves were on tenterhooks. Then we settled down to playing our parts, and soon it was over. The applause was thunderous. Our play received wide acclaim and we were asked to repeat it half a dozen times at various venues. We reveled in the unaccustomed light of instant fame, which brought some recognition to our school.

Our Sixth Form teachers often complained that our fifteen-member class was too boisterous, and that, as prefects, we set the worst example ever to the student body. One classmate kept telling me we were probably the best set of students St. Hugh's ever had. The competition among us was always very keen for the first ten places in the school exams, often with differences of only one point between one place and the next. My schoolmate was right, as the results of the Higher Schools Exam, our final exam, bore out. Not only did the class achieve one hundred percent passes, but Diana Lindo did win the Jamaica Scholarship for Girls. Everyone at St. Hugh's was jubilant and the president of the school board entertained us as guests of honor at a garden party at his home.

Oddly enough, Barbara Straughn, our star actress of *Market Women* fame, was not allowed to enter Sixth Form to sit the Higher Schools Exam. Any candidate wanting to continue her education was carefully vetted by the headmistress and staff. After all, the reputation of the school was at stake and Barbara's results had fallen short of what was expected. So Barbara transferred to another school, sat the exam, and passed. When Mrs. Landale was told of Barbara's success, she had the gall to exclaim, "We did not just get fifteen out of fifteen passes. We got sixteen out of sixteen!" We were appalled. After all that Barbara and her acting had done to put St. Hugh's in the spotlight, we felt she should have been given a chance. She was a bright student but probably had not devoted enough time to academic subjects because of her repeat stage performances on behalf of the school.

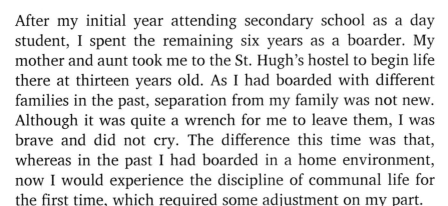

After my initial year attending secondary school as a day student, I spent the remaining six years as a boarder. My mother and aunt took me to the St. Hugh's hostel to begin life there at thirteen years old. As I had boarded with different families in the past, separation from my family was not new. Although it was quite a wrench for me to leave them, I was brave and did not cry. The difference this time was that, whereas in the past I had boarded in a home environment, now I would experience the discipline of communal life for the first time, which required some adjustment on my part.

The hostel, located at No. 4 Leinster Road and a five-minute walk from the school, was managed by three old maid sisters, the Cotterells. Miss Gigi, the eldest, was in charge. Miss Mae, a retired teacher from St. Hugh's, was quite the disciplinarian. She kept in contact with her friends on the teaching staff and thus was able to discover which girls had received order marks for bad conduct or refused lessons for poor work, which precluded them from going on weekend outings. Miss Edith, the youngest sister, was largely innocuous and usually ignored us. All three sisters appeared really old to us. They were tall, well-built ladies who dyed their hair blue, wore corsets, and earned the nickname "the waist touchers" since their breasts seemed unable to defy the force of gravity.

The hostel was a rambling house two doors away from the main gate of the long winding driveway leading to the school. The hostel had been converted to accommodate about thirty students, who came mostly from rural areas. While private rooms were allocated to the Cotterell sisters, the two largest rooms were converted to dormitories for the senior and junior girls. Each dormitory was lined with rows of double-decker beds, with wardrobes and chests of drawers interspaced between. It took me a while to get used to only a small area around my bed as "my space." We had to share the wardrobes and each girl was allotted a single drawer for folded clothes, intimate items, and toiletries.

With only one bathroom, there was a very strict schedule for bath times, with some students bathing in the morning and others before bedtime. A single washbasin located in an accessible area just outside the bathroom could be used when someone else was occupying the bathroom. The rules included keeping the washbasin and the bath scrupulously clean. We cleaned them before and after use. Each person was allotted fifteen minutes to complete her daily ablutions as well as these chores.

Homework sessions, presided over by Miss Mae, took place in the converted garage and lasted a mandatory two hours each afternoon. St. Hugh's burdened us with an overload of homework, and if any of the lazy students claimed she had none, Miss Mae gave an assignment to memorize a Bible passage or a collect taken from the Anglican prayer book.

Other afterschool activities included piano lessons, given by Miss Mae to some of the girls who paid extra for this service. A roster listing a half hour's practice daily for each music student was posted, with some girls practicing in the morning and others in the afternoon. As I was a pupil of Miss Violet Mills, whose studio was off campus, I was not given a favored time on the practice schedule but I did get my full half hour. The first person to practice at six a.m. each day was Hope Murray, a senior student who later became Head Girl at the school. An excellent pianist, she treated us to the strains of Beethoven's "Moonlight Sonata" or "Für Elise" first thing in the morning.

Before dinner we were allowed to go out on the back lawn and play rounders, a game that dated back to Tudor times and was a forerunner of baseball. We hit the ball with our bare hands and then ran the bases around to home, hoping the bases would not get stumped. Stumped meant that a player hit the base with the ball before the runner reached it, resulting in the player being called out. Some of the stronger girls could send the ball high over the fence, thus earning home runs. We enjoyed more leisurely activities too. At the front end of the lawn stood a wide, spreading almond tree. We picked the ripe almonds, devoured the fleshy fruit, and then, when the brown nut was exposed, cracked the outer casing with a huge stone to reach the prized nut.

Seating in the dining room was rather tight, but our meals were tasty and nutritious despite the fact they were the result of institutional cooking. One of my favorite dishes was stewed ox-tail with lima beans on a bed of white rice. The meals the Cotterells provided us were not fully appreciated until my later school years, when a new matron took over running the hostel and was far more parsimonious in the servings.

Parents were allowed to send goodies and treats for their offspring from time to time, and sent canned salmon or chicken and crackers and the like. These treats, known as "tuck," were kept in a designated area of the pantry, with highly regulated times when we could partake of them. We boarders shared our treats with everyone in the dormitory and that is where I learned to share with others. We were not allowed to keep food in our dormitories. Besides the lack of space there, food would have encouraged ants and even rodents in our sleeping area.

"Lights out" was strictly enforced, and not even a whisper was allowed after our nine p.m. bedtime. At exam time, those of us who felt the need for more time to review the areas covered in the curriculum still managed to study after lights out. We continued with the aid of a flashlight under cover of a blanket, sometimes until the wee hours of the morning. Luckily for me,

I never got caught. The extreme pressure to do well, which began after coming first in class in my initial year and fueled by my intense competition with Diana Lindo, continued.

Most Saturday afternoons we were "let out of jail," provided it was not Lent and we had not incurred order marks or refused lessons at school. Sometimes a group of us strolled up the road to Bruce's, the local soda fountain, for ice cream and patties, the Jamaican version of empanadas. Bruce's patties were the tastiest, with flaky pastry enclosing hot, spicy ground beef that burned our lips. We alternated bites of patty with licks of sweet, cold, soothing ice cream in whatever delicious flavor we desired—chocolate, vanilla, strawberry, cherry, or even more exotic flavors like mango, coconut, guava or soursop.

Sometimes we were allowed to attend matinee movie performances at the new air-conditioned, fully enclosed Carib Theatre about half a mile away. In those days few movie theaters were enclosed like the Carib, although their impressive façades seemed to belie this fact. Only the balcony and box sections were under cover, while the cheaper sections were under the stars. Matinee performances were impossible at these venues, which could only put on showings after dark. Needless to say, whenever a shower of rain poured down, people stampeded for cover along the sides.

One afternoon in my first year, Janet, one of the older girls, approached me. "Do you want to come with us to the matinee on Saturday to see *Ships Ahoy*?"

"Sure," I replied, pleased that as a newcomer I was included in the group. "Where is it showing, and who's in it?"

"Esther Williams is starring, and it's at the Ward Theatre downtown," she replied.

"Okay, I'll go," I said.

Several of us got permission from Miss Gigi, hopped the

bus to downtown, saw the movie, and had a wonderful time.

"Wow!" I enthused as we were leaving the theater in the gathering dusk. "That was a good musical! Esther Williams is one of my favorites!"

To my surprise, Janet had a look of foreboding. She said, "The movie ran longer than I thought, and it's quite late now. We're going to be in big trouble with Miss Gigi."

"Why should we be in trouble?" I queried.

"She thinks we went to the Carib. She wouldn't have let us take the bus to go downtown," Janet said. Then she advised, "You know what, girls, don't say anything! Just let us all say that we went to the pictures."

Here I was facing a real quandary for the first time in my life. I was usually very obedient. I pondered, would it be worse to lie to Miss Gigi by omission or to betray my schoolmates?

Night had fallen by the time we returned to the hostel. The three sisters were waiting like sentinels at the front door. I felt as if I were going before the Judgment Seat of God, where we would be judged for all our misdeeds. With great trepidation, we stepped into the hallway.

"Where on earth have you all been?" growled Miss Gigi.

"We went to the pictures, Miss Gigi," we all replied in unison.

"You could not have gone to the pictures. I phoned the Carib, and the show was over hours ago," she stated flatly.

We were caught out, but we stuck doggedly to our story. Indeed we had gone to the pictures, though not at the theater designated for us. Miss Gigi and her sisters interrogated us for hours, together and singly, but they always received the same reply, "We went to the pictures."

They never found out where we went that Saturday afternoon. For punishment, we were grounded for the remaining school term. Looking on the bright side, the

Lenten season was upon us shortly thereafter, when, with the exception of seeing *The Ten Commandments,* starring Charlton Heston, no one was permitted to go to the movies anyway. In the end we really fared quite lightly, given the magnitude of our transgression.

The deeply religious Cotterell sisters made sure that all household members gathered in the drawing room for prayers every evening after dinner. During Lent season, we were forced to attend weekly services at St. Luke's Parish Church in addition to regular Sunday services. On all Sunday mornings, dressed in white, we traipsed single file along the city streets for about a half-mile to the church. Most of us were embarrassed at standing out so strikingly. Passersby, as well as the congregation at St. Luke's, must have been thinking, "There go the St. Hugh's boarders!" We hated the attention we attracted.

Looking back, the years spent at the Cotterells were not all that bad, certainly better than what was to come. However, for the first time I had to endure sharing life with many other girls in close quarters. I had to learn to share goodies sent by my mother, and endure even stricter discipline than I had been subjected to at home. The regimentation of meal times, bath times, and lights out took some adjustment on my part, but, like in army situations, camaraderie developed among us boarders.

Two years later Miss Gigi and her sisters ceased operating the hostel, and Mrs. Williams, mother of Mrs. Saunders, our math teacher, provided boarding. This meant we had to move to a new location on Marescaux Road, farther away from the school but still within walking distance. The large two-story house, with a mahogany staircase near the front of the building and a smaller spiral staircase to the back, showed evidence of past grandeur. There were several good-sized rooms, as well as balconies upstairs and a veranda downstairs. The building was set in spacious grounds, with a semi-circular driveway lined by tall crepe myrtles.

One would have thought that with the grander house, we boarders would have more personal space. This was not to be. Mrs. Williams—whom we secretly nicknamed Matrona, was so bent on cost cutting and maximizing profits that she took in too many boarders, resulting in serious overcrowding. On our arrival, the beds were packed so tightly that we girls could not access them from the sides and had to scoot onto our beds from the ends. My mother was so appalled by the conditions that she wrote a letter of complaint to Mrs. Landale, headmistress at St. Hugh's, who, after visiting the hostel, demanded a minimum space between each bed.

Apart from the dormitories, two rooms were occupied by Matrona and her husband, whom we called "L'Aveugle," since he was almost completely blind. In addition, Mrs. Saunders and her husband lived in the house for a while. Since she always carried news between the school and the hostel, she earned the nickname "The Buzzer." From time to time, Matrona also rented a room to temporary visitors—for instance, when a circus from Cuba visited Jamaica, the tightrope walker stayed at the boarding house. We girls were all agog with excitement when the dark, handsome young Cuban man came to reside among us. To my great disappointment, I could not converse with him since I studied French and knew no Spanish. I do remember that he called me "Rosamaria."

Another form of Matrona's cost cutting was the reduction in the size and quality of the meals. At the Cotterells, the food was nourishing, tasty, and provided in adequate amounts. At Mrs. Williams' establishment, we might have been seriously malnourished had it not been for the tuck our parents sent us regularly. There was such a sense of comradeship among us that we shared whatever was sent from home. If eight girls occupied a room and one possessed a single polished red American apple, that apple was evenly divided into eight portions so everyone got a taste. Although I did not have a best friend among the boarders, I was closest to the girls with whom I shared a room. We suffered together under adverse conditions and I have kept in touch with four or five of them to this day.

Once, at breakfast, we were disturbed by a commotion from an elderly gentleman, a temporary boarder, whose loud and vociferous complaints caught the attention of the entire dining room. "What is this?" he fussed. "Here I am, a big man, and all I get for breakfast is a big white plate and one little sardine in the middle of it!" He carried on for quite a while. We chuckled quietly among ourselves, as the man had gained our sympathy. We were only too accustomed to a serving of one small sardine as our protein intake, but we were juveniles. We could understand that a big man would be extraordinarily upset with such a paltry breakfast.

With such poor nutrition, it was perhaps not surprising there often were outbreaks of serious illnesses. Whenever I felt a scratchy throat, I gargled diligently with a solution of water with dissolved aspirin or, failing that, salt water. During a mumps epidemic at the hostel I was one of the few girls who did not succumb to the disease. Even Matrona contracted mumps, but refused to admit it. She did not quarantine herself and tried to hide her fat jaws by tying a scarf over her head and neck, while continuing with the business of running the boarding house. Sometime later, one of my roommates fell gravely ill, and ended up in hospital after her parents came to collect her. She was away from school for ages. On her return we learned she had suffered from rheumatic fever. Several years later, while in college, she found out that her heart was damaged. Nobody told her or any of us of the dangers of rheumatic fever, and in my mind I always attributed my friend's heart problems to the poor conditions at the hostel.

During my teenage years I was a voracious reader. I was an omnivore when it came to reading, devouring everything that came into my possession. All girls were compelled to borrow books from Miss Kingdon's library at school. Reading classics such as Dickens' or Robert Louis Stevenson's novels was mandatory, but we also were allowed to borrow lighter fare, such as the Nancy Drew and Hardy Boys detective novels. I learned to wade through Sir Walter Scott's *Ivanhoe,* made easier by watching the movie starring Robert Taylor and Elizabeth Taylor. Once I navigated through the heavy areas, I actually enjoyed the book. Having discovered Jane Austen's novels, I reveled in them. Georgette Heyer's eighteenth century historical novels counted with Miss Kingdon as classics, even though the tongue-in-cheek romantic episodes did not sound authentic to us girls. We lapped them up, often passing them on to each other before returning them to the library. They were so easy to read, each girl finishing one in a day. We also patronized the public library down the road, where we picked up the cheap romantic novels, particularly the Mills & Boon series. These trashy books were not the best examples of literature and I could not read such stories now, but this was a stage we all went through.

I continued my music lessons with Miss Mills, who possessed the Licentiate of the Royal Academy of Music certificate from England. An accomplished pianist, Miss Mills was a spinster living alone at her studio. From the start I realized that the two most important things in her life were her pampered poodle, Candace, and her treasured baby grand piano, which she treated like a person and which occupied pride of place in the center of the room. In fact, it dwarfed everything in the room, there not being much space left for other furniture. Those of us who were her students received our lessons on the baby grand, and it was where we performed our carefully practiced pieces before the music examiner who came out each year from Britain. In preparation for these exams, Miss Mills had the baby grand finely tuned, after which divine tones emanated from its depths as our nimble fingers moved over the black and white keys. Once, when Hurricane Hazel threatened Jamaica, I went as usual after school for my lesson, only to find the baby grand all wrapped in tarpaulin, with only the tiny castors on the feet peeping out. Miss Mills declared resolutely, "I'm sorry, you're not going to have a lesson today. Hurricane Hazel is approaching. I have already wrapped up my baby grand. I'm not about to unwrap it for you. You'll have to come back another time." So I traipsed back to the hostel and recounted Miss Mills' reaction to my roommates, who guffawed gleefully. In those days we had so many false alarms with hurricane warnings that we tended to ignore them. Hurricane Hazel never did hit Jamaica.

However, other natural disasters occurred occasionally. One evening in 1956, we senior girls were upstairs in the rear of the boarding house, gathered around a table sharing a snack. A parent had sent canned chicken, which we were enjoying with crackers. As I was about to put a cracker to my lips, a sudden and violent tremor shook the old building to its foundation. I realized we were experiencing an earthquake, a phenomenon in Jamaica from time to time, and waited for it to stop. Maybe as a delayed reaction on my part, I put the snack in my mouth and starting chewing. This time, the shaking did not stop. It seemed to go on forever. As I chewed, I stared, mesmerized, at the wooden wall panels as the spaces between them opened and closed repeatedly. Then the lights went out. Still the earthquake continued, and now the screaming erupted. The younger children, six-year-olds attending St. Hugh's Preparatory School, were the chief screamers. Those of us who were school prefects rounded up the little ones and stood in the threshold leading to the rear balcony. Even after the earthquake stopped, fear of aftershocks gripped us and we felt safer in the threshold, which was reputed to be the strongest part of any building. In the dark, we repeated The Lord's Prayer, which helped to calm the younger ones. Through the balcony I could see Camp Road below in the distance, with a trail of car lights winding along the curving road. Had the occupants felt the earthquake?

Matrona called out from downstairs, "Are you girls all right?"

"Yes, we are!" we shouted back.

"Come downstairs!" she instructed.

"We're afraid to take the spiral staircase. It's too danger-ous!"

"Then find your way to the front staircase and come down," she ordered.

We groped our way in the pitch-black darkness to the front staircase, and slowly and carefully inched our way down. We quickly exited the building. Outside was quite dark, with only the beams of the car headlamps along Marescaux Road providing intermittent light. We spoke in hushed voices, maybe because we had not recovered from the shock of our experience.

Through it all, we were in deathly fear of a strong aftershock. Outside was definitely safer, I thought, avoiding beams and debris that might fall on our heads. On the other hand, outdoors was not always immune from disasters. I remembered the story of Lewis Galdy from Montpelier, France, who had lived in the town of Port Royal, which guarded the entrance to Kingston Harbour. During the devastating earthquake of 1692, when half of Port Royal sank beneath the waves, the earth opened up and swallowed Lewis Galdy. Then in the next few seconds, the earth opened again and ejected him into the harbor. He swam back to land and lived for many years after. This fantastic story is inscribed on his tombstone in the cemetery at the church that replaced the old one, which had sunk into the harbor. The legend persists that during stormy weather the old church bell can be heard ringing from the sea floor. I prayed silently that the ground would not open and swallow us. After a very long time, Matrona ordered us back inside. Needless to say, we did not sleep too well that night, but mercifully there were no more tremors.

Also in that final year of high school, as a prefect in Sixth Form, I spoke out to the headmistress on behalf of the younger boarders at Mrs. Williams', who had many more school years ahead of them and could fear retaliation if they were to make complaints. I had nothing to lose and so became their champion. I approached Mrs. Landale and was interviewed privately in her office, where I outlined the hostel's less than desirable conditions, including poor nutrition and taking in male guests at what was supposed to be an all-girl hostel. Mrs. Landale chided me for making allegations and so I saw no tangible result from my speaking out. In our day minors did not question authority either at home or at school. When I was fifteen, if it seemed as if I was challenging my aunt, she would say, "If you think you are grown up, then you need to leave this house and take care of yourself." Knowing that I could not do that, I bit my lip and remained silent. Therefore, when Mrs. Landale refused to act, for reasons best known to her, I just accepted her decision.

I speculate now that she was reluctant to confront Mrs. Williams, the mother of one of her best teachers, and perhaps go through the disruption of finding someone else to operate the hostel.

Frustrated and burned out by all the years of rigorous studying, I was ready to leave school. However, I had no idea what I was going to do next. What was to be the next chapter of my life?

Lechmere McDonald Cox

CHAPTER SIX | $\mathcal{F}$athers, Two

$\mathcal{I}$ was fourteen years old and in my third year at St. Hugh's when Lech came into my mother's life. His full name was Lechmere McDonald Cox. As a manufacturer's representative for a prominent German firm, he traveled extensively in Europe, North and South America, and the Caribbean. He met my mother at the Melrose Hotel in Kingston as she was by this time at the front desk. He became captivated by this pretty redhead with a sweet, caring manner and, although he continued on his travels, he never forgot her.

Mum had had a few boyfriends whom she met through her job at the front desk. One in particular, a Scotsman named Archie, was particularly keen on her, and I got to meet him. As he was in Jamaica for a while, I presumed he was there on contract with an engineering firm, since Jamaica was expanding rapidly at that time. I, at twelve years old, did not like him and I had a difficult time deciphering his thick Scottish brogue. Archie tried hard to get in my favor by giving me gifts. For my birthday, he sent me leather-bound copies of *Treasure Island* and *Rob Roy,* which I dutifully read. However, I was not into boys' adventures, much preferring the contemporary Nancy Drew series. I also was slightly afraid of Archie. He was a daredevil who drank too much. His breath always smelled of Scotch whiskey, he smoked like a chimney, and encouraged my mother to do the same. Years later, I overheard Mum relating to Aunty how the top-heavy black Ford he drove when they were out clubbing one night overturned while attempting to negotiate a corner. Archie, drunk, was driving too fast, and the little car keeled right over. Luckily, neither of them was hurt. Archie promised to marry my mother but he went away and, although he wrote for a while, eventually they lost touch. I was relieved.

When Lech first came into my mother's life, I thought, "At least he is a West Indian, not a drunken white man like Archie!" The son of a prominent family on the island of St. Vincent, he grew up there, although he was born in Barbados. Tall, handsome, and distinguished, he was in his forties but appeared considerably younger. He was often the life and soul of a party, loving to tell stories of dramatic incidents in his travels. However, there was a dark side to Lech, and the relationship between us did not start off well.

After an absence of a couple of years, Lech returned to set up a business in Jamaica and sought out Mum at the Melrose Hotel. He was not free to marry because, although he had long ago left a wife and three children in Barbados, he was not divorced. He and Mum rented Aunty and Uncle Bert's two-bedroom bungalow on the premises of No. 17 Kew Road. When I was home on holidays from boarding school, I still slept in my bedroom in the big house.

Lech got permission from the Palmers to start a business of raising chickens in the backyard. They were kept in a coop near the fence, fed growing mash, and electric lights were kept on continuously so they would keep feeding and grow big very rapidly. The trays under the coop that collected the droppings were meticulously washed downed twice a day, but still the odor made Aunty sick. Some animosity developed between Lech and the Palmers and, to avoid any further rift, Mum and Lech moved out. After they rented a house about half a mile away, I was expected to live with them whenever I was home from boarding school.

By then Mum had left the Melrose Hotel, after thirteen years service, and acquired a job at the Courtleigh Manor Hotel. For the first time since I was a babe in arms, I had my mother around all the time, and this made me happy. However, my relationship with Lech was rocky, to say the least. We were not accustomed to living together as a family. I saw him as a stranger who was taking away my mother. We were both competing for her attention, and Lech was very competitive by nature. My poor mother was in the middle, pulled in different directions.

Perhaps Lech detected my underlying resentment of his presence because he would suddenly start shouting at me for reasons that were beyond my understanding. He would raise his voice, saying, "You are extremely out of order, very impertinent! Who do you think you are?" Taken aback, I tried to retaliate. Big mistake. His voice then rose several decibels to drown out my remonstrances. Unaccustomed to shouting matches, I could not handle this behavior. Considering that I was fourteen and he was the adult, he did not handle the situation very well. He never laid a hand on me, but his words were like daggers, very deliberately uttered to hurt. Many times I ran over to Aunty and Uncle Bert's, sobbing my heart out. Aunty and Uncle Bert were not particularly enamored with Lech, especially after the chicken incident. They knew Mum had been deeply wounded by my father's callousness and were afraid she would get hurt again. They tried to comfort me as best as they could, and agreed that Lech should not lash out with spiteful words that I had never before in my young life had to deal with. No curses were used but the effect of his words was just as hurtful.

In addition to these wild outbursts, Lech suffered from extreme mood swings. At times he was pleasant and fun loving, at others moody and anti-social, retreating into his den. He literally would stay in his room, refusing to come out to meet guests, and if forced to interact lashed out verbally at anyone who happened to be in his path. Lech also suffered from horrific nightmares practically every night, his screams filling the entire house, waking all the occupants. Later when we met his sisters in America, they confirmed what he had told us, that his father had been very hard and cruel to him as a child. His mother tried to protect him from his father's brutal whippings. The father's love and attention was, instead, lavished on Lech's older sister, while he tried in vain to win his father's approval.

Gradually I realized Lech was not going away, and we started to engage in activities as a family when I was home from boarding school. While his personality did not change—in those days no one in the West Indies knew anything about getting psychiatric help—we slowly came to be on better terms. A truce developed between Lech and me, although I truly considered my long-suffering mother to be a saint. She bore with his idiosyncrasies, yet she did not allow them to change her. She showered him with all the love and attention that he craved, and calmed him down during his worst nightmares. Life continued for us on a more even keel, with me spending weekends and vacations with Mum and Lech. Even the Palmers realized that he loved my mother deeply and they became the best of friends.

By the time I reached Sixth Form, I was allowed to go home most weekends. Matrona did not mind, since my absence enabled her to cut costs even further. Mum's two young nephews, whose parents were living in the United States, boarded with us for a while that year. Winston, Bevin, and I looked forward to weekend beach outings with Mum and Lech. We frequented the newly opened Gunboat Beach, the best nearest to Kingston, despite the fact that it lacked white sands. A narrow strip of land called the Palisadoes that encloses Kingston Harbour is accessed by a winding road leading to the international airport and ending in the historic town of Port Royal, which guards the harbor's entrance. On the outer side of the Palisadoes the waves are rough, whereas on the harbor side the water is as placid as a swimming pool. Gunboat Beach was opened on the harbor side during the 1950s, providing a respite for many Kingstonians who often took afternoon dips after work. Sand was brought in to cover the pebbles and almond trees were planted to shade the many benches dotting the property. The warm water was dark but clean, the only disturbance to its tranquility being the sting of translucent jellyfish. The calm water was conducive to my practicing my breaststroke, but I always kept an eye out for the jellyfish. Even a light touch from one of their threads left an angry red line of irritated skin. Gunboat Beach was then a popular spot for beach parties but declined in later years, and swimming was banned eventually due to the increasingly polluted water.

We also sometimes bathed in the Rockfort Mineral Baths on the south coastal road to the airport. Unlike the warm mineral waters of Milk River and the hot springs of Bath in other parts of the island, Rockfort's water was cold and refreshing. Small private pools were suitable for the elderly or infirm, whereas the large swimming pool with jets of water at strategic spots attracted the crowds. The boys and I cavorted in the water and had a whale of a time. The only drawback was our time spent in the pool was restricted to half an hour.

Another favorite spot Lech took us to was Cane River Falls, ten or fifteen miles east of Kingston. By then Lech had acquired a red Hillman Minx convertible with a black top. We all piled in and—with the top down, the wind blowing our hair, and the radio blasting—sped happily along the south coastal road. At our destination we piled out and, armed with picnic baskets, descended the rock-strewn trail leading down to the river. There were several huge boulders along the narrow riverbanks that provided surfaces to enjoy our picnic lunches. Facing us, where the river crossed a hard outcrop, a thin stream of water fell a few hundred feet with a splashing, clattering sound. As it was not a huge river, in the dry season water flowing in the rain shadow of the mountains was sometimes reduced to a trickle. We enjoyed bathing in the refreshing river water until late afternoon, when we would pack up, climb up the trail, and return home in the Minx. Many adventures were had in that little Hillman convertible. The only snag occurred when it rained. There was no internal switch to raise or lower the top, so at the first sign of even a drizzle, Lech stopped the car and there was a mad rush to raise the cover before getting too wet.

The very sheltered life of boarding school did not afford me the opportunity of meeting members of the opposite sex. Shy and retiring, I knew nothing of boys. In fact I was a little afraid of them. I believe Lech found my situation somewhat unnatural, so he encouraged my mother to allow me, at sixteen, to attend a co-ed summer camp. She was acquainted with a lady whose daughter, Marjorie, attended the Anglican

Summer Camp in Montego Bay and, even though I did not know Marjorie and had no desire to go to camp, I was sent.

It was a camp in name only. The former Fairfield Hotel in Montego Bay had gone out of business and was co-opted by the Anglican Church for use as a summer camp. We had single beds under a proper roof and a beautiful view from the hills overlooking Montego Bay. Marjorie, who was a day-student at another school, quite sophisticated, and knew her way around, pretty much ignored me. There were plenty of boys at the camp, but they too paid me no attention. After the obligatory sessions of prayers and workshops, the rest of the time was a big dance party. Rock 'n' roll was then the rage and the kids danced all the time. Not knowing how to dance, I just stood in a corner and watched. A couple of times we went to the beach. A bus picked us up and took us to the famous Doctor's Cave, with its powder white sand and limpid green water. This was the first time I had seen such a magnificent beach—the beach at Dunn's River in Ocho Rios was no match for it. In the evenings at sunset, I looked out the window and saw a pink sea, the burnished rays of the setting sun giving a rosy glow to the normally blue Caribbean Sea. I could not believe my eyes.

Still, my social isolation did not improve. By the following year, Lech felt I needed to learn some of the social graces befitting a young lady. When he and Mum went to the Rainbow Club, they had me tag along. At seventeen I did not really object to these outings, which gave me a little insight into life outside of my narrow world. I was allowed to have a crème de menthe or a crème de cacao to drink. Of more importance, I was taught to dance—not rock 'n' roll but dances like the waltz, the quick step, fox trot, and mambo. I would have been happier learning to jive. The daughter of a family friend taught me the cha-cha-cha, which I performed adequately, but on the whole I was ill at ease with my peers. One evening at the Rainbow Club, I spied my geography teacher, Miss Field, enter with her escort. Miss Field was my favorite teacher while I was in Sixth Form, and I did not want her to believe that I wasted time in nightclubs instead of studying. I do not think she saw me, and not wanting to be recognized, I kept in the shadows of the dimly lit club. I watched with interest as she danced the mambo, which she performed assuredly. This was how the adult world behaved!

When Mum moved to the evening shift at the Courtleigh Manor Hotel, she hired Doris to housekeep Monday through Saturday, cooking, cleaning, doing laundry, and buying food from the market once a week. I continued to be spoiled rotten, not learning to cook, sew, or engage in domestic activities as was expected of girls in the 1950s. My nose was always in a book. The only things I could do were clean the house and wash small personal items. In those days all laundry was done by hand, as middle-class households could not afford washing machines. Doris washed large items like towels, sheets, and blankets, wrung them manually, and hung them on the clothesline to dry.

One Saturday, Doris was off and Mum had to work, so I, who had no cooking experience, had to make soup for the first time. Mum told me what to do: put the marinated meat chunks in the boiling water, and when the meat began to soften, add peeled potatoes, onions, and carrots. I grabbed a kitchen knife—potato peelers were not known to us in those days—and awkwardly peeled the vegetables. I looked as if I had two left hands. Then it was time to make dumplings. I added a little water to flour, kneaded the dough, and rolled small amounts of the dough in my hands to make them. So far so good. I also remembered that Mum told me to add salt and black pepper to season the soup. As it boiled, I kept tasting. "Ugh," I thought, "rather insipid, needs more salt." I added more salt, stirred a little and tasted immediately. Still not satisfied, I added a little more salt, stirred and tasted again. I repeated this routine a few more times. No one had told me that it would take a while for the flavor to change. Eventually the soup ended up as brine, and I could not drink the broth. Lech bravely drank it all so as not to disparage my first attempt at cooking. Later he told my mother that the taps could not hold enough water to quench his thirst. This was an incident I never lived down, and many years later Lech still liked to entertain dinner guests with this embarrassing story. Strangely enough, I have become a decent cook, although I never achieved my mother's level of competence.

With the ribbing I got about my first attempt at cooking, I never had the courage to tell Mum what else had happened. While making the soup, I found what I was sure was flour in a plain brown paper bag in the kitchen cupboard. The dumplings I made had a translucent appearance while they were cooking. The more they cooked, the more slippery they looked. They in no way resembled the dumplings Doris put in her soup, so I tossed them out. When Doris returned to work the following week, I overheard her saying to herself in puzzlement, "Am sure ah lef' a bag o' starch in de cupboard, but ah can't find it at all!" She searched high and low. It was then I realized that what I thought to be flour was really starch, used to add body to cotton clothes, especially to bone-stiffen our crinolines. I never admitted what I had done. I was too embarrassed. It was a good thing that I threw out the dumplings. We were lucky to escape with our lives, as that type of starch was derived from the bitter cassava, a tuber like the potato, and deadly poisonous.

In 1957, Mum and Lech decided to start another business. Mum had gained years of experience in all aspects of hotel operation and had risen to the position of manageress of the Melrose Hotel by the time she left there. After her stint at the Courtleigh Manor, they decided to open a guesthouse in a rented property at No. 23 Constant Spring Road, a busy arterial road leading north from Kingston to the interior foothills. The roar of constant traffic night and day at first interrupted our sleep, but we soon got used to the din. The business was unimaginatively named The Odeon Guesthouse, since the Odeon Movie Theatre was located a couple of blocks down the road. Behind a spacious front lawn stood the main house, with a colonial style veranda that wrapped around the drawing room. There were four large bedrooms, a dining room, a kitchen, and two bathrooms which the guests had to share. Our family lived in a rented two-bedroom bungalow set behind the big house. In a pinch, the bedroom I used was sometimes occupied by overflow guests, and I then slept at the Palmers at Kew Road. Doris continued with us as housekeeper and cook, at an increased salary since she now had many more rooms to take care of, and she also had an assistant.

Some of the guests were short-term, coming from abroad for one or two weeks. I remember a colored family from Bermuda, whose accents sounded to me more American than British. A French-Canadian couple from Montreal spoke fluent English with hardly an accent, but kept talking to me in French after learning that it was one of my subjects in school. A Finn by the name of Berg spent quite some time in Jamaica on a contract job. He told us that in Finland children learned to ski as soon as they could walk. On Christmas Day, he and his Swedish fiancée went to the beach. It seemed odd to them to be able to swim at Christmas, at the height of the northern winter. Robin Schiele, a young Englishman, also spent some time in Jamaica while traveling around the world. He passed on to me his love of classical music. It was a revelation that young people could enjoy listening to such music and that it was not "work" like my music lessons with Miss Mills. Robin introduced Dvorak's "New World Symphony" to me, and every time I hear it now, I remember him. Manfred von Obenbach, a handsome young German with dark hair and startling blue eyes, visited from Venezuela. I did not even think of it at the time but his family could have left Germany after World War II, seeking a quiet life in South America. All in all, I found it interesting to meet various people at the guesthouse and learn about different countries and cultures.

The long-term residents, the bread and butter of the guesthouse, were mostly locals who needed a place to live. Many of them, like Mrs. De Lisser, had their eccentricities. A very large white lady in her sixties, she lay in bed most of the time. We privately dubbed her "the Berkshire pig." Then there was David, a young man from a wealthy Jewish family, who was born deaf. Having been sent abroad to learn to lip-read and to talk, he spoke in a droning monotone with no inflection at all in his voice.

One of my favorite long-term residents was Mr. Solomon, a retired Jewish businessman and a sociable gentleman who enjoyed a game of bridge. After dinner, the foursome of Mr. Solomon, Mum, Lech, and I would sit down to a game on the veranda. Mr. Solomon considered his moves while puffing away on a Royal Crown Jamaica cigar, its aroma filling the air around him. I loved the scent of his cigar and he always comes to mind whenever I smell the scent of a good one. Mr. Solomon loved winning and usually did. I did not find out till later that he was superstitious, always choosing to sit at the card table facing south. The only time I ever remember him losing was when, for some reason, he was not sitting in his favorite position.

Mrs. Cochrane was an eccentric English lady who held the delusion that she was continually being assailed by insects. Aerosol cans were unknown then, so Mrs. Cochrane traveled everywhere with her faithful flit gun. A flit gun consisted of two cylinders joined together like a T. The short cross-cylinder contained a reservoir of the poisonous and malodorous chemical DDT. The long cylinder, with a piston and a pump handle, sprayed the fine mist of mosquito killer. As Mrs. Cochrane kept her beloved flit can with her at all times, she used it everywhere. She assiduously sprayed the corners of the room, under the table, under the bed, in closets and cupboards, sometimes she even flitted her own legs. No one was aware at the time of the deleterious effect of DDT, which was banned from use in later years.

One Sunday evening when Lech decided to drive us to the Kingston Parish Church downtown to attend the evening service, Mrs. Cochrane, who was Anglican, came with us. It was a rainy evening so only a few congregants were in attendance. Just when the service was at its quietest, when prayers were being offered during the Holy Communion, we heard "Shh, shh, shh." There was no mistaking that sound of the flit gun as Mrs. Cochrane surreptitiously sprayed her feet. Even though she tried to be quiet, that swishing sound shattered the stillness of the service. We pretended Mrs. Cochrane was a total stranger and that we had nothing at all to do with her.

One of our last residents was Mr. Shanks, a member of a wealthy Scottish family noted for the manufacture of toilet bowls and tanks. Although perhaps in his thirties, Mr. Shanks was not careful in his personal grooming. His hair was frequently disheveled and his shirt often not tucked into his pants. Obviously he and exercise were not friends, as evidenced by his pudgy mid-section and his flabby arms.

One day he did not appear at the dinner table and Mum went looking for him. She knocked on his door several times, discreetly at first, but then progressively more loudly. No response. She called out, "Mr. Shanks! Mr. Shanks!" Still silence. She slowly opened the door and peeped in. No sign of Mr. Shanks. She looked high and low. Then she saw legs sticking out from under the bed. It turned out that he was under the bed, completely unresponsive. We thought he was in a drunken stupor but, in fact, he had suffered an epileptic seizure, a condition he had not made us aware of. Eventually he regained consciousness and we all breathed a sigh of relief. At the time there was no known treatment to mitigate the disease. There were a couple more epileptic episodes afterwards, and we would just have to wait for him to snap out of the condition. On one occasion Mr. Shanks had an attack when we arrived at the parking lot of the upscale Blue Mountain Inn, about two miles up the hills overlooking Kingston. We had formed a party to dine at this famous place that people raved about. I thought, "Not again; there goes my opportunity to experience the Blue Mountain Inn." Fortunately, this time he recovered quickly, and we entered the establishment.

After having negotiated the narrow ascending road with its hairpin turns we found the ambience of the Blue Mountain Inn pleasantly appealing to all the senses. We stepped into the tastefully decorated main room and were immediately led outdoors to tables and chairs in the garden, under trees subtly lit with all different colors—reds, blues, greens, and yellows. As we arranged ourselves at a table, the serenity of the scene made a great impression on me. We were fanned by a light, cool breeze while behind us a small mountain stream burbled past, with lights strategically placed against rocks and boulders. To crown this experience, a magnificent panoramic view of the city of Kingston lay beneath us, with the twinkling lights of houses and street lamps appearing like jewels in the velvet darkness. These lights were Earth's answer to the stars in the night sky. We were awed by the sight. As we dined on the fine cuisine, we were entertained by the beguiling, tastefully subdued syncopated rhythms of a Jamaican mento band, the indigenous music of the island. The wonderful evening was forever etched into my memory.

The couple of years when Mum and Lech ran the guesthouse were among the happiest in my life. More time was spent with my mother than previously, and I had grown used to sharing her with Lech. When home, I helped out with some of the duties of running the establishment, and meeting and conversing with people from diverse countries widened my horizons considerably.

With wanderlust in his veins, Lech soon tired of being in one place too long. In 1959, he traveled to New York, where two of his sisters resided, and was followed soon after by my mother. They settled illegally in Stamford, Connecticut, where Mum's niece lived.

The guesthouse, while not wildly successful, had been a going concern when they decided to abandon it and depart for the United States of America. They found a Mrs. Smith, who seemed knowledgeable about the hospitality industry, to manage the business temporarily while keeping the profits for herself. I still remained in the cottage behind the main house. By then I was out of school and had a temporary job in the Jamaican Civil Service, but also assisted Mrs. Smith in the running of the guesthouse. However, the business took a nosedive when it became apparent that Mrs. Smith was only looking out for herself. First she fired Doris, our long-time housekeeper, without finding a good replacement. The reputation of the establishment began to sink. As the money dried up, she set her sights on Mr. Shanks, who still resided there and whom she recognized as being well-heeled. As an epileptic who had never worked a day of his life, he was supported completely by his wealthy family. Mrs. Smith, who was either widowed or divorced, wooed Mr. Shanks and next thing I knew they took off and got married.

In the meanwhile, I had been apprising Mum and Lech of the goings-on at the guesthouse and they decided to liquidate the assets. A family friend was asked to handle the auction, but he was not savvy about such transactions and I, at nineteen, was totally ignorant of such things. Everything went for little or nothing—the furniture, including the beds; the linens; the tableware, and dinner and tea sets. With Mum and Lech away, it was a sad day for me. Everything connected with the guesthouse was gone, and I had nothing by which to remember it, not even a photograph. Years later when I was married, Aunty presented me with two large serving dishes, with a gold rimmed navy blue and white Chinese design, which she had salvaged from the dinner set. These are all that remain with me now from the guesthouse.

Even when we were still occupying No. 23 Constant Spring Road, the writing was on the wall but I did not realize it at the time. I used to sit for hours on the front veranda, watching bulldozers clear the land on the opposite side of the road. I was amazed at how quickly large trees that took decades to grow were destroyed. The land was graded and construction began. This was to be the first of the shopping centers lining a couple of miles of this major road. The momentum eventually reached our side of the street. Years later when I revisited Jamaica, I could barely recognize the spot where the guesthouse had stood. I looked over at Tropical Plaza, the first to be constructed and where I had watched those trees being uprooted by the bulldozers, and then glanced directly across the road. Completely unrecognizable! Just another plaza with an array of shops.

Rupert Newton Smellie

In the 1930s, Rupert Newton Smellie, a young, handsome government clerk, was assigned to St. Ann's Bay on Jamaica's north coast. He often visited Brown's Town, about eight miles away in the hills. Brown's Town—with its cool, healthy climate and salubrious breezes, and far from the mosquito-infested, disease-ridden lowlands—was considered by the British as the Riviera of the island. The crème de la crème of Jamaican society settled there, many residing in large colonial-style houses with beautiful gardens filled with roses, gardenias, bougainvilleas, anthurium lilies, and orchids, among other gorgeous flowering plants. Brown's Town was the home of a top-notch girls' boarding school, St. Hilda's High School, which had a name for turning out the most refined young ladies in the island, except for those educated in the mother country itself, Britain.

In this hotbed of Jamaican society Frances Anderson, my mother, found herself when she landed her first job in the catering department at the prestigious Huntley Park Hotel. After the death of her stepmother and the decline of her father to drink and despair—during which time he lost the house, the farm, indeed everything—she was taken in by the English parson and his wife, Reverend and Mrs. Cover. In their home she had learned the necessary culinary skills that equipped her for the job. Frances made several lifelong friends among the young ladies of Brown's Town and attended many parties, and during this period of her life she did not care about the consequences of her actions. She met and fell in love with dashing, ambitious Rupert Smellie and soon found she was with child. A wife and family would have interfered with his ambitions to further his education, so he refused to marry her, even suggesting that she have an abortion. When Frances refused, he washed his hands of the situation, had nothing further to do with her, and gave no support to the young mother.

In Jamaican society at that time, a double standard existed. Although illegitimacy was widespread among the masses, it was frowned upon by the middle classes. Yet many single women from good families were raising children, and little was said publicly about it. Men, many of whom were regarded as upstanding pillars of society, were expected to have their affairs, with no one batting an eyelid. My father, my mother, and I were all products of this society.

When I was about six, I had asked my mother, "Why don't I have a father? I want a baby brother or a baby sister. Why can't I have one? I want to have a daddy like everyone else." Mum said nothing, but when my questions became more persistent, one day she told me fiercely, "Your father is dead!" That stopped all my queries. Until I was about twelve, when called to be examined by the woman on the veranda I passed on my way home from school, I thought he was dead.

How did I feel when I first learned about my father and his family? Disinterested, and somewhat uncomfortable. There was no curiosity on my part to know more about him, especially after Mum revealed that I was unwanted by him. If he did not want me, I had no interest in finding out more about him or intruding in his life.

I met my father for the first time when I was sixteen years old. A series of events led up to the inevitable meeting. Mum and I had a chance encounter with my father's brother Bertie, who worked at the *Daily Gleaner,* the Jamaican newspaper. He and my mother chatted pleasantly, and for the first time I realized that my father was part of a family, that he had brothers and sisters. Later I met another brother, Syl, with his wife, Dolly, and their son, Dalton. Mum remarked that Dalton was the spitting image of my father, with the same cocked-up top lip. From time to time thereafter I visited Uncle Syl and Aunt Dolly, who were very family-oriented and lived not too far away from us at Kew Road. Throughout the years, Mum also had kept in touch with her friend Colly Chevannes, who happened to be related to my father's wife and worked as a postmistress in various country post offices throughout the island. I liked Aunt Colly, a big-hearted lady who enjoyed life and laughed a lot. When we visited her, it pleased me that she noticed and talked to me. In those days, children were seen but not heard. Aunt Colly paid attention to me and never failed to send me a gift on my birthday.

Between Aunt Colly and Uncle Syl and his family, my father received reports of me and my progress, that I was doing well in school and had won a scholarship to St. Hugh's. During my early teens, Aunt Colly repeatedly told my mother that my father wanted to meet me, but Mum adamantly refused to allow it. After all, he had not wanted me and never gave her any support. She had brought me up as a single parent, of course with the help of the Palmers and my surrogate mothers. Now that my father heard I was growing up nicely, he was changing his tune. What gall!

It was Lech who urged my mother to allow our meeting to take place. I do not know what arguments he used, but I imagine he empathized with my father. He too was estranged from his wife, who lived in Barbados with his three children, whom he saw rarely. My opinion was not sought as to whether I desired this meeting.

One evening when I was sixteen, a stranger came in a big car to take me for a drive. This stranger was introduced to me as my father. He was a brown-skinned man of medium height who had short-cropped dark hair with flecks of gray beginning to show and a cocked-up top lip, the trademark of the Smellies. I got in the passenger seat and he drove around. He did not take me to any particular destination. Looking back now, it must have been as difficult for him as it was for me. Not knowing how much my mother had told me, he must have been uncertain about the kind of reception he would get. He was as reticent as I was. It could not have been easy for him to have that first conversation with this unknown daughter of his, and I certainly did not help him. I cannot remember what we spoke about—desultory things I suppose. I did not volunteer much in conversation. I did not ask or even think, "Where were you for the first sixteen years of my life?" because, to tell the truth, I had not missed him. My beloved Uncle Bert fulfilled the role of father, and I felt comfortable, safe, and happy with the Palmers.

My father finally asked, "Would you come and spend a day with us?" He was referring to his wife, three children, and his mother who lived with them. I said okay and it was arranged.

On the appointed day, I was picked up and taken to the family residence on Sharrow Drive. There I officially met my stepmother, my two half-sisters, Avrill and Barbara, and my half-brother, Ruddy. My grandmother and my father's unmarried sister, my aunt Lucy, occupied a separate wing of the house. The day itself was rather uneventful. No one was gushing, and perhaps it was best that way. With Avrill being three years my junior and the other two even younger, the gap in our ages seemed insurmountable; we did not have much in common, just the same biological father. I felt like the outsider I was. It was simply a visit to a family I was getting to know for the first time.

I was told to call my stepmother Lena, but I never could bring myself to address my father as Daddy, or my grandmother as Granny. So I just did not call them by name. They probably realized they had to draw me into the family slowly. My stepmother tried to get me to commit to spending some part of the holiday season with them. "Would you come and spend Christmas Day?" she asked.

I thought about Mum and Lech, Aunty and Uncle Bert, and Mama Jen, and knew I could not leave them on that special day, so I made an excuse.

"How about Boxing Day?" she queried.

Boxing Day, the day after Christmas, was also a big holiday. I recalled that old family friends, the Stiebels, had invited Aunty and me to their party. There were nine Stiebel siblings, and when they and their spouses and children gathered at the patriarchal home, twenty to thirty people were in attendance. Aunty and I were the only outsiders invited, and since Aunty and Uncle Bert were godparents to two of the Stiebel children, we were considered honorary members of the family. I shook my head in response to Lena's question. "I'm sorry," I said. "I have a previous engagement." Anyway, I did not particularly want to go to the Smellies for the holidays.

Lena persisted. "Are you available on New Year's Day then?"

I considered a while and realized I had run out of excuses. Very reluctantly I said, "I'm free on that day."

I spent New Year's Day with the family, and every year thereafter I was expected to spend one day of the holiday season with them. Later, when I knew my stepmother better, I realized Lena was a good woman who did want to integrate me into the family. Years later, after I was married, she counted my children among the number of her grandchildren.

In 1959, after Mum and Lech left Jamaica, I found myself back at Kew Road with Aunty and Uncle Bert. In my job as a temporary clerk in the Jamaican Civil Service, I was now able to contribute towards the household. In the 1950s it was not common practice for unmarried women to live on their own in rented apartments. The wisdom of the day was that there could be only one reason an unchaperoned young woman would do so: to receive male visitors, a recipe for loose living resulting in a loss of her good reputation.

At that time, my father's influence, which up till then was practically nonexistent, or at most minimal, began to exert more weight on my life. I received news that my grandmother had died and although I had not known the old lady very well, I was expected to attend the funeral. Jamaicans hold the widespread sentiment that family members need to get to know one another and it is the duty of everyone, wherever possible, to attend all family occasions, especially weddings and funerals. My father picked me up and, together with Lena and their children, drove to the parish of St. Catherine, where the funeral was held. Here was the family home of the Hylton clan to which my grandmother belonged. I do not remember much about the day, the ceremony, or the place. It was a small village much like any other in the Jamaican countryside. What I do remember was that it poured rain, and my new white pumps sank into the squishy red soil at the burial site. My shoes were so soaked and permanently stained that they were utterly destroyed and had to be thrown out. I felt more regret at losing my new white shoes than by the loss of my grandmother.

Upon obtaining a permanent position as a clerk in the civil service, I was transferred to the payroll department at the Treasury. This was a job I hated with a passion. Figures were not my strong point and working non-stop all day calculating them gave me headache. Besides, the young man who headed the department made romantic overtures towards me and I was not interested. I took over the desk of this young man upon his promotion, and he became my immediate boss.

When he indicated I needed to come into the office over the weekend to catch up on work and that he and I would be the only ones there, I was immediately suspicious. He warned me that payroll had to be completed on time each month, otherwise all employees would be in an uproar. I was reluctant to work Saturday and Sunday, as we were salaried and there was no overtime pay. It was just overwork. I faced a dilemma. Should I refuse to work over the weekend and thereby lose my job, or go to work and face the possibility of having to fight off my boss? I really did not know this fellow very well. I did show up at work, but my face was set like thunder. My grim look must have intimidated him because he did not touch me, and we got the work done. Still, the pressure of having payroll ready on time each month, with the correct deductions, weighed on me. I did make some friends at the Treasury and sometimes we participated in social events, but I was dying to leave that place.

During my stint at the Treasury I saw quite a lot of my father since the building was right next to the Income Tax Department where he was the deputy commissioner. He encouraged me to visit his office during my lunch hour. What did I get to know about my father? He related easily to his staff, to people he met, even to the man in the street. He was very reticent about his private life, and there was awkwardness in our relationship. Neither of us brought up the topic of my mother or the events of long ago. These were never discussed, so I never ever heard him say, "I'm sorry." My father was a proud man, and I guess I was willing to let sleeping dogs lie. He was acknowledging me as his daughter now, and even then there was a striking resemblance between us. He was not particularly religious, but I would say that education was his God. It meant a great deal to him, as he perceived it to be the route to future success and upward social mobility. Ambitious and intelligent, he continued studying, racing up the ladder in the civil service, and eventually attained the position of Income Tax Commissioner.

I soon realized that my passport to reaching the administrative grades in the civil service, and therefore command a better salary, was in obtaining a bachelor's degree, and I turned all my energy into gaining acceptance to a university. I sat the entrance exam for the University of the West Indies at the Mona Campus in Jamaica. No response. Then I applied and got accepted to the University of Hartford in Connecticut, which was not far from where Mum and Lech resided in Stamford. They undertook to put me through college and I figured I also could make some money working at vacation jobs.

With plans to attend university in the USA, I began to prepare for travel abroad, obtaining a passport, applying for visas, and acquiring warm clothes. On one of my visits to my father's office, he asked me, "What are you planning to do with your life?"

"I am going to attend university," I replied. "I have already been accepted by the University of Hartford, not far from where my mother lives."

"Why don't you consider England instead?" he asked.

"But I don't know anyone in England," I protested.

"Let's see," he said, and proceeded to draw up a list of pros and cons on a note pad on his desk. Under the heading of University of Hartford, he listed "Near Mother" and "Could work part-time." Under British university, he listed "Much lower cost," and "Degree recognized all over the world." He went on to point out that the American dollars my mother was willing to invest would go a much longer way in England.

"So this is how his mind operates," I thought—he doesn't allow his heart to rule his head. Viewing these factors from such a cerebral viewpoint, there was no doubt left in my mind as to which carried greater weight. I remained silent for a while, my mind awhirl with confusion. Seeing my hesitation, my father continued, "I can introduce you to a lady who is familiar with Leeds University. You can talk with her and she will tell you more about the place."

I agreed to meet his friend, Miss Dennison. Having received her master's degree from Leeds, she taught nurses at the University of the West Indies. I had never heard of Leeds, as the British universities popular to Jamaicans were Oxford and Cambridge, plus the University of London and the University of Edinburgh. Miss Dennison assured me that the redbrick universities such as Leeds and Manchester enjoyed a good reputation and were not as costly as big-name schools like Oxford and Cambridge. The meeting convinced me to switch, which proved to be a turning point in my life.

It was as if it were meant for me to go to Leeds University. My application to enroll in October 1960 was made in March of the same year, at the eleventh hour so to speak. The ease with which I was accepted was overwhelming. Despite the fact that I was no longer going to study in Connecticut, my mother made no objections. Indeed, Lech must have encouraged the change, as he was such an Anglophile. I booked air travel in September to Idlewild Airport (the former name for John F. Kennedy International Airport) in New York City. That allowed me to spend a week with my parents in nearby Connecticut before crossing the Atlantic.

My father's main influence was the advice he gave, which turned out right for me. Was it divine providence? I think so. The only time he ever gave me money, £50, was when I departed for England. I never asked him for money, never even wanted his money. The relationship we had was not financial. It was obvious he was well respected in government circles, indeed in Jamaican society. Being accepted as Rupert Smellie's daughter was enough for me, and I believe he was proud of me.

When my mother finally allowed my father to have a relationship with me, I had acquiesced, even though I did not seek or initiate it. Why did I go along? Perhaps it was not in my nature to hold a grudge, and it seemed my mother had given her blessing. She was able to overcome her bitterness and forgive him. If I had been up in arms against my father, my life would have taken an entirely different turn. I am not unhappy with the path taken.

I lived to see the day when my father showed the emotion of regret. In 1970, he was diagnosed with pancreatic cancer. Then living in Trinidad, I took three weeks off from my job to visit him as he lay dying in the hospital in Jamaica. My stepmother, Lena, let me use her car so every day I went to his bedside. On a liquid diet because he could not keep food down, he looked weak and gaunt on the hospital bed. Conversations were often interrupted when he had to bring up phlegm, which he spat into a little cup. Then one day he revealed to me that he had received a letter from my mother in America. A tear rolled down his cheek. Choking up, he asked me to give her a message. He paused a bit. After a while, he said, "Tell her thanks for the letter, but as you can see, I am not in a position to reply." On the surface I accepted his explanation, but wondered why he could not dictate a response. Then I thought about how very private a person he was, and there was nobody, absolutely no one, that he could have dictated that letter to … not his wife, not his daughters or his son, not me—especially not me.

My mother had written him a letter of forgiveness and therefore he could die freed from the weight of his past guilt.

England

Lupton Hall – where I resided for 3 years

It was September 1960 and I was aboard a British Overseas Airways Corporation (BOAC) plane on the overnight flight crossing the Atlantic Ocean, en route to London's Heathrow Airport. BOAC was the premier British airline, and I had just departed from Idlewild Airport on my way to study at Leeds. Just about a week before then, I had left Jamaica for the first time, first to visit Mum and Lech in Connecticut.

At that time Jamaica was still a British colony and, as proud subjects, we Jamaicans idolized all things British, including the monarchy, the British Empire, and the game of cricket. Two of my uncles had served in World Wars I and II in support of "the mother country," a term used to describe our special relationship with Britain. Now I was on my own way to "the mother country."

The British BOAC crewmembers were impeccably dressed and addressed me very politely. "Tea or coffee, madam?" they asked, giving me a little jolt of surprise. Nobody had ever referred to me as "madam" before. After dinner, the lights were dimmed to allow the passengers to settle down to sleep. However, I could not sleep. The excitement, the uncertainty and strangeness of the journey had me on tenterhooks. I was not accustomed to sleeping on a chair, no matter how comfortable the seat or how far it reclined. So I only dozed fitfully, often waking with a start when the plane lurched or dropped slightly in an air pocket. In my wakeful moments, I thought back on my life and how I happened to be on that plane at that stage of my life.

Even though I was about to enter a new and strange environment, I was not unused to being away from home and family. I thought about my parents in Connecticut, who were making a tremendous sacrifice to put me through college. It had been good to see Mum and Lech again, even though for only a brief visit. They had equipped me with good winter clothes to withstand the raw English weather—a couple of smart woolen suits; a long, heavy black winter coat reaching my knees; boots; and what I called my Little Red Riding Hood jacket, even though it was not red throughout. This hooded jacket had broad vertical strips of red, black, and gray from the crown of the hood to the hem encircling my hips. It definitely made a fashion statement.

On that BOAC flight I also thought about my father and the unpredictability of life. Ironically, it was he—who did not want me in the first place and had never supported me—who had influenced me to enroll at Leeds University. Through my introduction to Miss Dennison I had been persuaded to apply, even though I did not know a soul in England, and had no family or friends there. As I sat on that transatlantic flight I wondered, what was I getting myself into? Would I make the grade?

Looking out the window I could see the brightening dawn. Streaks of light appeared as we approached Heathrow. I could see a walled castle, which looked very medieval. (Later I discovered it was Windsor Castle, the private residence of Queen Elizabeth II.) The landscape looked very green, with paddocks, orchards, and arable land. As we zoomed in even closer, I saw rows of houses with steep, hipped roofs and attics with tiny windows, and miniscule gardens. Finally we landed and boarded a bus that shuttled us to the terminal.

I had been thoroughly coached by my father and Miss Dennison as to what to do on arrival at Heathrow, so I followed their instructions to the letter. After retrieving my suitcases and going through immigration and customs, I sought directions to the correct platform for the train to Waterloo Station, where I would be met. I was in some trepidation as to how I would find my way around London, so three different persons had been asked to meet me, one being a friend of my father's and the other two who were pals of Miss Dennison. Two of the contacts showed up, and one of them, a lady, shepherded me into a black taxi to shuttle me to St. Pancras Station, to catch the train to Leeds. Everything was so new in my introduction to London but I was far too nervous to sit back, relax, and observe much. I did, however, notice the red double-decker city buses and the red telephone booths I had heard so much about.

The taxi itself was quite unusual. This black vehicle, specially constructed for carrying passengers, was probably based on the prototype of old horse-drawn carriages. The driver sat alone in the front compartment, separated from the back by a sliding glass window through which, when drawn open, he could speak to his passengers. The seatless space in the front beside him was used for luggage and could hold a surprisingly large number of bags. In the rear compartment where my companion and I sat, a bench seat facing forward could comfortably hold three passengers. In addition, facing backward behind the front compartment were two drop-down seats to accommodate two more passengers. I marveled that such a compact vehicle could comfortably hold five passengers plus the driver and still have plenty of room for several pieces of luggage.

On arrival at St. Pancras, I thanked the lady who assisted me, then boarded the train and settled in a compartment where an English gentleman was already seated. After we greeted each other briefly, he retreated behind his newspaper. I sat on the opposite seat but not exactly facing him. I looked nervously out the window every time the train stopped. Having no idea how long the train ride would take and not being completely attuned to the British accent of the conductor who called out the names of the stations, I wanted to be sure I was ready to disembark at Leeds. We passed Peterborough and Nottingham, where Sherwood Forest of Robin Hood fame is located. As we were pulling out of Nottingham, the gentleman, who must have been studying me from behind his newspaper, suddenly spoke. "May I ask where you are getting off?"

"Leeds," I replied. "I'm going to study at the university there."

"I'm surprised you took this line from St. Pancras, which goes through Sheffield to Leeds. It is much longer. The more direct line leaves King's Cross and passes through Doncaster."

Encouraged by this gentleman's interest, I blurted out, "I just arrived at Heathrow this morning. I don't know a soul in Leeds and I don't even know where I'll be staying yet, because of my late acceptance. I did not get a place in a hall of residence so will live in lodgings with a landlady, but I have no idea who she is or where she lives."

The gentleman said, "I am familiar with Leeds because I went to the university there, but I'm getting off at Sheffield, which is the next stop." He paused a bit and then advised, "What you need to do when you get to Leeds is to go to the No. 2 bus terminal, which is the bus which goes by the university. You will find a taxi stand there. Take a taxi to the Parkinson Building at the university, but tell the driver to wait. Go inside to administration and find out the address where you'll be staying. Then the taxi will take you and your luggage where you need to go."

Breathing a sigh of relief, I murmured, "Thank you so very much for your help and advice."

He continued, "My name is Wilkinson and I'm a chemist. I'll give you my telephone number. If you have any problems at all, give me a call."

I thanked my lucky stars. Mr. Wilkinson seemed like an angel sent down from heaven to help me. Following his invaluable advice, I arrived at the administration building at four-thirty p.m., just in the nick of time because the office closed at five. The staff was expecting me but had not been aware of my exact arrival date. The address of my lodgings was given and the taxi proceeded along the narrow cobbled streets past redbrick row houses typical of the industrial north of England. All the buildings were blackened with soot from the nearby coalmines. There was a drab sameness in the appearance of these houses, with all the entrances and doors looking alike. Even the streets had names that were very similar. The address I was looking for was No. 22 Ebbertson Terrace—but there were Ebbertson Street, Ebbertson Place, Ebbertson Circle, and Ebbertson Close, all within close proximity of one another. I realized one had to be really careful to have the exact address because otherwise one could surely end up being truly lost.

Having found the correct house, the taxi driver rapped the door-knocker loudly—there was no door bell—and the door opened, revealing Mrs. Gordon-Smith, my landlady, who welcomed me warmly. I cannot adequately express my relief and thankfulness to have survived a long, tiring, nerve wracking journey across the Atlantic, and to be received into a warm house with a good meal and a hot relaxing bath.

At twenty years old, I was still somewhat unsophisticated and naïve, ill prepared to face the culture shock of living in "the mother country." The university had arranged for two other girls and me to share "digs," which was what students called the lodgings. I was the first to arrive at Mrs. Gordon-Smith's, who was a native of Austria and lived with her husband and teenaged daughter. The husband was a gentleman from The Gambia in West Africa, and seemed to be a perennial student. I often wondered if he ever graduated. There were two other couples that lodged with our landlady but we rarely saw them because they did not share meals with us.

On the night of my arrival, as we sat around the fireplace—there was no central heating—Mrs. Gordon-Smith advised me, "You can have a bath at any time, but you have to let me know in advance, as the water is heated when the fire is lit." I had a bath on that first evening. On the following evening after dinner we sat around the fire again and, after some desultory conversation, I said, "I think I'll have my bath now." The landlady hesitated a little and then, to my great astonishment, said, "Well, you know, there is only enough hot water to provide one bath per night, and other people in the household need the chance to bathe too." When I counted the number of people in the household, I realized, with horror, that I could have a bath only once every ten days. Coming from the Caribbean, where we are accustomed to the ritual of a daily bath, this situation was anathema to me. Each day I had to make do with what I called a "dry clean"—I filled the washbasin and used a washrag to try desperately to cleanse my entire body.

My two roommates arrived the day after I did. Mildred, a medical student, seemed a typical, sensible English girl like the heroines of the many English schoolgirl books I had loved to read in high school. She was fair, had rosy cheeks, listened to classical music, and had a quirky sense of humor. When she heard an amusing comment she often said, "Tickle me!" However, Mildred was serious and hardworking, as medical students had to maintain a high standard in order to pass their exams. Jackie, my other roommate, was a pretty brunette who was barely eighteen and seemed more frivolous and adventurous, foolhardy even. Both girls, as with most of the British students, were the recipients of government grants that covered the cost of their university education as long as they maintained good grades. I was a little jealous because it seemed they did not sufficiently appreciate the opportunity afforded them. Certainly my mother and stepfather were making terrific sacrifices in order to put me through college. Many took the government help for granted and often wasted their time. So many of my friends from back home would have jumped at the opportunity that Mildred and Jackie and others were given.

My roommates and I shared an unheated room in the attic. In fact, the only room in the house with heat was the living room, where a roaring fire was lit each evening. We each had a single bed, covered with three or four blankets. I was perpetually cold, not only because of the September weather but because Mildred cracked the skylight for ventilation, and the skylight was directly over my bed. This was when I learned about hot water bottles. Made of rubber, these were filled with hot water, then tightly corked and placed between the sheets. I possessed two, and each night I placed one at the head of the bed and the other at the foot. Then I moved them at intervals to positions closer together until they met in the middle. After the bed was warm enough to slide between the sheets, I kept the bottles around my body all night. In the morning, however, I ejected them with a cry of disgust because by then they were freezing cold.

Orientation at the university went well enough but I never forgot a statement made to us newcomers by one of the professors. He said, "Look to the person on your left, and then look to the person on your right. One of you will not be here by the end of the first term." He probably made the same statement each year to the incoming freshmen, but it made a deep impression on me.

It took me a long time to get used to the various buildings on the large campus. In fact, it could hardly be called a campus in the traditional sense of the word. The main Parkinson Building housed the administration, the library, and classrooms on the second and third floors. The Students Union Building contained the refectory, two small cafeterias, other good-sized rooms, and showers for men and women. In addition, there were classrooms scattered in various buildings along nearby cobbled streets. These were public streets, so the presence of these buildings interspersed with private residences showed that the university had far outgrown the original campus. We only had ten minutes to get from one class to another, and sometimes had to race at a rapid speed from one end of the university to the other in order to get to class on time.

By October, it was growing far too cold and damp for me. The days shortened and the shadows lengthened, so that by three in the afternoon it was already dark. The sun barely showed up in the sky. When it did, it was veiled by clouds and fog, its pale, sickly, jaundiced light giving off no heat whatsoever. Not wanting to face the cold raw weather if I did not have to, I was not inclined to accept social invitations, but whenever I did, I usually enjoyed the occasion. The Warden for Overseas Students got individuals and organizations, such as churches, to invite us to tea or to parties. One evening as I was leaving one such party, I stepped out the door and found myself flat on my back. This surprised me because I was clad in my trusty boots bought in the United States. It turned out that invisible "black ice," a term I had never heard of before, had frozen on the ground. Luckily only my pride was hurt and two of my hosts accompanied me, supporting both my arms, until I was safely aboard the bus. Thereafter, I learned very quickly how to walk in icy conditions.

One afternoon, bundled in a scarf and the long black coat that reached my ankles, I was bracing myself for the brisk fifteen-minute walk back to my digs. Just then two young men approached. One of them called out, "Hullo there! Are you from the West Indies?"

Anxious to escape the biting wind, I replied, rather impatiently, "Yes, I'm from Jamaica."

The other young man interjected, "I'm from St. Kitts!"

A small chuckle escaped my lips as I said, "You're from one of the small islands."

The young man who had first hailed me said, "My name is Ainsley Borel and I'm from Trinidad." Then they hurried off. (Years later I learned from Ainsley that after this encounter he had advised his friend, who was really Ghanaian, "Never ever tell anyone that you're from St. Kitts! Say that you're from Jamaica, Trinidad or Barbados. Nobody respects St. Kitts.")

Sometime later on campus, I again met Ainsley. He invited me to join him and his friends in the cafeteria for lunch. He told me he was pursuing a bachelor of commerce degree on a government scholarship from Trinidad & Tobago. At our first meeting I had barely looked at him; now in the warmth of the cafeteria I realized he was a tall, dark, and handsome young man. He was smartly dressed in a suit and tie, no oversized chunky sweater for him. His dark hair and moustache were neatly trimmed and his skin looked as smooth as black velvet. "So he's good looking and he's bright ... mmm!" I thought.

Ainsley alerted me to the fact that one of my old schoolmates from St. Hugh's was pursuing a course in fashion design at the Leeds Polytechnic College. Her name was Amy Repole and she was in her second year. Although Amy and I had attended school together, she had been one grade ahead of me and we had not been particular friends in school. The hostel where I had boarded then was next to Amy's house and we girls often talked to her through the chain link fence. We also both took piano lessons after school from Miss Mills' Academy of Music down the road. The annual Overseas Students Party was coming up and, after talking on the phone with Amy, we agreed to meet there.

Preparing for the party was quite an exercise because I had not paid too much attention to my appearance since my arrival in Leeds. I pulled out my two-piece, black-and-white houndstooth wool flannel suit and got my accessories together. Then came the question, what to do with my hair? I had not found a hairdresser since my arrival. In desperation, I sought information from a Sierra Leonean couple that rented a room from our landlady. The wife informed me there were no black hairdressers in Leeds, but said she would assist me by ironing my hair with a hot comb. I could then put my hair in rollers overnight, producing a beautiful curl by morning. After she was done, to my total dismay my hair could not even bend to fit into the rollers. It had been loaded with grease and ironed too straight. I looked like someone who had just arrived from the Indian sub-continent. (I believe I fooled even nationals from India and Pakistan because, for several weeks after that, young men from those countries tried to strike up conversations with me.) My two English roommates came to the rescue. They poured cologne over my locks, and even then just managed to remove only some of the grease. Nevertheless, they saved the day, and on the night of the party, as I sashayed out of the digs to meet Amy, my everyday appearance had been greatly transformed. I felt and looked good.

When Amy and I met at the party she welcomed me like a long lost sister. She was pretty, vivacious, pleasantly plump, and stylishly dressed. We had an enjoyable time at the party, which included a concert with performances rendered by various groups or individuals from different nations. The West Indian boys, with Ainsley as the leader, contributed a couple of calypsos, playing guitar, xylophone, and maracas. I won a box of chocolates in a raffle, the first time in my life that I had ever won anything. I insisted that some of Amy's luck had rubbed off on me. The boys kept crowding us, asking for chocolates and generally making a nuisance of themselves. I believe they were attracted to two beautifully turned out West

Indian chicks, of which there was a paucity at the university.

After the party was over, Ainsley suggested we go to the Wednesday night hop, which was held in another room in the Students Union. The hops were dances held on Wednesdays and Saturdays. Ainsley asked me, "Do you know how to jive?" When I hesitated, because indeed I was not well versed in the dances of the day, Amy burst out, "Sure, she can jive!" So we went to the hop, Amy pairing with Ainsley's friend Rodger and I pairing with Ainsley. He showed me how he did the jive and I believe I was a quick learner because we managed just fine, with no stepping on toes.

Thereafter, we partied every weekend, something I was not used to, because up till then I had led a pretty sheltered life. Amy had me come to her digs first so she could doll me up and spray me with loads of perfume "to catch Borel," in her words. When indeed Ainsley and I started a relationship, whenever Amy saw us together she shouted, "Lovebirds!"

Amy had a number of talents. On Ainsley's request, she shortened my long black winter coat and, as an accomplished seamstress, had the expertise to do a proper job. Also, after I related the fiasco of my first hairdressing experience, she offered to do my hair since she was expert in using the hot comb and tongs to iron and curl my tresses. Many a Saturday, Cislyn Baptiste—a Trinidadian friend who also attended the university, and I spent the whole day at Amy's. She would declare, "The hairdressing salon is open!" and then proceed to make our hair beautiful. I would make a pot of rice and red beans and chicken fricassee, the only two dishes I felt competent enough to cook. Of course a whole lot of girl talk went on.

Cislyn had known Ainsley in Trinidad when he was a nineteen-year-old. Even though he himself had just graduated from high school, he was hired to teach physics for a few months at Bishop Anstey, the respected all-girls Anglican high school she attended. It had been the very first time a young male was allowed within the confines of that female institution. She recounted the reactions of the young ladies and how they gave this young man, who seemed shy in their presence, a hard time. I reveled in all these stories because by then Ainsley and I were dating. Cislyn became "my riding partner," one of my closest and dearest friends. She, Amy, and I went to many parties and dances together. We were very much in demand because there were few women students of color pursuing higher education, and we were greatly outnumbered by the hordes of African male students. Even among the West Indians the boys far outnumbered the girls.

Two months after starting at Leeds, I received news from my father that I had been granted a bursary to study at the University of The West Indies in Jamaica. Although the award was late, I considered that it would relieve my mother and stepfather of the financial burden of funding my college education. I consulted with the Tutor of Women Students, Miss Joyce Bloxham, telling her of my intention to return to Jamaica. A large, imposing woman with an almost masculine appearance, Miss Bloxham was rather intimidating. She spoke deliberately. "If you intend to go back to Jamaica," she advised, "you need to leave immediately, because so much time has already been lost." I sent a cable telegram to my parents in the United States and packed up.

My roommate, Mildred, felt it was a shame I was leaving before seeing much of England. "You haven't even visited an English castle," she declared. She kindly offered to let me spend a week with her parents, who lived in Essex just outside of London, so I could visit some of the historic sites in London prior to my departure. I gave away items I would no longer need, including my Red Riding Hood jacket to

Amy, and said goodbye to my new friends. The night before leaving, I met Ainsley for the last time. He sang to me a song by Frank Sinatra, "We'll Be Together Again:"—*"No tears, no fears—Remember there's always tomorrow—So what if we have to part—We'll be together again ... Your kiss, your smile—Are memories I'll treasure forever—So try thinking with your heart—We'll be together again ..."*

I giggled because I found it funny, yet touching and romantic. I was genuinely sorry I was leaving Ainsley just when we were getting to know each other. The things he said, plus the words of the song made me believe he had deep feelings for me. Why would he sing that song to me if he did not mean it?

During the week I spent with Mildred's parents, I boarded the train each day for London and toured nearly all the famous sites. I spent half a day at the British Museum, marveling at the Egyptian mummies, and then realized it would take me about a week to really see everything that interested me in the museum. I toured the Tower of London, Westminster Abbey, and the Houses of Parliament. I witnessed the changing of the guards at Buckingham Palace, visited Madame Tussauds's famous wax museum, the Tate Art Gallery, and finally Trafalgar Square, where Lord Admiral Horatio Nelson's statue towered over the pigeons.

While I was still with Mildred's parents, I received a distraught phone call from my parents in Connecticut. "Why are you going back to Jamaica?" sobbed my mother. Her voice was choked with tears. "You know we are prepared to see you through school."

My stepfather cut in, "The education you receive in England will be far superior to what you would get in Jamaica!"

Mum asked, "Would you consider going back? We spoke with the Warden for Women Students and she is prepared to take you back."

My stepfather continued, "You have already started at Leeds. You must go back immediately!"

I was quite aghast at their reaction and realized that their love for me far surpassed thoughts of the financial burden they had taken on. So I returned to Leeds.

When I landed in front of Amy's door she nearly dropped dead with shock. She was kind enough to return my Red Riding Hood jacket. The next day I encountered Ainsley in the cafeteria. He looked as if he had seen a ghost. His friends later related his reaction to my return—on reaching his digs that evening he said to them, "You can't guess the terrible thing which happened today."

"Did your mother die?" they asked.

"No," he replied.

"Did your father die?"

"No," he answered, "Worse than that!"

"Then what happened?" they asked in unison.

"The woman has come back!" he stated flatly.

Ainsley would never have expressed his feelings for me so early in the relationship, including singing Frank Sinatra's "No Tears, No Fears," if he thought there was a chance of my returning, but the die had been cast. We started dating again.

In my first year I pursued a general arts degree with studies in geography, history, French, and economics. In my second year, I changed to combined studies, dropping economics and French. Economics was foreign to me, since I had never done it in high school and the numerical section of the course did not come easily to me. Old Professor Brown was knowledgeable but did not impart his knowledge very well. His classes often became a free-for-all, with students throwing paper darts in the classroom. He mildly asked them to refrain from "launching intercontinental ballistic missiles," which elicited hilarious laughs from the class.

Naturally, learning could not happen in such an environment, so we were happy to find Professor Brown's book in the campus bookstore. We thought our problems were solved and that we did not even have to attend class because his lectures were all in his book. His books sold out but, unfortunately, we were no more enlightened by reading his *Introduction to Economics* than we'd been in the classroom. A smaller tutorial class of eight to ten people still did not help, because I was lacking sufficient background in the subject. I was therefore extremely grateful when Ainsley offered to tutor me personally. He suggested two simpler textbooks, which turned on a light bulb in my brain. During these personal tutorials he often got angry because he felt I was not concentrating enough on what he was saying. Maybe I was daydreaming or mooning over him. Nevertheless, to the surprise of all, including myself, I did pass economics at the end of my first year.

In the meanwhile all was not well in the digs. Apart from the bath situation, the atmosphere was volatile, sometimes even traumatic, due to Mrs. Gordon-Smith. She was given to fits of rage, alternating with periods when she was as sweet as pie. We could never be sure of what mood she would be in each day. Looking back now, I realize that, being Austrian, she might have suffered terribly during the Second World War, and also that she most likely had a bi-polar condition. My two roommates and I found ourselves in Miss Bloxham's office, lodging complaints against our landlady. Miss Bloxham, dressed in the tweed suit she wore perennially— even in summer, always presented an intimidating appearance and it was not without some trepidation that we approached her. However, her bark was worse than her bite and she proved to be kindly disposed toward us. She was horrified to hear of our experience and arranged to have us immediately transferred to halls of residence, where spaces had opened up. The three of us were separated to enter different halls. I went to Lupton Hall, a women's residence about a mile away from the university on Wood Lane.

Lupton Hall, the smallest of the halls and accommodating about thirty-six students, consisted of a main building and an annex situated two hundred or so yards away. These were former manor homes, surrounded by spacious grounds with gardens and, in the case of the main hall, a croquet lawn. I started off in the annex where three other girls and I shared a room large enough to accommodate four single beds, one in each corner. Even better, the coal-heated furnace provided abundant supplies of hot water for bathing and for central heating in the winter. I reveled in the fact that I could now take unlimited baths and I no longer needed the hot water bottles. The radiators were the perfect places for drying small items of hand-laundered underwear. Each room was also provided small electric space heaters to supplement the heating of the often-drafty rooms.

The hall provided us two full meals seven days a week, and on weekends we were provided materials to prepare afternoon high tea in our rooms. High tea was more substantial than just a cup of tea and a cookie. We often got cold cuts to make sandwiches, tinned fruit, and a slice of cake. Favorite items often included in the fare were crumpets—very large English muffins, which we stuck on forks and held next to the electric heater to toast. The delicious toasted crumpets were then slathered with butter and strawberry jam before being devoured greedily. We were allowed to invite guests for tea and the English girls usually invited their boyfriends. Ainsley came over only once because he was uncomfortable with the setup. He much preferred that we meet privately, rather than in the same room with people he barely knew.

Despite the disadvantage of having to walk over to the main building for meals, we rather liked living in the annex since we were not under the nose of the warden of the hall. The annex had a sub-warden, Miss Chester, who was younger and more lenient than the warden. Whenever we went out in the evening the rules required us to sign out, stating where we were going and the estimated time of our return. Curfew was eleven p.m., after which time the doors were locked. I discovered the English are masters in using double meanings. On one occasion someone gave the destination of "South Pacific" in the sign-out book. At that time the movie *South Pacific* had recently been released and she had in fact gone to see it. Another time someone wrote, "I've locked up Miss Chester." Because the comma after "locked up" had been omitted it looked as if our sub-warden, Miss Chester, had been locked up.

In my second year I moved over to the main building, where I shared a room with only one roommate. In my third and final year I occupied my own tiny room in the attic. Space was so tight that I had to approach the bed from the foot in order to get under the blankets. Third-year students were given more privacy, not only because of seniority, but also for more freedom to study without the distractions of a roommate.

The public areas of the hall included a spacious drawing room to the front, on one side of the foyer, with a dining room behind it. On the other side of the foyer were located the warden's quarters. A large bay window graced the front of the drawing room, enabling as much light as possible to enter. Beneath it was upholstered banquet seating, a favorite place for us students to sit. In addition, the room was furnished with several large, comfortable armchairs atop a large Persian carpet, some bookshelves holding a small library, and an upright piano that graced a corner of the room. By the time I reached my third year I was playing the piano again, just to relieve stress, and had arranged to have my music books, with Beethoven's sonatas and Chopin's nocturnes, sent to me from Jamaica.

The dining room held four or five long tables, each accommodating eight. Most people scrambled to get an early seat so they would not have to sit at the head of the table. The person at the head had to play the part of "Mummy," that is, cut and share the dessert, usually a pie, and most often rhubarb pie as the garden produced an overabundance of that vegetable. If the server did not succeed in dividing the pie equally, she ended up with the smallest piece, since she served herself last.

Once a month we were encouraged to invite faculty members to dinner, and then we had to dress more carefully and be on our best behavior. Aperitifs were served in the drawing room before the meal and we were expected to make small talk with our guests, something that was terrifying for me.

As my relationship with Ainsley deepened, we spent more time with each other. He invited me to a number of balls, the first and probably the best being the Engineering Society Ball. "This society throws the best balls!" he exclaimed. "It's a real formal affair. You'll have to wear a long gown. What color are you planning on wearing?" On the night of the ball, to my surprise, he presented me with a white carnation corsage, which contrasted beautifully with my sky-blue gown. He looked sharp in a black tuxedo, with a matching white carnation pinned to his lapel. The engineers set up ingenious mechanical decorations all over the Students Union. There were four live bands in different rooms. Our favorite was the traditional Big Band that reigned over the refectory. There we quickstepped or fox trotted our way in an anti-clockwise direction around the dance floor. When we were ready to let our hair down, we gravitated toward one of the smaller rooms downstairs where a steel band beat pulsating rhythms.

Sometimes we did simpler things, like rowing in the park or taking in a movie. At other times Ainsley invited me to his digs at No. 20 Consort Terrace, which he shared with five other West Indian boys. Most were Trinidadian, but one student, Nick, was Guyanese. Nick was affronted when he heard the others referring to me as "Smellie." He admonished them, saying, "She is a nice girl. Why are you disrespecting her by calling her that?" "That is her name!" they replied, and Nick was dumbfounded. Other Trinidadian students who resided elsewhere spent so much time in these digs that they could have been residents. No. 20 Consort Terrace was quickly dubbed "The Trinidad Embassy," as it was a good spot for "liming"—hanging out.

Their landlady was too old and frail to provide meals; besides, her cooking was too insipid for the palates of her boarders. So the compromise was made that she bought the food and the boys cooked their own meals. Ainsley was an excellent cook, and taught the others who had fewer clues as to what went on in a kitchen.

The Trini boys were fun loving, and spent much time telling jokes, listening to music, or drinking beer or harder liquor. Many a party was held at "The Embassy." In fact, if nothing else was going on elsewhere there would be a party at the digs, it seemed every weekend, and often with Cislyn and me as the only girls present. The boys made up their own band, playing and singing the latest calypsos from Trinidad, with Ralph Knight on the guitar, Rodgerson Joseph on the xylophone, one of the boys playing the shak-shak—maracas, and Ainsley singing. Because they needed a heavy metal section to keep the rhythm, they borrowed the landlady's iron fireplace pokers to perform the job. The rest of the group each grabbed an empty bottle and a spoon to beat the rhythm. Having been taught by the others, I joined the percussionists with the iron or the bottle and spoon. The neighbors complained to the landlady about the noise, but to no avail. She remembered she had once been young, and gave the young men all the freedom they desired, allowing them to make all the noise they wanted.

Despite the ups and downs when I first arrived in Leeds, I settled down and became comfortable in my new environment. Looking back now, I can laugh at some of these experiences, although at the time they were not so funny. The transfer to Lupton Hall stabilized my living conditions and I made friends with my English roommates. Additionally, finding a core of West Indian students provided me with a place to meet others of similar culture and background. Cislyn and Amy became lifelong friends. Most of all, Ainsley, the most eligible bachelor among the male students, became my mentor, my friend, and my lover. What more could I ask for? I was in a state of bliss.

CHAPTER EIGHT | The Vacations

As my first year at Leeds University came to a close, I needed to plan for the summer. Once the university was on vacation the hall of residence closed and I had to find alternative accommodation. This was another opportunity to explore a new place. During my first Christmas vacation I had accompanied Amy to Manchester, to spend the holidays with her cousin. At Easter, one of my roommates invited me to her home in Exeter, Devonshire, a beautiful part of England in springtime. But what to do during my first summer?

During my first-year French classes, I struggled with speaking the language. I had done well in French in high school, but on arrival in Leeds found that the English girls were way ahead of me. Having the opportunity to visit France during their high school years, they were far more fluent than I. Perhaps, I thought, I could improve my language skills if I spent the summer with a French family as an *au pair*. Arrangements made through the Students Union put me in touch with a family in southern France. When classes were finished, I caught the train to Dover in order to take the ferry to Calais. This was the first time I would be on a boat and I looked forward to the experience of an overnight crossing of the English Channel.

On the ferry I made the acquaintance of a French girl traveling alone, who showed me the ropes. "Let's go on deck," she advised. "The fresh air will help prevent seasickness." As we left the harbor, we looked back in the approaching dusk to view the famous white cliffs of Dover.

On reaching open water, the boat started to pitch from side to side as huge waves tossed the vessel. It was a much rougher crossing than I anticipated. The English Channel has quite a reputation for violent crossings, but this was August, not even in the middle of winter when one could expect strong winds and turbulent seas. Finding my sea legs, we remained on deck for quite a while. Despite the violent rolling, I felt good. No feelings of nausea. In the morning, experiencing the first pangs of hunger, I descended to the dining room for an early breakfast of bacon and eggs, toast, coffee, and juice. As the ferry continued to roll from side to side on the towering waves, fixed metal holders with various sized holes were placed on the tables to keep the plates, cups, and cutlery from sliding off. I gazed with wonder at this. After eating, some passengers got sick. I then went below deck to use the restroom, holding onto walls and railings to keep my footing as I inched my way. Here there was vomit with its sour stench everywhere—on the walls, on the seats, and on the floor. If I were going to be sick, it would have happened then. Luckily, I had a strong stomach and was able to resist the desire to retch before I beat a hasty retreat to the fresh air on deck.

After going through customs at Calais, I caught the train to Paris, where I changed to another train going to the south of France. In our correspondence, my host, M. Du Gauquier, gave me all the necessary instructions for connecting with the correct train, and I followed his instructions to the letter.

The train dashed through the French countryside passing castles, rivers, bridges, and farmland, including golden wheat fields, and eventually climbed the foothills of the Central Massif. Finally I arrived at my destination, Figeac, where M. Du Gauquier awaited me. Figeac was the nearest town to his home in Capdenac, a tiny village situated in southwestern France.

Toulouse was the big city in the area, and if one continued south, one would reach the Pyrenees and the Spanish border.

On arrival at his house, M. Du Gauquier introduced me to his wife, their five-year-old son, Jean Marie, and to his wife's mother, who also was a member of the household. Only he spoke some English, but they all formally shook hands with me. This was a typical European habit, as each morning thereafter they greeted me with a handshake and the query, "Ça va?" ("How are you?"), and asked if I had slept well. As members of the family, they kissed each other on both cheeks as part of their morning greeting.

My job was to teach English to young Jean Marie and to converse in English with M. Du Gauquier, and for this I would be paid. The husband and wife were teachers in the Central African Republic, coming home to France during the long summer vacation. Mme. Du Gauquier's mother lived in one wing of the large house year-round. My supersized room occupied another wing, which previously had been inhabited by M. Du Gauquier's now deceased parents.

After freshening up on my arrival, I joined the family for dinner, not realizing this was quite a lengthy and leisurely exercise lasting two or three hours. Even a simple family meal consisted of several courses—first salad, followed by hors-d'oeuvres, then in turn the entrée, dessert, crackers and cheese, and coffee. The interval between each course allowed the food to begin the digestion process while the next course was being readied for the table, and of course conversation flowed as we sipped our wine. Even five-year-old Jean Marie had wine mixed half and half with water. That first evening, the family's leisurely style of eating was a bit of a shock for me. I was worn out from traveling for a night and a day and, on top of the physical exhaustion, having to converse in French for such a long time at the dinner table was tiring. I did not think in French but formulated my thoughts in English and then tried to translate them. All that work for my brain literally gave me a headache.

The following morning I had a chance to explore the house and the property on which it stood. The house itself was a mansion. It was the only large residence in Capdenac, a settlement dating back to Roman times. Capdenac was situated on a puy, a volcanic plug that was the remnant of an ancient volcano. All sides except one of this steep-sided hill dropped precipitously, making it an excellent defensive site in historical times. Most of the old Roman wall remained intact and, as a history and geography buff, I was thrilled to experience places I had learned about in my studies. I was told the house once belonged to the Duke of Sully, who lived in the seventeenth century and was a statesman assisting King Henry IV in the rule of France. It was he who developed the celebrated wine cellar below, from which M. Du Gauquier brought his wines each evening to the dinner table. Sometimes *vin ordinaire* was served, at other times excellent red and white wines. The other homes in the village were modest and occupied by the workers in the area. I recall a villager walking on the narrow street from the bakery with a long baguette under his arm. I guess the perspiration made it taste all the sweeter.

The Du Gauquier property included a vineyard and a plum orchard. On one occasion, Jean Marie, his grandmother, and I walked down to the vineyard and plucked green grapes. They were small and sweet but seeded, and I was still munching on my bunch when I noticed the other two had already devoured theirs. I was laboriously spitting out the seeds while they just ate the entire fruit, grinding the seeds with their teeth. Surely the seeds could get stuck in the appendix, causing acute appendicitis? Or was this an old wive's tale still accepted by gullible me? We also reaped sweet delicious black plums so Madame Du Gauquier could make fruit preserves, referred to by the French as *compôte*. Of course, as we gathered plums, perhaps more entered our mouths than the baskets.

Mme. Du Gauquier did all the cooking, sometimes but not always with the assistance of her mother. I would offer to help but I guess the lady of the house sensed my inexperience because my tasks were usually simple—setting the table or helping with the clean-up. I also prepared the salad, breaking the leaves of the various greens into bite-size pieces, and washing and drying them. Putting them in a sieve-like covered container with a long handle, I shook the contraption for at least ten minutes until all the water escaped.

Madame was an excellent cook. Although when I first arrived my appetite was small, by the end of my stay I ate like a horse. The lady of the house would say to me at first, "Rosemarie, tu manges comme un petit oiseau." ("You eat like a little bird.") Later in my stay she was saying, "Tu es tres gourmande." ("You are very greedy.") I do not believe she meant greedy in a negative way because she was happy to see me enjoying her meals. As an appetizer, she often served *jambon cru,* which translated literally as "raw ham." I could not believe the ham was uncooked because it tasted so delicious, but later realized it was smoked and therefore fully processed. Their steaks and roast beef were always cooked rare, with the blood oozing out, something I was unaccustomed to. Mme. Du Gauquier allowed me to cook my portion longer since I had no intention of eating raw meat. I did let on to Madame that I was not particular about potatoes, whether cooked well, indifferently or badly, having tired of the ubiquitous tuber as a staple food in our residence hall. Madame prepared new potatoes impeccably, swaddling them in butter, and I became a fan. "I thought you said you don't like potatoes," she exclaimed. I replied, "I don't usually and not in England, but I enjoy how you prepare these."

Much of my time was spent with Jean Marie, playing and singing to him, telling him stories and pushing him in the swing. However, my communication with him was mainly in French. Maybe because of my inexperience I could not get him to learn any English words. The only person with whom I spoke English was the master of the house, but he was often not around. As I communicated in French with the other household members on a daily basis, my language skills improved considerably. By the end of the month I was almost fluent. It seemed to me I got the better end of the bargain because no hard work was involved and I was getting paid, to boot. In England I had heard several horror stories of au pair girls being treated shabbily, like servants, and forced into heavy drudgery, doing the cooking and cleaning as well as babysitting. Fortunately, none of those things happened to me.

The icing on the cake was the fact that the family traveled considerably around the countryside during their summer vacation at home, and I accompanied them wherever they went. We visited Toulouse, a grand southern city with a magnificent cathedral. After the family shopped in some of the big department stores, we had lunch in an excellent restaurant. It was a gastronomic experience. A wide-ranging selection of appetizers, on separate platters, was set on the table and we partook of what we desired. I had no idea these were only starters and I helped myself to all—sardines in an olive oil sauce, and sliced tomatoes in a balsamic dressing and prosciutto. Then we had soup and a green salad, followed by fish. All these tasty dishes were accompanied by fresh-baked bread, and I went to town on the feast. Nearly sated, I was astonished when the entrée of baked chicken with sides was served. Needless to say, I could not give full justice to the last dish. All I kept repeating was, "Le peuple de Toulouse mange beaucoup." ("The people of Toulouse eat a lot.") The sumptuous meal left a lasting impression on me. I was used to taking everything placed in front of me at the residence hall, where the meals, though ample, did not go overboard in variety or quantity. I did not realize I could limit partaking of all the dishes, and certainly overate that day.

The family made other memorable trips in which I was included. As their home was in short proximity to a famous limestone region, we had the opportunity of visiting a number of caves. The first were the caves at Lascaux, the site of ancient caveman drawings. Along the dimly illuminated walls I saw an outline of a horse, its mane flying high. In another place was a bull with an arrow in its heart, surrounded by stick figures with bows and arrows. I was completely in awe to be standing in a place where early humans had lived and worked and left their mark.

We also visited Le Gouffre de Padirac, a world-famous limestone cave in the Dordogne region of France. This became my personal wonder of the world as I viewed, from the rim, this chasm, which is approximately 325 feet deep, with a diameter of about 115 feet. The cave, fitted with stairs descending nearly to the bottom, was well lit with electric lights. Carefully, we picked our way down, not wanting to lose our footing. On reaching the first level down, I was amazed to see several chambers with stalactites, stalagmites, and columns—the limestone formations I had studied in geography class. We descended further, to an underground river where we embarked on a flat boat. The guide poled the craft while explaining in French how this subterranean river was formed. Soluble limestone developed sinkholes, down which surface streams flowed and traveled for miles underground like this one did. Water dripped from the roof of the cave onto us in the boat, and I, concerned about my hair, promptly donned a plastic rain hat for protection. Typically geared toward tourism, the authority managing the tour took a photo of the boatload, which was offered for purchase. Although I looked a bit silly with my rain hat I bought a copy as a souvenir of my visit. I did not really care too much about my appearance in the picture because had my hair got wet it would have been a disaster.

The Du Gauquiers, having learned that as a geography student I was interested in seeing the Tarn Gorge, one of the most famous limestone gorges in the world, arranged for us to make a trip there. It was thrilling to actually be in a place I had only read about and studied for an exam. The road winds its way beside the Tarn River, where the rock faces of the valley rise perpendicularly in many places. At one point we saw cliff dwellings, their facades resembling regular houses, with windows and what looked like doors. I imagine these were fake doors, as real ones could not be used for entry or exit. Entry to these cave dwellings was from the side away from the river valley, and I think all the work of construction was done from the inside. Outside was such a steep and dizzying drop that I doubt people ever accessed the dwellings from the valley side. Maybe, like builders of skyscrapers in New York, they had used scaffolding to construct and clean the exteriors on the rock face. Some of the dwellings were inhabited well into the twentieth century. The windows, which provided light and ventilation, looked like any sash window typical of the 1950s and '60s and were often veiled by pretty chintz curtains. Cave dwellings with curtain-framed windows—that seemed odd to me.

Finally, the Du Gauquiers took me to the caves at Roquefort, renowned for the making of bleu cheese. When first introduced to this cheese I found it extremely potent. When I learned that only a tiny amount was needed to nibble with slices of French bread, I liked it. Learning of my partiality to Roquefort cheese, the family thought it fitting I should see where it was made.

The only negative experience I had at the Du Gauquiers was no fault of theirs. A young man, a fellow teacher on staff at their school in the Central African Republic, visited. After dinner he showed a home movie of African children dancing in their inimitable style to the beat of accompanying drums. I watched with interest and smiled at the joy in the children's faces. Then we all retired to bed, I going to my huge room that took up an entire wing of the house, where my single bed was placed against the wall along the far end, well away from the door. As usual I fell asleep immediately.

Suddenly awakened by a flashlight shining on my face, there was the visitor staring at me. My immediate reaction was to scream as loudly as possible. Fear gripped me as I realized no one could hear me. The house was huge and each wing somewhat isolated, but I kept on screaming. I tried to raise the volume of the shrieks coming from my throat. The commotion must have deterred him. He extinguished the light and fled. I heard his retreating footsteps in the darkness. Finally I heard the door close.

My heart pounding wildly, I turned on the overhead light and moved to the door with the intention of locking it. However, the latch would not hold. In an old house like that, some things did not work very well. What to do? What if this man tried to come back again, especially since the household had not been disturbed? Looking around frantically, I spied the heavy antique dressing table. That would do, I thought, and tugged and pulled it until it was wedged against the door. I lay down again but did not sleep a wink for the rest of the night.

The following morning, Mme. Du Gauquier asked, as usual, how I had slept. Having thought about it and prepared my statement in my mind, I seized the opportunity.

"Madame, I did not sleep well at all last night. Your visitor came into my room and awoke me by shining a flashlight in my face. I screamed for help. Did you not hear my screams? He left the room but I was so afraid he would return that I could not sleep after that."

Madame and her husband were extremely distressed to hear my report. They left my presence to question their guest. Soon after, they returned to tell me what he said: he had gotten up to use the bathroom, somehow got disoriented, and entered the wrong room. I knew this was not true. If it were, why would he have used the flashlight? Why would he have not stammered an apology and retreated immediately? They added that he was leaving right away. I breathed a sigh of relief even though I realized that a plausible excuse had been concocted for everyone's benefit. I did not see him that morning or ever again. I was simply thankful for the Du Gauquiers' quick and decisive action.

Finally my month was up and it was time to leave sunny France for cloudy, gray England. Still, it was a good thought that I would be speaking English again. The Du Gauquiers had been perfect hosts. I never felt as if they were my employers, and I always had the nagging feeling that they got the worst of the bargain. On leaving, they recommended I take an early train so I could spend a day in Paris touring some of the famous sites. Having been given a detailed itinerary to follow on exiting the train station, I first visited the Gothic cathedral of Notre Dame, and then walked through the Tuileries Garden to the Louvre. It was then I realized that this museum was so huge there was no way I could see everything in one day. I did, however, view the famous painting of the Mona Lisa, noting that a few art students were attempting to copy the masterpiece. Thereafter I did some shopping, purchasing a beautiful necklace with coral pink stones and a matching bracelet. After a light lunch—I didn't eat much, because the meals in Paris were expensive—I tried to cross the Place de la Concorde, which was a real madhouse. This is a huge roundabout with perhaps eight avenues radiating from it like a star. The French drive crazily, refusing to yield to anyone, including pedestrians, and cars race around on a first-come, first-served basis. After managing to dodge the racing cars, I strolled up to the Arc de Triomphe, built by Napoleon Bonaparte.

In Paris I became acutely aware of a couple of young men while wandering around by myself; they tried to pick me up. In Notre Dame an Asian man tried to get me to join him for coffee. At the Tuileries Garden I sat on a chair for a while to watch the swans. As a woman approached me, a man nearby handed her coins and said something to her that I did not understand. Then he told me, in English, that I was supposed to pay for the chair but that he had done so. He proceeded to ask if I would have dinner and then a night of sex with him. What gall! Did he think I was a prostitute? I quickly rose from the chair and offered to repay him but he refused to accept. Indignantly I told him I had to catch a train shortly, to return to England, and beat a hasty retreat. What was wrong with these Frenchmen? This had never happened to me in London during the week I spent visiting the famous tourist sites.

The return crossing of the English Channel was uneventful, certainly not as rough as the first time. By then I felt I was an old pro, and had gained valuable experience by taking this trip alone. While I was maturing and learning to be much more self-reliant and independent, it was good to be back in jolly old England, where there was no danger of being interfered with and where I was comfortable speaking my native tongue.

The next vacation was Christmas of 1961. The university gave four weeks for the holiday, during which time most of the English girls who rented flats while at university went home. My friend Cislyn, who resided in another hall, suggested that we sublet a flat together for the holidays, and we obtained one from two former Lupton Hall residents. The Trinidadian boys were jubilant about our decision. During that month we were living in greater freedom, and they knew they could visit at any time. For once the tables were turned and they showed up at our flat practically every evening.

The first evening they helped us with the move. One of the things I did immediately was feed coins into the gas meter, which powered the electricity in the flat. Then I turned on the water heater so Cis and I could have a bath before bed. While we were having dinner, the lights went out. We could not understand what had happened. I had fed five shillings into the meter, and the girls we sublet from had said they used approximately five shillings per week for electricity. Then I remembered that I had left the water heater on. The water was piping hot but we were plunged in darkness. The problem was that neither Cislyn nor I had any more shillings. Finally Ralph, one of the boys, produced a shilling and the lights came back on. In the ensuing days he kept us supplied with shillings; in fact he declared he was paying an extra two-pence for each shilling that he acquired, but we assumed he was joking.

Cislyn and I got Christmas jobs delivering mail from the local post office along routes. Never before in my life had I felt so cold. The temperatures were so low that it was said to be too cold to snow. Despite wearing the trusty winter boots I acquired in America, my toes felt like frozen meat. My fingers were equally numb since my fleece-lined leather gloves did a poor job of keeping in the warmth. Letters were pushed through slots in each front door, and then fell to the foyer floor. The tips of my gloves often got caught in the springs of the slots, so that after a couple of weeks my fingers were peeking out through holes and even colder than before. The Yorkshire people were warm and friendly, many of whom invited me in for a cup of tea. Never have I appreciated a cup of tea more than then!

At the end of each work day, Cis and I wearily trudged home, arriving at our cold flat at about the same time. Each day we attempted to light a fire, usually without success. We tried everything—fire lighters, pieces of wood shavings, kerosene oil—and fanned and fanned as smoke wafted, yet still the coals refused to ignite. If we managed a glimmer of flame it would die out quickly. We were obviously extremely inexperienced in getting a roaring fire going.

During this frustrating exercise we kept our coats on while consuming several cups of tea to warm to ourselves. Most times we gave up on the fire and concentrated on preparing dinner. We knew the boys would arrive soon, and inevitably they were given the job of getting the fire going. (One thing we noticed was that if any coals were left over in the fireplace from the night before, they ignited readily. It was towards the end of our stay in the flat that we made a discovery. There was water in the cellar where the coals were stored, which dampened them, and that was why they refused to ignite.)

Once the fire was lit and we finished the evening meal, we sat cozily around the fireplace and turned off the lights. As we sipped our drinks in the darkened room, we stared with fascination at the dancing flames. The whole atmosphere delighted the boys, who referred to our abode as "kinky scenes." Most often they stayed till the wee hours of the morning, telling jokes, listening to music or, for those of us who had partners, just snuggling. When the boys left around two in the morning, we encouraged them to tiptoe down the creaking stairway that led past the landlady's flat downstairs and out the front door. One morning, as they were descending quietly, Ainsley stopped and loudly declared, "Why are we trying to sneak out like thieves in the night? I refuse to sneak out!" Then, to our horror, he tramped noisily down the stairs. Luckily for us, the landlady must have been sleeping soundly because we received no complaints.

Before leaving the hall to go on Christmas vacation, one of the English girls, Ruth Coggan, had approached me. "I hear that you are staying in Leeds for the holidays. Would you like to come for Christmas dinner with my family in York?"

I was quite flattered because her father was David Coggan, the Archbishop of York. "I'd love to," I replied, "but I'll be sharing the flat with my girlfriend and would hate to leave her alone on Christmas Day."

"She'd be quite welcome to come as well," Ruth said, which cheered me. After checking with Cislyn, we happily accepted the invitation.

What we did not know was that the boys had every intention of inviting us for Christmas dinner. Ainsley and his friends were planning a big feast for us, and their disappointment was clearly evident when we declined. So we compromised. We lunched with them and then traveled to York for an evening meal with Ruth's family. Ainsley and the boys produced quite a spread—baked turkey, stewed chicken, roast pork, pigeon peas, rice, and what Trinidadians called "mayonnaise." This is basically a potato salad that also includes diced beets and carrots mixed with mayonnaise and French's Yellow Mustard. About two tablespoons of this mixture was dropped on a lettuce leaf, presenting an inviting picture on the serving plate. The lunch was very tasty as Ainsley was a talented cook, having learned by watching his mother. We had to cut short our enjoyment of the meal to catch the three o'clock train to York.

Dinner at the archbishop's residence was a different experience—a traditional meal followed by time spent sitting in front of the massive fireplace with a Yule log burning. I had never before seen such a huge log in a fireplace. What surprised me was that Archbishop Coggan himself attended to the fire. There was no butler to do the job for him. The archbishop was a gentle and humble man who carried no airs. I should not have expected anything less because Ruth was one of the most beautiful Christian girls I had ever met, a reflection on her parents and upbringing. Ruth's father later became Archbishop of Canterbury.

We had a final misadventure in the flat that Christmas. We used the bed linens belonging to the girls we sublet from, and when it was time to wash the sheets we gathered them together with our personal laundry to take to the nearby launderette. All seemed well until we took the clothes out of the washer. The previously white sheets were now pink! In our inexperience we had thrown them into the washer with Cislyn's red dressing gown. We looked at each other with alarm when we saw this catastrophe, then immediately went shopping to buy replacement white sheets. It was with great embarrassment that we told the girls what happened, but they took the news with equanimity. I do not know if the new sheets were of similar quality to the original ones, but at least the pink sheets were still useable and they received an extra set.

All in all the 1961 Christmas vacation in the flat, with its ups and downs, was a memorable experience for Cislyn and me. We learned fortitude in working our jobs delivering the mail. Some small domestic lessons were also learned, such as lighting a coal fire and not mixing colors with whites in a wash load. We became more acutely aware of the cost of living independently, and feeding shillings into a gas meter made us more frugal. In the residence hall, we had taken for granted what seemed like an inexhaustible supply of hot water, where we could take as many baths as we wished. Now we realized that utilities were amenities with a cost. Above all, we took back the truth that we needed to treat those we held most dear with consideration, which is why we ended up eating two Christmas dinners so as not to offend our friends. We enjoyed some freedom in the flat, but we also understood that with greater freedom came a keener sense of responsibility.

During the following Easter vacation, Cis and I made a trip to Dublin, where she had a friend studying at Trinity College. We spent the first week at the Trinity College dorm, and therefore had the opportunity of touring the oldest university in Ireland, dating back to 1592. The library housed some ancient manuscripts, including the *Book of Kells,* an illuminated manuscript of the four Gospels of the New Testament in Latin. Created by Columban monks about 800 AD, it is considered one of Ireland's finest treasures. We felt a sense of awe on viewing pages on display in the library. The illustrations and calligraphy were so beautifully and intricately executed, the flourishes in the capital letters a wonder to behold.

We toured the fair city of Dublin, situated at the mouth of the River Liffey, visiting the ancient crypt of Christ Church

Cathedral and climbing the steps of the spiral staircase to the top of Nelson's Pillar, which dominated the city. That monument, honoring Lord Nelson, has since been replaced by the Spire of Dublin, which was constructed to herald Ireland's place in the twenty-first century. Perhaps the most famous spot we visited was the Guinness Storehouse. Cislyn absolutely loved dark, bitter ales, but I preferred lagers and pale ales. Back in Jamaica we enjoyed Guinness stout mixed with evaporated and condensed milk, a supremely delicious drink. Having been afforded the opportunity to visit this world-renowned brewery, of course I had to take a pint of the bitter brew, even though consuming it in a pure unadulterated form was not my favorite activity.

Unfortunately we were poor students on a limited budget and were unable to tour most of Ireland, including the wild beauty of the western counties. We did venture on a bus tour to the nearby town of Dun Laoghaire, where I remember standing on a promontory overlooking the cobalt waters of the Atlantic. Light rain floated to earth gently but persistently. It rained constantly in Ireland but lightly enough not to interfere with daily activities, and all this moisture contributed to the bright green of the tender grass—the most beautiful emerald green I had ever seen. Ireland is not called "The Emerald Isle" without cause. We also managed a day-trip by train to Belfast, as we wanted to see something of the north. Our time there was very brief, but I do remember driving past the University of Belfast. Our trip occurred almost a decade prior to the Troubles, the warring unrest between the Protestants and Roman Catholics, so it was all perfectly safe for us.

Our second week was spent at the YWCA in downtown Dublin, right in the heart of all the city's action. We could always tell when the pubs closed each evening because the noise outside exploded exactly at eleven p.m., when the last hangers-on were kicked out. On the sidewalks the drinkers lurched from side to side, singing Irish ballads at the tops of their lungs. If we happened to be on the sidewalks at that time, we had to be prepared for the passing drunks to bump into and bounce off us.

While in Dublin, Cislyn's friend introduced us to a number of young, handsome, and ambitious West Indian guys studying at local universities. Cislyn was especially taken by an attractive young man from the island of Dominica. The fellows showed us a good time, especially since there were few West Indian female students around. Every evening on retiring to the hostel, we sang exultantly, "In Dublin's fair city, where the *men* are so pretty," and then proceeded to compare notes. It led us to wonder why we chose Leeds rather than Dublin because, with few exceptions, there was a dearth of "talent" among the West Indian men in Leeds.

All too quickly our Dublin vacation came to an end. It was time to return to Leeds and reality.

Cislyn and I had one more jaunt together. We made plans for the Whit Sunday weekend, which occurs late in May. This is a big three-day weekend in England at the end of spring when the weather begins to warm up. Spring was my favorite time of year, allowing me to enjoy drier weather. Skies then were mostly clear blue, sometimes dotted with small puffs of white cumulus clouds. The temperatures were so hot that Cis and I decided to visit Bridlington Beach, about sixty miles away on the Yorkshire coast. We caught the coach wearing our spring jackets, carrying our swimsuits just in case we felt like swimming or sunbathing. The beach was crowded but we found a spot. Cis and I looked at one another. Were we thinking the same thing? We were decidedly cold as a brisk onshore wind blew off the North Sea. We were shivering in our spring jackets and there was no way we were going to remove them, let alone don swimwear. To us Caribbean

BRIDLINGTON—1962

Rosemary and Cislyn at Bridlington Beach

girls, this experience was by no means our idea of "going to the beach." Immersing our bodies in the sea was out of the question, but we decided to test the temperature of the water with our big toes. The shock of the ice-cold seawater, which felt like water from the refrigerator, gave us a nasty jolt and we beat a hasty retreat. As we were making our way back to the coach, Cislyn cried, "Look out!" We both moved away from each other but not fast enough. A cameraman had bounded up in front of us and snapped a picture. The photo showed us in our jackets on opposite sides of the picture, frowning slightly. Although it was not our best shot, we each decided to buy a copy to remember the experience of Bridlington Beach.

The summer vacation of 1962 was one where I made big plans. I was going to Italy alone. My riding partner, Cislyn, was preparing to spend a year in Spain, a requirement for her as a Spanish major. I hardly saw Amy anymore, as she was taken up with her Sierra Leonean boyfriend, Rodney Fergusson Williams. In fact, they were planning a wedding on short notice, as Rodney's course was completed and they were both leaving soon for Sierra Leone. Unfortunately, I missed their wedding as I had already paid for my trip to Europe. As

Ainsley was officially my boyfriend, I tried to persuade him to accompany me on the trip but he refused.

This tour, arranged through the Students Union International, was a low-cost trip with travel by ferry and train and accommodation in youth hostels. Ainsley's excuse was that if he could not go in style he would rather not go at all. I had no intention of giving up my desire to see Italy, and having gained confidence from my previous trips, I decided to go on my own. It was not that I would be completely alone because I would be traveling with a student group, even though they were strangers to me.

On the train from Leeds to London, the starting point of the tour, I discovered I was acquainted with another student on the trip. It was somehow comforting to know someone else on the tour although we did not stick together all the time. His name was Ram Singh, an engineering student from Trinidad. Ram was not a part of the Leeds' in-crowd of Trinidadians but, as an officer on the student council, was well known at the local students union. He always talked big. The West Indian crowd chuckled behind his back because of his predilection towards the use of "green verbs"— meaning the lack of agreement between subjects and verbs in sentences. He was the recipient of a Shell Oil Company scholarship, but perhaps engineering was not his forte as he had trouble passing the exams. Ram did have his strengths. He probably would have excelled in another course, such as law, because he liked to talk and, except for small grammatical slips, did have the gift of the gab.

In London we boarded a train that took us to Folkestone, where we ferried across the English Channel to Le Havre in France. From there we proceeded by train to Luxembourg, where we changed to another to Italy. The entire journey took a night and a day. As poor students we could not afford sleeping compartments, so when night fell and most passengers, who could, left, we were grateful to have more space. We spread out so two students occupied each compartment, with each of us having a banquet seat. We lowered the shades to the outside as well as to the main corridor. As we were able to stretch out our full length on the seat, our sleep was comfortable.

On waking and drawing back the shades in the morning, I peered outside and was delighted to see that we were crossing the Alps. We whizzed past magnificent scenery— majestic snow-capped peaks, narrow lakes of deep blue, green meadows reminiscent of scenes in *The Sound of Music*, and the occasional chalet. At one stop, a burly man and his wife joined us in our compartment. They spoke no English but were very friendly. They pulled out a yard-long loaf of bread, which they cut up and filled with salami slices. They must have noticed our hungry faces because they offered us some. They also shared their sparkling mineral water, which we found refreshing as by then we were descending on the Italian side of the Alps and the temperature was rising rapidly. As we journeyed further we noticed the landscape was decidedly drier and the vegetation sparser. The trees—whether they were cedars, poplars or pine, seemed carefully arranged, standing straight up in rather solitary splendor between red-roofed buildings.

Finally we arrived at our destination, Florence, or Firenze as the Italians call this beautiful historical city. We stayed at a youth hostel where I shared a room with three other girls. The summer warmth was rather oppressive, especially in the afternoon. One roommate was Aisha Patel, an Indian girl I got close to. Since we both came from tropical climates we had no problem adjusting to the temperatures, and it seemed natural to hang together. Our two other roommates, however—being English, were especially overcome by the heat. While the room we shared was equipped with a fan, there was no air conditioning so they were forever soothing their reddened skin with washes of cool water. As water was at a premium, most of us dwelling at the hostel took just one shower per day.

The first morning after our arrival, we took a guided tour of the magnificent city, which reached its heyday in medieval times and is considered the birthplace of the Italian Renaissance. We toured the Uffizi Museum, the Boboli Gardens, and the Palazzo Pitti, which was the seat of the powerful Medici family in the mid-1500s. We also visited a couple of churches, including the Cattedrale di Santa Maria del Fiore— the Cathedral of St. Mary of the Flower, which dwarfed all the other buildings in the city. We took photos of the Ponte Vecchio spanning the River Arno. As we ambled along a narrow winding street, we spied a statue in the middle of the roadway. It was the famous *David* by Michelangelo. I could not believe my eyes! Yet art surrounded us on all sides and had become a part of the city's everyday life. (Long after my trip, the *David* was vandalized and defaced in 1991.) After restoration it, sadly, had to be placed inside a museum for safety. The guide also took us to a jewelry workshop where the most exquisite and delicate silver filigree work was being made. Although we admired the workmanship, I do not remember any sales taking place because, after all, we were students on limited budgets.

As we were trying to keep up with our guide who walked at a clip, we spied a sidewalk vendor selling watermelon, a sight for sore eyes. Aisha, Ram Singh, and I made a beeline to the stand with the intention of quenching our thirst on that hot, dusty day. No one else on the tour seemed to know watermelon. They were more familiar with honeydew and cantaloupe. The vendor had long, thin slices of luscious red fruit, dotted with black seeds, backed by tough green skins. The slices were skinny enough that we could chomp on the fruit without getting juice over our entire faces. Each slice was very cheap, costing the equivalent of maybe a nickel. Above all, the fruit was kept on ice so the slices were cool and refreshing. Seeing our enthusiasm for the watermelon, the English students decided to try it. Having devoured the red juicy fruit, we were left with the skins in our hands and searched diligently for a trash bin. After quite a while and failing to find a suitable receptacle, we asked the guide to direct us to one. Can you imagine our surprise when she replied, nonchalantly, "You can just drop them anywhere in the gutter. We Italians are quite dirty." Still, the feast so delighted us that each day we kept our eyes peeled for the vendor. In fact, we even learned the Italian word for watermelon, *cocomero.*

There were a couple of days when we roamed the city on our own. We soon found our way to the street market where many beautiful and relatively inexpensive products were displayed. There were handicrafts and many other wares, but we were especially beguiled by the leather goods. I bought a large tan bag of elephant leather, so durable that it lasted for several years. At that time I do not believe elephants were protected, and there was not yet a movement to educate people about the evil of killing these magnificent animals for their skins and their tusks. I bought the bag without a thought about the elephant that died so I could have it, just like how I ate beef or chicken without thinking about the animal slaughtered to provide me with meat.

The vendors were rather handsome young men who spoke some English and bantered and bargained with us. Their products were very cheap to us because at that time the Italian lira was worth much less than the British pound. The thousand-lira note was as big as a handkerchief, yet was valued as a small fraction of a pound. I could not wrap my head around the amount of paper I received in change. It barely fit into my wallet.

Two of the vendors in the market made dates to take Aisha and me riding on their scooters. We accepted their invitation readily enough. Scooters were a popular mode of transportation in Italy in the 1960s, as one may remember from the movie *Roman Holiday* with Audrey Hepburn, and I looked forward to my first scooter ride. When my young man came to collect me, I was wearing my Jamaican cotton dress with a voluminous skirt and crinoline. In those days young ladies rarely wore pants. I had seen Italian pillion riders seated sidesaddle, so I gathered up my skirts as best as I could and sat sidesaddle behind him. I held him tightly around the waist with one arm as he raced the scooter up a hill overlooking the city of Florence. With the other hand I tried to keep my billowing skirts in check. I was slightly apprehensive about going out like this with a stranger, but then I thought I was not entirely alone, as Aisha was on the other scooter behind her young man and they were ascending about the same time. When I could not see them, I quietly panicked until my fears were allayed by their appearance on the hill. At the summit we got off the scooters and surveyed the magnificent view of the city spread out below. It was evening and the sun had not yet set, so we had a superb view of the cathedral towering over the red-roofed buildings. We also saw the Ponte Vecchio—the Old Bridge, spanning the River Arno. After a while we descended and the young men treated us to gelatos, the Italian ice cream with silky-smooth exotic flavors such as coconut, mango, and watermelon. The date turned out to be rather enjoyable and nothing untoward happened, as the men were quite respectful of us. Now that I am much older and wiser, I see that things could have gone horribly wrong, but I am glad they did not.

On one of our free days, some of us took a bus trip to the principality of San Marco, not far from Florence. It was quite small and I wondered how politically independent it was from its larger neighbor. Its chief source of revenue was from the issue of its own postage stamps, and of course tourism was its prime industry. Ram Singh and others went on to visit Pisa. I sorely wanted to go too but had to watch the pennies.

The tour continued to Rimini, a noted seaside resort on the Adriatic coast. I had never heard of Rimini before then, but it seemed to be a favorite vacation site for Europeans, especially Germans. We stayed in a small guesthouse close to an extensive white sand beach stretching for miles along the coast. The accommodation and meals were far better than at the youth hostel in Florence. Here a number of interesting Italians were guests spending their summer vacation at the seaside. One young student, Paolo, spoke good English and liked conversing with us. I was amazed at the wealth of his knowledge, including the cultures and religions of India, especially Hinduism. He kept referring to Aisha as "Maharani," which translates as a princess or the wife of a maharajah. Another visitor, a handsome older guy, seemed familiar with the territory as he spent his vacation each year at Rimini. Heavily tanned, he spent most of his time on the beach where he loved to joke with young people. For photographs, he surrounded himself with us girls, the young and the beautiful, declaring himself the Sultan of Rimini with his harem.

Many hours were spent each morning on the beautiful white sand beach along the blue-green water. Ram Singh took a color slide photo of me posing in my green Jantzen one-piece bathing suit. There was also a black and white picture of me taken with a young Italian staying at the guesthouse, his arm draped around me in a rather proprietary manner. Together, the photos dazzled the Trinidadian boys when I returned to Leeds.

After lunch we all took siestas to avoid the afternoon heat. In Italy businesses were sensible enough to close from noon to four o' clock each day, and then re-opened until about midnight. Dinner at the guesthouse was an extremely heavy meal, with a first course of pasta followed by an entrée and dessert, and of course accompanied by the house wine, a heavy red wine that had a soporific effect on me. To counteract the after-dinner drowsiness, each night we walked along the beach for miles and miles, passing shops, cafés, restaurants, and nightspots. I made friends with a guest from Milan, Sandra Angeloni, who was my guide on the nightly walks. Since neither of us was familiar with the other's native tongue, we communicated in French. Sometimes we stopped and listened to singers crooning in the open-air cafés. On one occasion I attempted to sit on a chair to listen to a singer belting out "Dimme Quando Tu Verai." Sandra quickly stopped me. She said I would have to pay if I did that, and I remembered my experience in Paris on the bench at the Tuileries Garden. Not being able to take a seat did not diminish my pleasure at listening to the singer. I just adored that song, which had risen to popularity in Europe long before it hit the charts in Britain and America, so much so that I got Sandra to explain the meaning and also write out the words in Italian. Months later after my return to England, I sang that song while reminiscing on my trip to Rimini.

One evening Sandra told me about pizza, an Italian dish I had never heard of before. Desirous of trying it, I was warned by Sandra that we would have to allow our dinner to digest and have it quite late at night. So at about eleven p.m. we each ordered a slice of pizza. Can you imagine my consternation when I was handed an enormous slice of dough, the size of a hand towel, with a sprinkling of cheese? In Italy, pizza was the poor man's food. Needless to say, I was not really impressed. It was far too heavy and there was not much in the line of toppings. It was not until I was re-introduced to pizza in New York, where it was served with cheese, pepperoni, and a plethora of other delicious toppings, that I became an ardent convert.

It was during my third year at Leeds that my father arrived in London to pursue a twelve-month course preparing him to take over as Income Tax Commissioner. I planned to take the overnight train to visit him for a weekend, after consulting with two of the Trinidadian boys who had made the trip previously. They assured me the journey was quite safe and I only had to be careful to sit in a compartment filled with people. The trip to London was uneventful and the weekend pleasant. The return trip, however, was far different. I chose a compartment filled with a number of students who engaged me in conversation. All went well until they alighted from the train in Nottingham, leaving me alone in the compartment with a Greek-Cypriot man.

As soon as they departed the Cypriot dimmed the lights and lowered the shades in the compartment. He then said, "We can each have an entire seat to lie down and sleep." Feeling a bit doubtful, I thought about finding another compartment, but rationalized that it was way past midnight and people would be asleep already. I remembered that on my European trip I had done the same thing so decided to stay. I stretched out on the seat, clutching my handbag even though I only had a couple of British pounds on me. The man asked me several leading questions. "Where are you getting off? Where are you from? Are you a student? You must be on a scholarship. Your parents must be wealthy to be able to afford paying for your education. Why are you clutching your bag like that?" I grew more and more nervous.

Then in the gloom of the compartment I spied something in his hand that glinted like a piece of metal. Immediately I sat bolt upright. The man enquired, "Are you scared?"

Stupidly, I said, "Yes."

Then he went on, "This is my penknife that I keep in my pocket."

My heart started thumping. I thought, "What have I got myself into? How could I have been so foolish? This is the end!"

Then he explained, "I was lying on it and it was uncomfortable, so I took it out. I always keep it for protection because I was in London and I didn't know whom I would meet there."

At that time, when the island was seeking independence from Britain, there was intense fighting between Greek and Turkish Cypriots so what he said seemed to make sense. I pretended to accept his explanation and lay still on my seat. My mind, however, was very active. The thought of leaving the compartment popped again in my mind, but what would I find in another one? What if I jumped out of the frying pan only to land in the fire? So I remained, but did not sleep a wink. I kept my eyes intently on him as he lay opposite to me.

Eventually we reached Leeds and I breathed a sigh of relief. It turned out he was also leaving the train at Leeds. To give the young man his due, he did take my bag to the taxi-cab. I was thankful to arrive at my destination safe and sound, but I never, ever took the night train after that incident.

Other than the visit to my father, in my final year I pretty much laid low since I had much catching up to do for the final exams. During the Christmas break, however, when I could not stay on campus, those of us who were geography students went on a field trip to Scotland. Over a three-week period we toured the lowlands, crossed the Firth of Forth, touched the cities of Fife and Aberdeen, and ended up in Edinburgh. Our return trip passed through the huge industrial port city of Glasgow and wound its way through Cumberland and the Lake District before returning to Leeds. While on the trip, the other students stayed up late studying every night, despite our weariness after a full day of assignments. I did no such thing. I had a couple of old school friends in Edinburgh attending the university there and every night we got together for dinner or parties. On my return to Leeds, catching up seemed even more hopeless.

Graduation in June 1963

By the beginning of my third and final year at university I began to panic. Too much time had been frittered away during my second year, and with no pressure from end-of-year exams I had not concentrated enough on my studies. I had a growing sense of foreboding that I would pay dearly later. The rocky relationship with Ainsley had not helped. He had graduated and had gone off to London to be articled to a firm of accountants before taking his professional exams. Our relationship had gradually worsened over the year. We were still on speaking terms, but he had a number of girlfriends, chief of whom was a German girl he had started dating in Leeds during my second year.

Basically he and I were quite different. I was shy and naïve, whereas Ainsley was the ultimate extrovert, fun loving, magnanimous, and constantly surrounded by friends. Differences in religion added to the difficulties. I was Anglican and he Roman Catholic, and I sensed in him a somewhat intolerant attitude. Also, he liked having his own way, and when he thought I had wronged him I was given the silent treatment. A hurt look in his eyes would show something was amiss, but it seemed I was expected to telepathically divine the reason, which was maddening. I did not have much experience with men and my fierce independence meant that I would never let on when I was hurt by him. There was a basic lack of communication between us, so our relationship was a tempestuous on-again, off-again affair. When it was off, I went out with other men just to show I did not depend on him. After all, he was not the only fish in the sea. Privately I thought no one else measured up to him, but I would never have admitted that to Ainsley. Throughout all this Cislyn was my chief confidante. I would tell her, "I'm finished with him for good!" She listened sympathetically but only made non-committal remarks. When it was on again, Ainsley or I would call the other and we went on from there without any discussion or resolution of the problem, and certainly no apology on either side.

By the time Ainsley left for London we had grown far apart, although there was no open rupture. In the big metropolis, he felt free to play the field. However, Ainsley was not my greatest concern since I was entering my third and final year. I faced the seemingly insurmountable task of catching up with my neglected studies.

By the time the four-week Easter vacation arrived, the situation was dire. I could not leave Leeds because I had mountains of revisions to get through, so I stayed at the Methodist International House. There I met a young graduate student who influenced me positively. Although he made only a cameo appearance in my life, the advice he gave me was a turning point. He said, "When I was preparing for my finals I studied ten hours a day."

"Really!" I replied. "So I guess you didn't eat or sleep much."

"I had three meals a day and got eight hours sleep each night," he declared.

"I couldn't do that," I said doubtfully.

"Oh yes, you could do the same," he urged, and he told me how he did it.

I thought I would give it a shot. I had nothing to lose. Each day from Monday to Saturday I rose at six a.m. After breakfast I took a brisk fifteen minute walk from the International House to the library, arriving there for its opening at nine a.m. I knocked off for an hour's lunch at midday, and returned for an afternoon session at the library till five p.m. After the walk back to the House, a brief rest, and dinner, I tried to do another three hours of study in my room, until ten p.m. I did not always make the ten hours each day but got close to it. Sunday was my day of rest, when I did not so much as open a book. One Sunday my mentor took me to hear Handel's "Messiah" being performed at a local church. Another Sunday he invited me to a Chinese restaurant, where he taught me how to use chopsticks. It turned out he had spent his early years in China, where his parents had been missionaries. By the end of the Easter vacation I had covered a lot of ground, for which I had to thank the friend who inspired me.

I sat my final exams in June, after which I had a particularly nail-biting experience. Usually I do not worry about an exam after it is over but this time I was summoned for an interview with the external examiners. Normally this occurs when one's results are on the borderline between pass and failure. It was with great trepidation that I entered the room. I do not recall the questions I was asked or how I conducted myself in the interview. What I do remember was that when the results were published a few weeks later, I had obtained an Upper Second Class degree, one step below a First Class degree. In fact, I had received the highest marks in my department, beating all those students who had stayed up late every night while we were on the field trip in Scotland. On graduation day, several parents looked at me with what seemed like envy. Were they wondering how a young girl of color from the colonies could have dared to surpass their little darlings in the final exams?

The irony of the situation was that when I walked down that aisle to pick up my Bachelor of Arts degree in Combined Studies in Geography and History, the only family member in attendance was my father, the person who had not wanted me in the first place, who had made the trip from London. I was saddened that Mum and Lech, who had sacrificed so much for me to achieve this goal, were not able to attend. Their status in the United States was not legal and they could not leave the country until their papers were in order.

Having graduated in the summer of 1963, what was my next move to be? My wish to become a librarian prompted me to apply for an internship at the Goldsmith's Library in London. While awaiting their reply I joined a students' camp tucked away in a rural part of Cambridgeshire, where I engaged in the extremely boring job of sorting strawberries. The red berries were emptied onto a conveyor belt and as they moved along we pulled out the bad ones. We workers were at first thrilled to be able to pop any amount of luscious fruit into our mouths. No one stopped us, perhaps because the managers knew that very soon we would get sick and tired of strawberries. Indeed, by the end of my stint at the camp I did not want to see another strawberry in my life!

At the camp, I struck up a friendship with Jill, a blonde English girl a couple of years younger than I, who occupied the bunk bed above mine. One evening after work Jill had a bright idea. She said, "We're not far from Cambridge. Let's go there on our day off on Saturday."

I had never before visited Cambridge and the idea appealed to me. "But how are we going to get there?" I asked. There was no public transport in this very rural part of Cambridgeshire. People either walked, as we did in the evenings to the local pub down the road, or drove their own cars or lorries (trucks.)

"We could hitchhike," Jill suggested.

I had one previous experience hitchhiking, with Cislyn when we visited Ripon Abbey in Yorkshire. Hitching there had been easy but on the return journey the road was absolutely deserted. We had to walk about five miles to Ilkley where we caught a bus back to Leeds. "Have you any experience hitchhiking?" I asked.

"Yes, I have," Jill replied, "and it's not difficult."

I agreed to go, ignoring any lingering doubts in my mind.

Bright and early on Saturday morning we set off for Cambridge and had no difficulty getting there. We got a ride as far as Ely, where we stopped to admire the beautiful cathedral. It was a bright summer's day with blue skies dotted with little puffs of white clouds. There was plenty of traffic on the road so we easily got transport.

Cambridge was a wonderful experience for me. As a history buff I enjoyed walking through the ancient halls of academia, two of the most memorable being Magdalen College and King's College. We wandered the spacious green lawns and crossed a little bridge over the River Cam, the site of the hotly contended annual rowboat races between Oxford and Cambridge.

At about four in the afternoon Jill suggested it was time to head towards the outskirts of the town to hitch a ride back to the camp. We felt optimistic because the earlier trip had been so easy and the sun was still shining brightly, high in the sky. A number of vehicles breezed past, not bothering to stop. Eventually a lorry slowed down and stopped some distance away. We ran towards it and told the driver our destination. On hearing where we were headed, he said he was not traveling that far but could take us a part of the way. Glad to at least get started on our return journey, we hopped into the cab beside him.

We exchanged a few pleasantries, telling him we were students and that I was from Jamaica. However, as we drove along I began to feel uncomfortable. I sat in the middle of the bench seat beside the driver, who kept throwing furtive glances at my bosom. At twenty-one years old, I was fairly well developed, unlike youthful, boyish looking Jill who sat on my other side. I grew more and more uneasy.

Then it seemed the driver made up his mind as to his next move. He remarked, "You know, you will not be able to get a lift to the camp when I drop you off because it's getting late. No traffic will be going to such a small village at this hour."

Of course, this horrifying thought had not occurred to Jill or me. We were babes in the wood and the driver obviously thought so too. He continued, "I could take you back to the camp but not in the lorry. I will have to drop it off at my house first. Then I can use my car to give you a ride."

Jill kept silent. Fear clutched at my heart. I did not like how he had looked at me. Was he fabricating a story to gain control over us? I had visions of us being abducted and raped. Nevertheless, it seemed there was no other way out of our dilemma. There was no other way for us to return so I had no alternative but to accept his offer. I thought, "Rose, you got yourself into a jam again. How could you be so foolish?" I tried not to let him see how scared I was, but silently I was praying.

Despite our apprehension, it turned out the driver did as promised. He did not interfere with either of us and indeed was a Good Samaritan, dropping us safely at the camp just as night fell.

The various incidents where I took stupid chances could have ended very badly, and from hindsight I believe God was continually looking after me even though I did not know it at the time. I was young and perhaps too gullible, but then it was another time and another age. I was lucky to come out of these situations intact, yet without these experiences life would have been a little tamer and not so rich.

I was accepted at the Goldsmith's Library in London. Unfortunately, the internship did not turn out as expected and that six-month period was one of the most miserable times of my life. The employee assigned as my mentor ignored me completely. He neither talked to me nor coached me, and finally relegated me to an attic floor to work on moldy, moth-eaten books for days on end. Was he a bigoted racist? I did not know, because he refused to engage in conversation with me.

Just as a number of predestined circumstances had directed that I go to Leeds, even allowing me to return there in my first term after attempting to leave, now the signs were pointing to the need for me to depart. The time was fast approaching for me to leave "the mother country." Having applied furiously for jobs at home in Jamaica, I was offered a position as an administrative cadet in the Jamaican Civil Service.

This time I elected to cross the Atlantic by boat, first to spend a couple of weeks in New York with my parents before flying to Jamaica. The transatlantic liner I sailed on was the *SS France,* the newest and fastest at that time. It crossed in four days, surpassing even the *RMS Queen Elizabeth,* which needed five days to complete the journey. The passage in mid December was rough, and huge waves buffeted the large ship. However, I was unfazed and quickly found my sea legs. From past experience I knew I would not get seasick. Perhaps some unknown ancestor of mine had been a sailor.

I shared a cabin with an older woman who spoke no English. It did not matter. Little of my time was spent there as I only entered to sleep, bathe, and dress. Too many interesting activities took place on deck or in the public areas. Every night after dinner I went dancing. As there were twenty-six Spanish jai-alai players onboard, I had no lack of partners. We did not talk either, because they did not know my language and I did not speak theirs. My various partners tried to teach me the *paso doble.* Whenever I made a mistake I pretended the lurching ship and constantly moving dance floor were the chief culprits. That trip on the *France* was a supremely satisfying experience, one I never forgot.

My student days in England had come to an end. Apart from earning a degree, I had learned a few lessons in the school of life. I had grown in maturity and independence. Perhaps there was a little sadness that things had not worked out between Ainsley and me, because he was my first true love. However, I was not about to sit and mope. I was young, intelligent, healthy and strong, and blessed with a good education. There was no looking back, only the future to look forward to. Little did I know then that my sojourn in England was a pivotal time that would change the direction of my life story.

New York

| # *Free, Single, and Disengaged*

Rosemary and her mother, Frances

By December 1963 I was back in Jamaica. It gave me a warm, fuzzy feeling to be in the land of my birth. To this day whenever I land at the Norman Manley Airport in Kingston and view the purplish-blue mountains in the distance, a lump always forms in my throat. I could not believe how much I had missed the sunshine and warmth, the clear blue skies, the sea breezes, and the glorious sunsets. I did not even mind the dust, the flies and mosquitoes, or even the bad manners of so many of the people. I was just so glad to be home.

In other ways, however, my feelings were mixed. During my sojourn in England I had grown up and become independent, but now at twenty-three years old I was back at Kew Road, living with Aunty and Uncle Bert. While I loved them dearly, it really would have been better to have my own apartment. In the 1960s it still was unheard of for young single women to live on their own. Society did not look kindly on that. Why would a young lady want to live alone if it were not to receive male visitors, and who knew what kind of behavior would go on behind closed doors? Living with my aunt and uncle was not that stringent, though. The hardest part was not having my own house key. Maybe it was a matter of security, but as far as they were concerned only the master or mistress of the house possessed a key. I dared not even ask for one. Nobody forbade me from going out or even staying out late, and the old folks were determined to rise out of bed whenever I arrived home, be it one-thirty a.m., four-thirty a.m., or at any other time. They rose willingly, did not seem concerned about the lateness, and hoped I had a good time—but I was still not getting a key to let myself in. I felt badly about waking them from their slumber and luckily I did not go out too often, certainly not every night. The gap between the generations had widened and there was nothing I could do about it.

My first employment was as an administrative cadet at the Ministry of Agriculture, located in one of the most beautiful settings in the island—Hope Gardens. These gardens were a crown jewel during the administration of the British colonial government. I remember, as a child, attending picnics there on public holidays, and on Sunday evenings the police band, dressed in flamboyant uniforms reminiscent of colonial India, performed concerts from the circular bandstand. When I started at the Ministry of Agriculture, Hope Gardens was still in pretty good condition and a zoo had been added. The ministry buildings were nestled between beautiful shade trees, and peacocks strutted all over the grounds, at times extending their long tails of iridescent blue, gold, and black feathers.

My job was easy but the work was boring. I felt myself settling into another rut. Life was a little lonely—many of my school friends were still abroad studying, my parents were in America, and although I dated a few men no one really caught my fancy. In fact, I still missed Ainsley. I found myself comparing any prospective beau to him and each and every one of them lacked in some attribute.

During my six-month stay in London after graduation I had not seen much of Ainsley. Desirous of keeping on friendly terms, he once or twice invited me to lunch. Of his many girlfriends his German fraulein appeared to be the favorite, because he talked quite openly about her to me, and told me of his plans to visit her and her family in Hanover in the summer. I pretended nonchalance even though my heart was breaking. It sounded to me that he was considering marriage—why else would he be going to meet her family? And why was he telling me this? Was he trying to make me jealous? Trying to get some reaction from me? I was determined that I would not run after any man with my heart on my sleeve. It was then I knew I had to get out of England as fast as I could and filled out innumerable applications for jobs in Jamaica.

It was my intention to cut all ties to Ainsley after leaving England, but the night before my departure he invited me to dinner and a movie. He seemed surprised and genuinely sorry that I was going. "So you really *are* leaving?" he kept repeating, as if he could not believe it. After a few more exclamations of disbelief on his part, I relented and promised to keep in touch. Subsequently, I wrote him about twice a year, at Christmas and for his birthday. I still missed him but could not afford to cry over spilt milk. He was probably very happy and I had to get on with my life.

The Smith sisters, whose mother boarded me as a child, lived across the road from Hope Gardens and I often visited them for tea after work. They always enquired of my progress at the ministry. When they discovered I was interested in joining the Jamaican Foreign Service, one of the sisters, Millie, put in a word on my behalf with a family friend, Sir Egerton Richardson, Jamaica's ambassador to the United Nations. After interviewing me, he decided he wanted me to join the mission in New York, and what Sir Egerton wanted, he usually got. A well-known and brilliant man, he was Jamaica's Financial Secretary for years.

After only six short months in Jamaica, I was off to New York, which suited me fine. Mum was still there, although Lech was not at the time. He had made an ill-advised sortie to Nigeria in the hope of establishing a business, only to have the venture collapse. He then ran for his life to England, where he had a sister. From England he was trying to return to America under sponsorship of another sister in New York.

On arrival in New York City, Mum and I quickly rented an apartment at 235 East 83rd Street on Manhattan's east side. This was a time of great satisfaction for us both, when we really had one-on-one time with each other. Mum worked as housekeeper and cook for a rich Jewish family on Madison Avenue. She was given quarters in the basement, which she occupied while on the job, coming home to our place on her days off. Our apartment, located between Second and Third avenues in an area known as Germantown or Yorktown, was conveniently accessible by bus or subway to reach the Jamaican Mission about forty blocks away, near the United Nations. I just loved to walk along the avenues and on 86th Street, where many small businesses, mom-and-pop establishments, delicatessens, bakeries, and other iconic shops assailed the senses, especially of smell and sight.

My time in that little one-bedroom apartment was one of the most idyllic periods of my life. We were on the third floor of a fairly small building, with seven floors and perhaps not more than ten apartments on each floor. Pretty soon we knew most of the people in our building. Big cities, where crowds throng the sidewalks, streets, and subways, have the reputation of being impersonal and lonely, with people caring little about strangers. I, however, did not have that experience in New York City. Shortly after we moved in, Mum and I found a note slipped under our door; it was an invitation to dessert and coffee one evening. The hosts were two girls in their twenties who occupied an apartment at the other end of our floor. Barbara and Ginger had invited everyone on our floor, as well as those on the floors immediately above and below us. Ginger was blonde, pretty, vivacious, and liked to have a good time. Barbara was a brunette who was easy on the eye and also very smart, having qualified as a librarian. They were opposite to each other in personality but we got along famously.

That first night we met several of the neighbors, including the young man who lived immediately below our apartment. He said, "I know exactly when you rise out of bed every morning, usually at seven a.m."

"Really?" was our surprised response. "How do you know that?"

"Because I hear you. I know when you are in the bathroom, too."

It was then that we became aware of the thinness of the walls and floors and realized we had to try to be more considerate of our neighbors. We both were amazed and horrified, and subsequently tiptoed around our bedroom until we installed carpets. Since we rented the apartment unfurnished it was our job to put in not only furniture and draperies but also carpeting. We acquired these things slowly, although we made the carpet a priority once we realized the problem.

We were very close to Lech's two sisters, Solita Cox and Cynthia Wong, who lived in Manhattan. Solita was a British-trained nurse who never married. However, she was the glue holding her family together, always displaying equanimity and the sweetest of temperaments. Solita shared an apartment with a friend on the corner of 49th Street and Seventh Avenue, almost opposite Madison Square Gardens. She just loved the hubbub and activity of a busy city, often walking down to 34th Street and browsing all day in the huge Macy's and Gimbels department stores. The latter was definitely Solita's favorite. More than once I heard my mother remark, "Sol spent the whole day in Gimbels and returned home empty-handed. She didn't buy a thing!"

Cynthia, the youngest of Lech's sister, was married to Frank Wong, a Chinese man. They produced three beautiful children—Junie, Stevie, and Tommy, who were then ages twelve, eleven, and nine, respectively. Since the Wong family did not live too far from us, their frequent visits gave us great joy, as the children were extremely warm and loving. Sometimes we took care of them after school while Cynthia and Frank were still at work. I frequently took them to the movies or to the park, and once we went to the ice rink at the Central Park Zoo—they skated while I watched from the sidelines; not being particularly athletic, I certainly did not want to take a chance and fall. In the summer we all often went to the beach or to Coney Island Amusement Park, and sometimes on a boat ride up the Hudson River to West Point or to the Bear Mountain picnic grounds in Poughkeepsie. Having family and close friends in New York made me feel right at home.

When Mum's birthday came around, I made reservations to take her to dinner at the Rainbow Room in Rockefeller Center. It so happened that Tommy visited that day. As the reservation time of five p.m. approached, Mum and I decided to take him with us. Although not dressed up, he was clean and, at the age of nine, he looked a lot younger because of his small size. Tommy was noticeably awed by the restaurant, where we had a magnificent view of the city against the backdrop of the setting sun. The staff, from the maître d' on down to the waiters, was captivated by Tommy, who was cute and asked inquisitive questions. Because the hour was so early, the restaurant was nearly empty and they danced attendance on us. I do not remember what we ordered, but what stayed with me was seeing Tommy's eyes pop open wide when the dessert trolley was rolled to our table for us to make our choices. The cart's three shelves were heavily laden with a variety of mouth-watering goodies. What to choose was a mind-boggling exercise.

One day while Lech was still in England Solita called asking for our assistance. Lech's son, Lennox, who was employed by British West Indian Airways in Barbados, and a fellow employee named Bentley were stranded at Kennedy International Airport. On their way to London from Barbados, they were bounced off the flight in New York for paying passengers. Young and inexperienced, they had insufficient money for hotel accommodations until a flight was available for them, and Lennox appealed to his aunt for help. Solita had space for one person and elected to have Lennox stay with her. She asked whether we could take Bentley. We had no objection, but Lennox had no idea of his father's connection to us, which presented a complication. In the end, we did agree to accommodate Bentley, and Lennox accompanied him to our place. The two young men had a lot of fun that evening. Lennox met and took a fancy to our attractive neighbor, Ginger. We stayed up late, talking, laughing, and joking, while the drinks flowed. The hour got so late that Lennox crashed on the sofa bed beside Bentley in the living room. He never once slept at his aunt's place. It was a long time after his return to Barbados before he learned that his hosts in New York were his father's girlfriend and her daughter. Lennox never forgot our kindness and several years later was instrumental in putting Lech in touch with a lawyer who handled his parents' divorce.

Some people declare that they dislike the hustle and bustle of New York City. I loved living there during the 1960s. When

I first arrived in the city, I consistently lost my way whenever I entered the subway system. Accustomed to the clear directions of the London Underground, I found it difficult to adjust to the New York subway lines. In fact, for a long time I used the city buses, despite the additional time it took to get to work. Eventually I found my way around the subways. I became accustomed to the wave of peak-hour crowds that propelled me into the subway cars and likewise on exiting, the wave of humanity that pushed me out onto the platform.

In November 1965 a wide-scale electrical blackout occurred, lasting nearly thirteen hours. It began shortly after five p.m., at the height of the evening peak-hour traffic. Most of the northeast of the country was affected, with power first failing in Buffalo, Rochester, and Albany, then spreading with a rapid domino effect to Boston, Connecticut, Vermont, Manhattan, the Bronx, most of Brooklyn, and eastern Canada. In New York City, thirty million people in an 80,000-square-foot area were without power, and more than 800,000 people were trapped in subways for hours. I have no idea how many thousands were trapped in elevators for the duration.

I was lucky to have a ride home from a co-worker who had driven to work that day. However, it took us nearly three hours to travel the forty blocks. The roads were a mess, especially since the traffic lights were not working. Civic-minded, experienced citizens began to direct traffic at some of the intersections. The subways could not run, and the buses were unable to handle the masses of people who had started walking home. When I eventually reached our apartment building, I then had to climb stairs to the third floor because, of course, the elevators were not functioning. At the time I did not realize how lucky I was to have such a short ascent. Later I discovered that Ambassador Richardson, who had a heart condition, lived on the twenty-fourth floor of his building and had to labor up to the top.

On entering our apartment, I found Mum sitting in the darkness, shivering in her winter coat. We only had a couple of flashlights and there was no power for heat. It being November, the nights were definitely chilly. My cousin Thelma Anderson, who worked in Manhattan, came to our apartment, as she had no transportation to her home in Jamaica, Long Island. The three of us spent the night huddled together in our coats and as many blankets as we could find. We had a gas stove so were able to make cups of tea, but we worried that the food in the freezer would thaw. It was then that I realized how dependent we were on electricity in our modern day society. It was fortuitous there was a large full moon. Under the usual brightness of all the city lights, street lamps, and neon signs, I had never before noticed the moon. Until we were plunged into darkness I had never before glimpsed the stars shining brilliantly. It took a blackout to discover that the moon and the stars shone even over New York City.

The power returned while we were dressing for work the following morning. As the subway system was still disrupted, Thelma and I decided to take the bus. The buses kept passing by, all filled to capacity. We started to walk while keeping a look-out if perchance a bus might stop to let out passengers and therefore be able to take us in. However, we had no luck. All the taxicabs were similarly full. We kept on walking and I was thankful there was no snow on the ground. After a while we found we had walked forty blocks and I was at the office. The walk turned out to be relatively easy since I was wearing my comfortable leather boots and conversation with Thelma helped to pass the time.

I was enamored by New York City. The lights, the glamour, the holiday season with decorated store windows and skaters at Rockefeller Center—everything enchanted me. I did it all, visiting the art museums, the Metropolitan Museum, attending Shakespeare in the Park, rowing on the lake in Central Park, and taking the Circle Line cocktail cruise around Manhattan, as well as cruising up the Hudson River to Poughkeepsie or Bear Mountain in the summer.

As the world's premier metropolitan center, New York is noted for its restaurants and its food, and the international fare intrigued me. I dined at fancy French restaurants, as well as Chinese, Greek, Arab, and Japanese ones. A favorite of mine was Chateau Madrid, which offered *paella* and other tasty Spanish fare, as well as classical guitar and flamenco dance performances. Once I was taken to the posh Plaza Hotel for a concert by the noted jazz singer Nancy Wilson. It was also a privilege to hear Tony Bennett and Miriam Makeba performing at clubs.

I visited all the tourist spots. At the Statue of Liberty I ascended the narrow spiral staircase to reach the arm, which was open to the public in the 1960s. It was a great thrill to reach the top of the Empire State Building, the world's tallest at that time. However, when friends and family visited from Jamaica I was expected to take them there, so by the time I had done the Empire State Building for perhaps the tenth time, I was completely jaded.

The Jamaican Mission to the United Nations where I worked was situated in a high-rise building near Third Avenue and 42nd Street, not far from the United Nations complex. Jamaica ran a tight ship, so the mission was small, consisting of the ambassador and three assistants, plus Angela King and myself as diplomatic attachés. Support staff, such as the office manager, librarian, and secretaries, was recruited from Jamaicans living in New York.

We worked together with the Trinidadians, the only other independent, English-speaking Caribbean country at that time. Although we were geographically considered part of the Latin American bloc aligned closely with the United States in voting, we had language differences with the majority of our neighbors. We took great interest in the Economic and Social Sub-Committee, where we joined the Third World bloc in an effort to help our products—bauxite, sugar, rum, and bananas—break into world markets. We tried to make our mark on the Human Rights Sub-Committee, since as a small country we had little influence on world geo-politics.

In many policy matters we joined the non-aligned countries, where we sided with neither of the two great powers during the Cold War. In 1964, the military arms race of the Cold War was raging. During the General Assembly sessions, our job was to listen to the speeches from the foreign ministers of the different countries and inform our country of any changes in policy. We wore headsets to listen to the simultaneous translation in five major languages: English, French, Spanish, Russian, and Chinese. While most of the speeches were boring and full of platitudes, we made sure to hear what was said by the "big guns," the five permanent Security Council members—the United States of America, the Soviet Union, Britain, France, and the Republic of China. (In 1964, China's seat at the United Nations was still occupied by the nationalist government located in Taiwan, which pre-dated the 1971 take-over of the seat by the communist People's Republic of China.)

I was introduced to the people I needed to know in the UN Secretariat, some of whom were Jamaican nationals. Soon I was finding my way around the General Assembly hall, different meeting halls, the delegates' lounge, and dining room. The highlight during my first General Assembly session was meeting Foreign Minister Golda Meir of Israel, who invited all the women delegates to lunch.

The social part of the job was huge and cocktail parties occurred on an almost daily basis, especially for Independence Day celebrations of the various countries. I learned very early to wear, each day, a basic dress that lent itself to a change of accessories. Slipping into fashionably high heels and adding an evening bag and diamante necklace and earrings, I was then well dressed for the after-work cocktail parties. Each morning the ambassador went through the invitations, deciding which staff members would represent Jamaica at which events. Among those I was assigned to attend were Nepal's celebration as well as Haiti's and Cote d'Ivoire (The Ivory Coast), where my French came in handy. Famed singer Miriam Makeba and political activist Stokely Carmichael attended one of the African receptions and we were thrilled when Miriam, whose nickname was "Mama Africa," entertained us with a few of her iconic songs.

I also met Tanzania's ambassador to Egypt, young man from Zanzibar, named Dr. Salim Ahmed Salim. He claimed to have visited Cuba and said he was friendly with Fidel Castro and Che Guevara. Although Cuba was Jamaica's nearest neighbor, only ninety miles north of our island, Jamaicans were not traveling to Cuba in those days. We were definitely toeing the line and obeying the bidding of Uncle Sam, which had banned travel to Cuba in 1960. I must admit some envy that Salim, from far-away Africa, had met these national heroes, who were brilliant leaders yet dangerous to the values and interests of the Western powers. In the 1980s, Dr. Salim became Tanzania's Minister of Foreign Affairs.

A member of Sudan's mission to the United Nations named Mahdi became one of my friends. He invited me to visit his ambassador's home one evening. The latter was celebrating the birth of his son, who arrived after several childless years. His wife was still in the hospital and although strict Muslims are not supposed to drink, he mixed a lethal cocktail of champagne and brandy, which he poured through a sliced orange filter and then proceeded to fill our glasses. The first one went down very well, but as fast as I drank, the ambassador topped off my glass. The bubbly began to go to my head and I instinctively started to slow down. "Drink up! Drink up!" the ambassador exclaimed. I wondered, "Is he trying to make me drunk?" There was I, a young, single girl in an apartment with two foreign men. I did not know what designs they had, and was determined not to pass out. So after about four large drinks, I insisted that I really had to leave. To his credit, Mahdi helped me get a cab because by then it was about two a.m. It was with great relief that I made it home safely. Maybe I was endowed with good genes for holding my liquor because my maternal grandfather had been known to be quite a rum bibber.

One of the perks of accreditation to the United Nations was the hospitality committee's offer of free Broadway tickets. Usually these were for the longer running shows and could be used if a delegate wished to entertain a VIP, such as his country's foreign minister. On request, the hospitality committee provided tickets, no questions asked, and I took advantage of the opportunity to see many Broadway hits, including *Funny Girl, Mame, The Odd Couple,* and *Man of La Mancha.* Although tickets for concerts at Carnegie Hall and the Lincoln Center were not included, I still jumped at the chance to attend those as well, even if I had to pay.

CHAPTER ELEVEN

Expanding Horizons

Shortly after my arrival at the Jamaican Mission in 1964, Ambassador Richardson summoned me to his office. He asked if I would be interested in a Carnegie Fellowship. I had never heard of this program. He quickly explained that the Carnegie Institute for International Peace was a non-governmental organization that awarded annual fellowships to young diplomats from newly independent countries in Africa, Asia, and the Caribbean. A Carnegie Fellowship involved two semesters of study at Columbia University's School of International Affairs, followed by three months of travel to various international capital cities. I jumped at the opportunity to take part.

Sixteen Fellows were stationed in New York, while a similar number of French-speaking members did a fellowship year in Geneva. The two groups would then combine when those of us from New York landed in Geneva and proceeded on the European leg of the tour.

The New York City program was managed by Reginald Barrett, an Englishman who was familiar with all parts of the British Commonwealth whose newly independent countries participated. He and his wife, Elizabeth, and their two teenaged children graciously entertained us at their suburban home in New Rochelle at the beginning and end of the program. Mr. Barrett was intelligent, gentle, and genuinely interested in different people and cultures. He had a unique ability to draw out and get the best from the individuals he came in contact with. Amply endowed with an oversized paunch, Mr. Barrett also enjoyed the good things of life—excellent meals, fine liqueurs, and good cigars. It was he who introduced me to Irish coffee after a superb meal; until then I had no idea coffee could be spiked with liquor.

Soon after I was awarded the fellowship, Probyn Marsh, one of our diplomats and a former recipient, advised, "You must meet Miss Ruth Jett. She is the person you need to know if you wish to thrive as a Carnegie Fellow." He then invited Miss Jett and me to lunch at a Chinese restaurant. She was an impressive lady of African-American descent. I believe she had native North American blood flowing through her veins because she was extremely tall and straight, at least six foot in height, and had an aquiline nose. Besides, her last name, Jett, and her sister's name, Jenny Peace, reinforced my belief in her North American antecedents. To my great regret, I never did ask her. Miss Jett was Mr. Barrett's right hand man, or should I say his girl Friday. As his executive secretary, she handled much more than the usual correspondence, including the day-to-day issues of the Carnegie Fellows. She was pleasant and helpful but she was also the powerhouse behind the throne.

Unlike the other Carnegie Fellows who resided in the International House nearby, I remained in the apartment I shared with Mum, commuting each day to Columbia University. We were a diverse group, representing Jamaica, Jordan, Kenya, Nigeria, The Philippines, Sierra Leone, South Korea, South Vietnam, Sudan, Syria, Tanzania, Tunisia, and Uganda. There were only three women among us, and I was the only representative from the Americas. The other two females were My Leung, from Vietnam, and Njeri, from Kenya.

The time spent at Columbia was a heady one. It was good to be in the halls of learning once more, although far different from what I anticipated. The whole concept and method of education was a far cry from my experience in Leeds.

We attended classes with Americans who had ambitions of entering the United States Foreign Service and had experience with such foreign languages as Arabic and Russian. We studied political subjects such as military alliances, NATO—the North Atlantic Treaty Organization, and the Cold War, along with international economics, which alas was still my bane. Since my country was geographically part of the Americas, it was considered part of Latin America even though we were historically, culturally, and linguistically different. Jamaica's alignment with the South American continent led me to do a course on corruption in Latin America. Considering that at that time Jamaica was stable, I did not feel the politics of the "banana republics" and strongman rule applied to us.

Studies in diplomacy were part of a graduate program we students were expected to handle on our own. There were no tutorials, although we could visit lecturers in their offices at specific times if we had problems. I found it strange that some students questioned the lecturers in class, sometimes even interrupting the presentations. Above all, it was strange to do three or four courses a semester, take mid-term and final exams, have the marks added to our aggregate at the end of our studies, and then be done with that course forever. In England we had fewer tests and all we learned during the entire year could come up in the end-of-year exams. It was a completely different system but I believe the American system produced more rounded individuals, who knew something of subjects other than their specialties. I was amazed that most students showed, in their conversations, they knew something of art, music, and science, topics outside of their International Affairs specialty. In the British educational system we specialized much earlier, in fact starting in our final two years of high school.

The Carnegie Fellows were not required to sit exams and obtain grades. Some of my colleagues barely attended lectures, much less took the tests. I did because I knew that if I did not undergo the pressure of exams I would just waste time and learn very little. However, the multiple-choice format of the testing was new to me; I was accustomed to essay type answers. Studying again was stimulating, though I confess I did not work as hard as I could have and therefore did not realize my full potential.

The excitement of meeting people of different backgrounds and cultures greatly appealed to me and I took great pains to get to know the other Fellows. I threw many parties in my apartment to which they were all invited. Our neighbors, Barbara and Ginger, were always invited, as well as my cousin, Thelma, and Faye Robinson—Bebe, my childhood playmate from Thompson Town days, who now resided in Brooklyn with her mother. We had wonderful times. On a couple of occasions the police came to shut us down because of complaints from other residents. We just took that in stride.

One November afternoon I stepped into the elevator at the School of International Affairs, on my way to visit the Dean's office. A young man entered at the same time and greeted me as a fellow student. While ascending to the top floor together, he asked, "How do you plan to celebrate Thanksgiving?"

"Oh," I replied, "we don't celebrate Thanksgiving in Jamaica, so it is just another day for me."

"What a pity!" he said. "Thanksgiving is the best holiday ever, better even than Christmas!"

We exited and went about our business. It so happened that in going back down we again found ourselves on the same elevator. He said, "I find it a shame that you don't know anything about our Thanksgiving. My name is Carl Schieren, and I'm a resident of the International House. I've invited some of the Carnegie Fellows to spend Thanksgiving with my family at my grandmother's house in Connecticut. I know it's short notice but would you like to join us?"

Taken by surprise, I hesitated. He went on, "Habib, the Carnegie Fellow from Tunisia, is coming."

"I'll have to think about it," I replied. "I'll let you know." Then we exchanged phone numbers. Later I contacted Habib, who confirmed that he was going on the trip. He said, "I know Carl. He lives here in the International House and he is a good guy. You have nothing to fear from him." So I agreed to go.

Twenty-four hours before our departure, Carl rang me to say, "All the Carnegie Fellows including Habib have backed out, and only one student from Ghana is still going. I don't believe you know him. I thought I'd let you know so that you'd have the option of backing out if you don't feel comfortable."

It was very gentlemanly of Carl to forewarn me of this new development. I thought about it for a few minutes while questioning him further. "He has to be all right," I thought. Taking a chance, I made up my mind. "Okay, I'll still go." Mum was obviously disturbed about my decision but did not try to stop me. I was twenty-four years old and she knew better than to question my judgment. She did, however, beg me to call her when we arrived at our destination.

Carl turned out to be impeccable in his behavior. The Ghanaian occupied the back seat and I sat beside Carl in the front. The only incident was the receipt of a speeding ticket for going over seventy miles an hour in his station wagon. We were all so engrossed in conversation that Carl failed to pay attention to the speedometer.

The weekend turned out to be a wonderful experience. Carl's grandmother's spacious house was painted white in the tradition of many New England buildings. She, as well as the extended family—Carl's parents, younger sister, aunts, uncles, and cousins, proved to be gracious hosts. The Thanksgiving dinner was sumptuous. That was the first time I ever tasted banana bread, which we Jamaicans never baked even though bananas were the island's second largest crop. I asked Carl's sister, who prepared the bread, to give me the recipe. Looking back now, I know I took a big chance but was glad for the opportunity to celebrate my first Thanksgiving in style. Even now at each Thanksgiving I still remember Carl Schieren and his family, and yes, I agree with him that it is better than Christmas. Certainly it is a longer holiday, due to the long weekend that always follows.

On another occasion Carl invited me to join a group of students for a weekend ski trip to Vermont. I had never before gone skiing and, despite my lack of athleticism, looked forward to this new experience eagerly. The successful Thanksgiving trip allowed me to feel quite comfortable in participating, so we piled into his station wagon and drove to Manchester, Vermont. We stayed in a chalet with oversized glass windows, giving access to magnificent picture-postcard vistas of the winter wonderland of the slopes outside. Using rental equipment from the ski lodge, three or four of us joined the beginners' class. I remember the Austrian instructor advising us to pay attention and follow all the rules so as to avoid breaking a leg or sustaining any other injury. "My God!" I thought. It had never occurred to me that I could get hurt! We headed to the baby slope for beginners, where I was outfitted with six-foot-long skis. Immediately, to my chagrin, I fell flat on my behind. When the instructor commanded me to rise, I found myself unable to move. The skis had crossed under my body and their entanglement immobilized me. I was red with embarrassment as the instructor helped me up. The first lesson had started inauspiciously for me.

We were taught how to ascend a slope by turning sideways and cutting the skis into the contours of the slope while going up. The next day the instructor took us further up the slope and showed us how to stop and to negotiate turns. The third day we were allowed to ascend on the ski lift to the top of the slope. Believe it or not, I made my way down without a catastrophic outcome, although it took me an agonizingly long time. The fastest learner was a Libyan. A natural, it looked as if he had been born on skis. What was remarkable was this trip occurred during the Muslim holy month of Ramadan, and he was fasting during the day. How he achieved what he did on the frozen slopes with no sustenance for energy and warmth, I could not fathom.

The temperatures on the mountain were the most frigid I had ever experienced. I had no thermal underwear or accessories, and was not about to buy those for just one weekend. Although thick woolen socks covered my feet, they proved utterly ineffective in maintaining warmth inside the rented ski boots, and my extremities felt like frozen meat. The pain of the thawing process was excruciating. From lessons learned in England, I knew better than get too close to the roaring fire in the lodge. I certainly did not want to lose a finger or a toe to chilblains, but never did I appreciate a mug of steaming hot chocolate as then. Despite the discomfort, I would not have missed the experience of skiing and had to thank Carl for affording me that opportunity.

Carl and his friends were stalwarts at my parties in the apartment. I believe Carl liked me and we did go out on dates, but he was probably too shy to reveal his feelings and it was likewise with me. We never even kissed.

The highlight of the Carnegie Fellowship program was the three-month, 1965 tour of capital cities in North America, Europe, and North Africa. Flying from New York to

Washington DC, I was dumbfounded when a length of red carpet was laid for us as we alighted from the plane. I had presumed "laying down the red carpet" was only a figure of speech and did not think there would be an actual piece of carpet for us to walk on. Accommodated in a first-class hotel that was centrally located, we could easily walk to most of the places on our itinerary. We sat in on a session of the House of Representatives and even boarded the underground trolleys lawmakers used to get around the huge building. After being treated to lunch there, we toured the White House, climbed the Washington Monument, and visited other national sites such as the Lincoln Memorial. A bus also took us to Arlington Cemetery, where we viewed the graves of the Unknown Soldier and President John F. Kennedy, who had been assassinated nearly two years earlier. In the evenings we were also entertained. I remember attending a performance of the Bolshoi Ballet and a garden party in Chevy Chase, Maryland, held in our honor.

From Washington we flew to Toronto, where we were accommodated in residences at the University of Toronto. We next flew to Ottawa, where we visited Carlton University, new at the time, and made trips to Niagara Falls and to Stratford, Ontario, to attend a Shakespeare play. The St. Lawrence Seaway at The Thousand Islands, and Upper Canada Village—a simulation of a pioneer village, were also on our itinerary. Then we flew to Ottawa where we sat in on a session of the House of Parliament and where I took a photo with a member of the Royal Canadian Mounties. We stayed at the prominent Hotel Laurentian downtown, where we attended a dinner with ministers in the Canadian government. One French-Canadian minister took a fancy to my Vietnamese colleague, My Leung, who was pretty and petite and proficient in French. She later confided that the minister spoke very old-fashioned French, citing that he referred to the movies as *la maison des images*—the picture house, instead of *le cinema* as the modern day French said.

The opportunity to visit all these interesting places, let alone as highly respected VIPs, was mind-boggling. As a geography student I was always drawn toward different peoples, cultures, and places. I do not know if I learned a whole lot but I certainly reveled in these new experiences, and there was more to come. After returning to our base in New York, we were to embark on a grand tour of European capitals, ending up in North Africa.

Across the Atlantic we flew, to Geneva, where we joined the French-speaking Carnegie Fellows who had spent two semesters studying there. Miss Jett was along, to chaperone us three young women as well as coordinate the tour and troubleshoot whenever problems arose.

A minor incident occurred as we were landing, something far outside Miss Jett's ability to resolve. Geneva is situated near the southwestern corner of Lake Geneva, and surrounded by the Alps and the Jura mountains. With very little room to make the usual wide circles while descending to the airport, the pilot had to drop the Swissair plane much more directly. As we were making the final descent, the plane suddenly lurched to one side and then began to climb rapidly. Luggage under the seats went sliding to the rear of the plane. This maneuver scared us all out of our wits. We had no idea what had happened since no announcement was made from the cockpit. However, the Jordanian Carnegie Fellow sitting by a window said he saw a small plane in our flight path, where it should not have been, and was visibly shaken. It was only the pilot's quick action of aborting the landing and swerving to avoid a collision that saved us. The next time around the landing went without a hitch. We all breathed a collective sigh of relief, but our nerves were well and truly rattled. As we collected our belongings, a member of our group found my butterfly-shaped gold ring, with five diamonds forming the body of the butterfly, on the floor. Given to me by my mother as a graduation gift, it fitted rather loosely and had slipped off my finger during the pilot's maneuver. In all the excitement I had not even missed it. I would have been devastated had it been lost.

Geneva was a beautiful, cool, clean city. We were accommodated in a modern hotel in a new section of town. After a night's sleep to overcome jetlag, we were ready the next morning to explore our new surroundings. Lake Geneva, a large body of deep blue water, was a sight to behold, with a *jet d'eau*—a geyser—erupting at regular intervals. Whether this was natural or manmade I did not know but it provided a mesmerizing focal point for us visitors. We toured the Palais des Nations, the headquarters of the old League of Nations during the inter-war period and which now accommodated specialized agencies of the UN, such as the International Labor Organization, the World Health Organization, and the World Trade Organization.

After a sumptuous lunch, we attended an afternoon session of the Economic and Social Committee of the United Nations. We sat in the visitor's gallery, which was divided into two sections, one on each side of the hall, and which placed us facing each other. The combination of the heavy lunch washed down with several glasses of wine, the afternoon heat, and the dry, boring speeches encouraged an overwhelming desire towards somnolence. The Carnegie Fellow from Sierra Leone, sitting beside me, was not about to fight the drowsiness. He donned his dark glasses, which he thought would prevent detection, and went to sleep. As his body relaxed he slumped on my shoulder. Embarrassment crept over me as the Fellows in the gallery opposite noticed and began to snigger. In vain I shook him, trying to get him awake. I was reluctant to make a scene and he was sound asleep, repeatedly slumping down on my shoulder. I could have sunk into the ground.

Later that evening—in fact, every evening we were in Geneva, we made our way over to the old town where all the restaurants and clubs were located. Here the nightlife buzzed with young people who enjoyed rock 'n' roll and we had a fabulous time.

From Geneva we flew to Paris. Immediately after we arrived, Mr. Park, the Korean Carnegie Fellow, found an excellent Chinese restaurant; the cuisine was probably the most memorable I had ever tasted. He had an uncanny ability to very quickly locate the first-class Asian dining places in every city we toured. Our professional itinerary took us to the UNESCO headquarters and the Quai D'Orsay, the nerve center of France's foreign affairs. We also did touristy things like visiting King Louis XIV's famous palace at Versailles and Les Invalides, where Napoleon Bonaparte is buried. We walked along the Rive Gauche, passing sidewalk cafés and artists in the bohemian Left Bank area, to Mont Martres. There we climbed the innumerable steps to the church of the Sacré Coeur, with its expansive, commanding view of the city. Most of all it was the fun things we did that made Paris so appealing.

From the moment we hit the streets of Paris, Chalaan, the Syrian Carnegie Fellow, became a different person. Whereas in New York he was always quiet and even a bit morose, here he was joyous and elated. Maybe recalling his carefree student days in Paris, Chalaan was instrumental in our going to the famous Moulin Rouge, to enjoy dinner and a show.

Occupying a huge, banquet-style table, we received VIP treatment. The Arabs among us suggested that instead of each person ordering individual glasses of scotch whiskey, which commanded an exorbitant price in Paris, we should order a bottle of champagne and split the cost. We did, and the six-liter Methuselah bottle lasted the evening, giving us a feeling of *bon esprit.*

As we dined, the cabaret show unfolded. What surprised ingenuous me was that all the females performed in all the various routines with bared breasts. In mixed company I felt rather embarrassed, but looking around, saw no one else thought anything of it. Particularly incongruous was a performance reminiscent of *My Fair Lady,* depicting ladies at the horse races wearing long gowns, gloves that extended to their elbows, and picture hats, while flaunting uncovered breasts. There was an underwater performance with a huge glass tank on the stage, in which topless swimmers went through their routines. The girls were young and pretty with uplifted breasts and there was nothing lascivious about the performances. Since everyone around me behaved as if there was nothing out of the ordinary I just settled down and enjoyed the show.

We stayed at the Hôtel Lutetia, an old and prestigious establishment in the Left Bank area. The three of us girls shared a room, which was adequate except for the private bathroom. It had only a washbasin and a toilet. To bathe, we had to reserve a bathtub in the general bathroom and at extra cost. Since Miss Jett had a tub in her bathroom, she generously allowed us to use it. I do not know how most of the men handled the situation, but on the morning when we were checking out, there was a little altercation at the front desk. The two Tanzanian Carnegie Fellows had taken daily baths, which they now were being asked to pay for. They refused, saying, "The Carnegie Endowment is supposed to pay for our full accommodation. See Miss Jett. She is to pay for our baths." Miss Jett was not happy with their behavior. I believe she, like we did, assumed that a private bath in the rooms included a tub or a shower. Thereafter, whenever we arrived in a new city, the first thing we did was to check the bathroom, to ensure we had a place to bathe.

From Paris we traveled to Brussels. This magnificent city is the headquarters of the European Union, comprising the European Commission—the executive government branch, and the Council of the European Union—the legislative institution. Our hotel was very near the Royal Palace of Brussels, but we never saw any members of King Baudouin's family. Touring the city, we viewed the statue of the Manneken Pis, which stands near a street corner. This famous, small bronze sculpture, created in 1619, depicts a little boy peeing into a fountain basin. We were told a legend about the sculpture. In the fourteenth century, Brussels was under siege by Spain. When the attackers could not overtake the city, they decided to set it afire. A little boy spotted the burning fuse and put it out by urinating on it, thus saving the city and becoming a national hero. Whether this story was true or not—there are several other legends—we all bought small souvenirs of the Manneken Pis.

Thereafter we proceeded to Amsterdam, the hub of our stay in the Netherlands, where we were accommodated in a modern hotel near the outskirts of the city. A boat ride through Amsterdam's canals ended with us dining at an excellent Indonesian restaurant overlooking the canal and which we had caught a glimpse of while on the boat. This was my first experience with Indonesian cuisine, which delighted and enticed me with its subtle and interesting flavors.

Independently, a group of us visited Rotterdam's large and important seaport. Also, we stopped at the town of Delft, a tourist mecca famous for producing a particular blue-and-white earthenware. I bought several small pieces, of windmills, Dutch clogs, and other curios. At the local market, Miss Jett bought Dutch cheeses, including Edam and Gouda. What was uncanny was that although neither vendor nor customer knew the other's language, they were able to understand one another. Many of the words and intonations were similar to English and this made me realize just how close our language is to its Germanic roots.

A trip to The Hague allowed us to visit the International Court of Justice, the primary judicial branch of the United Nations. Based in the Peace Palace in The Hague, its main function is to settle disputes between different countries and to provide legal opinions whenever needed by the General Assembly or any of its branches or specialized agencies. At the rear of the Peace Palace, we wandered through luxuriant gardens, which were dominated by a statue of Erasmus, a Catholic priest and humanist who lived around the time of the European Reformation.

Next we traveled to London, where we stayed at the prestigious Strand Palace Hotel in the heart of the city. Like the Hôtel Lutetia in Paris, where we had problems with our bathing situation, the Strand Palace was overrated, in my opinion. Again there were no private baths, so I had to let the staff know ahead of time whenever I wanted one, which they did willingly prepare and at no extra cost. They did, however, expect a tip. They also showed surprise when I requested a bath for each of the five days I spent in London.

We visited the Commonwealth Relations Office, which handled relations with members of the British Commonwealth, including those colonies that were now independent. As Jamaica had achieved its independence in 1962, we fell under this ministerial office. (In 1968, the Commonwealth Office merged with the Foreign Office, under the purview of the British Foreign Minister.) The other places we visited must have not been very interesting because I do not remember anything about them. In fact, my head was in a whirl because a new development was occurring in my life.

On leaving England in December 1963, I resolved not to keep in touch with Ainsley. However, on the night before my departure, when he invited me out, he seemed so woebegone and incredulous over my actual leaving that I relented and promised to write, which I did at Christmas and for his birthday in April. Knowing I would be in London for five days, I had written him this news. Immediately on my arrival at the Strand Palace Hotel, Ainsley contacted me. It turned out his office was not far away and we agreed on a time to meet. Seeing him again, I examined him carefully. His hair had started to recede from his forehead and a widow's peak had begun to appear. There were also a few gray hairs, but he was still a handsome young man. His dark skin was still as smooth as black velvet, and his nearly six-foot frame as trim as ever. He was dressed nattily in a dark suit with slim pants and a starched white shirt barely accented with a slim tie. A bowler hat and a finely rolled umbrella completed his attire. All these made up the uniform of workers in London's City district.

Ainsley seemed to like what he saw in me, too. I was slim, weighing approximately 120 pounds. My dark hair had been properly coiffed by my New York hairdresser and maybe I had an air of assurance about me. Ainsley seemed impressed that I was on this fellowship, with an opportunity to travel in style to so many countries. He was in awe that I was staying at the Strand Palace, which to me was not nearly as impressive as he thought it was. He invited me to join him and some of his friends at a pub after work. There I easily downed a few glasses of Johnny Walker Black Label and club soda, which had become my favorite drink in New York. I believe he was quite impressed with my capacity to drink—I had gained practice at the cocktail parties I attended at the United Nations.

Every single evening I was in London, Ainsley invited me out, whether to the pub or to dinner. On Saturday evening we attended a huge party at someone's home, and the place was jam-packed. A few Africans were there and attempted to dance with me. As Ainsley liked to spend time at the bar to have his drinks, he got his teetotalling friend, Eddie St. Hill, to keep watch over me so I did not go off with anyone else. Eddie liked to dance and kept me so occupied that no one else had a chance. Why this proprietary attitude on Ainsley's part, I wondered. Was he showing interest in me again? On my last evening in London, which we spent quietly together, he indicated that he wanted to start a relationship with me once more.

"What about your German girlfriend?" I asked. "I remember that you spent a summer with her in Hanover. It must have been serious since you were meeting her family, so I presumed you were contemplating marriage."

"No, I let her go," he replied. "I felt it was better not to marry a white girl, but to settle down with someone from the Caribbean. I see a future for you and me."

Ainsley was reticent with his words. I cannot remember him saying that he loved me. He did say that he was definitely interested in us getting married after he finished his studies. Still articled to a firm of accountants, he had passed most of the professional exams, but had a couple to complete before being certified.

"You do realize," I remarked, "this would be a long-distance relationship, which usually does not work out."

"We just have to try it and see," he replied.

I was persuaded because I liked what I saw in him. At twenty-six, Ainsley had matured considerably. We both had. I had gained much more confidence. He was less intolerant and domineering, and more compromising. He had learned to control his quick temper and his impatience, and was much more tolerant toward others. To tell the truth, even though I had dated different men, I had not encountered anyone who measured up to him in my eyes. He was a smart, take-charge sort of person, handsome and always neatly dressed, almost to the point of being a dandy. Also, he was an excellent cook, a plus with me because I loved good food. I promised that at the end of the tour I would return to London to spend a few more days with him before going back to New York. For the rest of the tour, I was elated. After seeing Ainsley again, there seemed to be a future for us together after all.

After our lengthy stay in London, we flew to Belgrade, Yugoslavia. In 1965, it was still a Communist country that unified Croatia and Serbia under the control of General Josip Tito. Although authoritarian, he was regarded by many as a benevolent dictator who managed to keep various ethnic groups coexisting peacefully in the federation. President Tito, together with Jawaharlal Nehru, India's first prime minister; General Abdel Nasser, president of Egypt; and Sukarno, the first president of Indonesia, were leaders of the Non-Aligned Movement, which kept their countries independent of the opposing sides of the Western Bloc and the Soviets in the Cold War.

In Belgrade, we engaged mainly in tourist activities. I do not remember visiting any government offices. For us the excitement was seeing a country that was officially socialist. It did not seem much different from other European countries.

The historical core of Belgrade is the Kalemegdan, an ancient fortress overlooking the Danube River at the confluence of its tributary with the Sava. Admiring the panoramic view, my observation was that the waters of the Danube were not the blue immortalized in Strauss' waltz, but rather an inky black. Strange! On the grounds of the fortress we listened to a concert of marches and polkas performed by a military band in full regalia. On another occasion, an evening's performance of music and dance made me realize how diverse Yugoslavia was, racially, culturally, socially, and religiously. Dances by Croatians, Serbs, Slovenes, Herzegovinians, and Albanians were performed, and all were different. I had not realized that the Muslim influence was so marked there, even though the Eastern Orthodox Church was still alive and well. Out of curiosity, we visited Belgrade's Orthodox Cathedral, where innumerable icons covered the walls. President Tito allowed religion to be practiced even though the majority of the young people, who were mostly communist, had no religion at all, neither attending church or mosque nor believing in God. Only a president of General Tito's stature was able to hold that country together, because of his political savvy, his military leadership, and because he was well-liked by all factions. After his death in 1980, the country disintegrated into its factionalized components.

Our next stop was Rome. My first memory, after landing at the airport, was holding on to our seats while traveling in a chartered bus towards the city at breakneck speeds. Normally drivers of public transportation move at a sedate and steady pace. Here, the Italian driver floored the gas pedal, and did not bother to decelerate when rounding corners. We Carnegie Fellows held our collective breath, only heaving a sigh of relief when we arrived in one piece at the hotel.

We made an obligatory visit to the Food and Agricultural Organization, a United Nations' specialized agency based in Rome. In that city I took the last of a series of inoculations against typhoid, which was required as we were to visit North Africa and I would not have been able to re-enter the United States without the vaccination. All the famous tourist sites were covered, including the Vatican, St. Peter's Cathedral, and the Sistine Chapel. We toured the Coliseum, where gladiators had fought as sport for spectators' entertainment; viewed the aqueducts along the Appian Way; and tossed our three coins into the Trevi Fountain while remembering the famous hit song by Frank Sinatra. We descended into the bowels of the dark and gloomy Catacombs, from which emanated a stale, musty odor, presumably from the thousands of decayed bodies buried there over the centuries. I felt rather uneasy while underground and was relieved to finally ascend and quickly fill my lungs with clean fresh air.

We Carnegie Fellows walked Rome's streets in a large group. With only three girls in our party, I recalled my earlier experience walking in Florence, when my female friends and I had been trailed by young men. I thought, "This won't happen here. After all, we are heavily escorted by males." But no, I was mistaken. A few hardy Italian youths had the gall to follow us. What was wrong with those people? At least they did not dare touch us. I had heard some horror stories of girls having their bottoms pinched by horny Italian men.

Rome was fine but I did not enjoy it as much as anticipated, maybe because our visit occurred near the tail end of the tour and we were becoming travel-weary. Believe it or not I still preferred Florence, my first introduction to Italy. A smaller, more compact city, it was surrounded by art and culture, and was more appealing to my senses. To me, Rome represented the power of that ancient empire, while the

Vatican and St. Peter's Basilica symbolized the power of the Catholic Church. The aesthetic beauty of the arts I saw in Florence seemed to work more toward peaceful pursuits than the acquisition of power.

Our final destination was Tunisia, North Africa, just a hop across the Mediterranean. The original people of the country were nomadic Berbers; later, Phoenicians settled on the coast and founded the city of Carthage, which rose to fame as Rome's chief rival. During the second Punic War between Carthage and Rome, Hannibal invaded Italy with his elephants and very nearly brought Rome to its knees. In the end Carthage was conquered and incorporated into the Roman Empire.

During our glorious ten-day stay, we were accommodated at a cultural center in the seaside resort area of Hammamet, not too far from the capital city of Tunis. At Hammamet there was a huge open-air stadium-like theater, with the seats facing the sea and the stage backed by the beach. Habib, the Tunisian Carnegie Fellow, passed on a little tidbit to us: During performances of Othello, the actor who portrayed Othello on his return home would approach the stage from the beach, giving a sense of realism to the play. Below the theater were rooms and facilities to accommodate visiting actors and there is where we stayed. The wide beautiful white sand beach was easily accessible, so whenever we had free time we took a dip in the blue waters of the Mediterranean. A small village sat at one end of the bay, about a mile away from the resort, and a couple of times we walked there along the beach to enjoy a cup of coffee with the locals.

One day someone brought a camel to our beach and several of us took a ride. The camel knelt down so I could mount its back. The exotic adventure of riding a camel was immortalized in a photo I still have today. The ride was very bumpy, bumpier than a horse ride, because of the camel's hump, which swayed slightly. If truth be told, I had nothing to do with getting the camel moving. A young man led it by the reins. Nevertheless, it was one of the most unforgettable experiences I have had.

The Tunisian government provided us with a bus to tour various parts of the country. In Tunis itself, the main tourist attractions were the ancient remains of Carthage and a large Roman amphitheatre, second in size only to Rome's Coliseum. The amphitheatre was not as intact as the Coliseum but still impressive. We toured the old part of Tunis with its narrow, winding streets and open-air markets displaying wares such as carpets, leather goods, and jewelry. What struck me as remarkable was the architectural uniformity—all the buildings were painted white, with wooden doors and jalousie windows painted blue. I presumed that the white paint reflected the sunlight, helping to keep the houses cooler. I never discovered why the doors and windows were all an identical color of blue.

One day the bus took us on a long trip into the interior of the country. No one told us what to expect. As the official language was Arabic (although the educated people spoke French), we Anglophones were at a disadvantage. Moving into the Mahgreb, further away from the coastal area, the landscape became more and more arid. Only when we arrived at an oasis did I realize we were in the Sahara Desert. Date palms and pomegranates grew, and we observed the canals of precious water that irrigated those fields. The oasis was not very big but it was amazing what that life-giving water could do.

Then we pressed on to visit the Great Mosque of Kairouan. Constructed in 670 A.D., it is the most famous mosque in the Muslim West, with the oldest standing minaret in the world.

The walls were covered with intricate mosaics typical of Islamic art. Long, covered walkways, reminiscent of the open corridors of ancient monasteries in Europe, surrounded the large central courtyard. Lunch was served to us in an area where the corridor widened into a room with an open side that allowed an unimpeded view of the courtyard. We sat on cushions on the floor around an extensive low table, laden with an abundance of food. We were served the national dish of Tunisia, couscous, a grain popular in North Africa. The couscous, combined with meat, potatoes, and vegetables, was heaped on large platters from which we helped ourselves. I found the steaming dish satisfying and tasty.

Generally I enjoyed the Tunisian cuisine, including a breakfast food called brique—a whole poached egg enfolded in dough and then fried. There was a trick in eating brique tidily, so the soft egg did not spurt out and splatter the plate or one's face. I never quite mastered the art.

One morning a colleague pointed out an article in the local French newspaper. The headline stated "Carnegie Fellows Mangent Crapeau," which translated to "Carnegie Fellows Eat Frog." Appalled, I figured I would have to sue that paper. I would never, ever eat frogs! Then I turned my thoughts to the previous day. We had been invited to lunch at the Ministry of Agriculture. I racked my brain trying to remember the menu. Oh yes, I recalled, it was couscous and I found it delicious indeed. The meat was chicken ... or was it? It dawned on me that what I thought to be chicken was in fact frogs' legs. Unwittingly, I had eaten this delicacy, so I had to bite my lip and remain silent.

During our stay in Tunisia, President Habib Bourguiba—considered the father of the nation because he led his country to independence from France—celebrated his sixty-second birthday. A gala was held at his palace, to which hundreds of people were invited, including us Carnegie Fellows. We dined on a sumptuous meal, washed down with several cups of mint tea. As a Muslim country, where imbibing liquor is forbidden, no alcohol was served at any official function, so we were noticeably wine-less and had to make do with mint tea. There was plenty of entertainment, notably a show with synchronized swimming in the Olympic-size pool. The evening concluded with a breathtaking fireworks display.

Finally our tour ended. It was time to leave Tunisia. While I might not have taken full advantage of all the opportunities available to me, the Carnegie Fellowship program broadened my horizons extensively. The tour allowed me to see international problems from other viewpoints, and develop camaraderie with a group of Third World individuals who were similar yet also different from me. We Carnegie Fellows became close-knit, and it was with some sadness that we said our goodbyes as we scattered, some to their home countries, others to take up tours of duty in host nations.

A short return to London was on my itinerary before flying to New York City. It so happened that Nacoulma, the Fellow from the Republic of Upper Volta (now Burkina Faso) was also traveling to London, so we sat together on the plane. As the minister-counselor, his senior position was second only to his country's ambassador. He basically took me under his wing, handling our very quick transfer in Paris. The change in Paris was so short that the bags would not arrive in London with us. It seemed he had taken a fancy to me because, while we were in Tunisia, he told me that he was married but that I would make a very good wife for his little brother. Of course I did not take him seriously. While approaching Heathrow, he invited me to share his embassy car into London. When I told him I had to refuse because my boyfriend was meeting me at the airport, he said Ainsley could come along too. Nacoulma turned out to be a kind, helpful person. He offered to pick us up the next day to claim the bags when they arrived at Heathrow, and then brought us back into London a second time.

Although Nacoulma's attention was dazzling, I certainly was not taking him up on the offer to marry his brother. An arranged marriage with a man I did not know in a faraway country might sound exotic but was asking for trouble. Besides, I had Ainsley.

But did I, really? I had reservations about long-distance relationships. How was this going to work out? We would have to see.

CHAPTER TWELVE | The Ultimatum

On an afternoon in March 1967, I was home after work, in my duplex apartment in the Meadowbrook suburb of Kingston, Jamaica. Staring at a letter I had just received from Ainsley, I kept re-reading it in the waning light. For the second time, he had failed the final professional exam to qualify as a chartered accountant in England. "This time," he wrote, "I shall have to wait one year, instead of six months, before I can re-take the exam. If you don't decide now to get married and come live in London, then we may as well forget about the whole thing."

I had been putting him off. I kept telling him, "Finish your exams first. Then we'll get married and go to Trinidad to live." Now I realized the man was serious.

I hardly noticed the rather large, bare room I was in, which contained a few sparse pieces of the mediocre furnishings typically found in furnished rentals. The duplex was shared with my friend Amy, her husband Rodney, and their three children, who occupied the larger unit. A typical bachelor-type pad, it was simply a place to rest my head. The front room of my side was used by Amy as her dressmaking establishment. Most of my waking time was spent with Amy and her family, with whom I shared meals, as my area had no kitchen.

Now, I had to examine my own feelings and make a decision. Yes, I did want to marry Ainsley. There was never really anyone else for me, even though I had dated a number of men. Dating Jamaican men was not my cup of tea. I found them to be thoroughly spoiled by their mothers, who treated them like princes. At twenty-seven, I no longer felt ill-prepared for marriage, and I had enjoyed a long, carefree period of young adulthood. Why, therefore, was I reluctant to return to England to start married life?

Ostensibly my excuse was the cold, damp, English weather. As a sun-loving creature, the endless, cloudy days depressed me considerably. Looking back, was there more to my reluctance? Probably. In the US, I had grown accustomed to the luxuries of apartment living in mid-town Manhattan. Even the middle-class homes in Jamaica had amenities rarely found in the more primitive atmosphere of British middle-class homes. Take, for example, washbasins in Britain. It was the norm to have separate hot and cold faucets, so every time one wanted to wash one's face, first one had to clean the basin and fill it with hot and cold water before one could complete the task.

These, however, were trivial matters. There had to be an underlying reason for my dilly-dallying. For me, marriage was a serious commitment. By 1967, I had known Ainsley for seven years. When we first dated while at Leeds, our relationship had been bumpy. Cislyn, my college friend and confidante, could testify to the numerous times our dating was on and off again. While we never had loud arguments, I often received the silent treatment from Ainsley, without any reason given.

The six-month I'd lived in London during the latter part of 1963 had been extremely unhappy for me. Apart from my almost non-existent social life, my job at Goldsmith's Library made me miserable. In addition to my woes at work, I had lived in a shabby area in southeastern London, which I hated. It was necessary to commute on the elevated trains, which I disliked immensely. The trains, which ran less frequently than the London Underground, ceased operations early in the evening. If I took in a show in London, often I had to make a mad dash to Charing Cross Station to catch the last train home. I tired of having to rush like that.

After Ainsley and I reconnected during my Carnegie Fellowship tour in 1965, we had settled into a long-distance relationship. Telephone conversations, being costly, were infrequent and brief. We corresponded by airmail, and I made a vacation trip to London in the summer of 1966. We had not actually discussed marriage until just prior to my return to New York after that vacation. Later in the year, I was promoted and transferred home to Jamaica, to the Ministry of External Affairs.

So there I was, several months later, sitting on my single bed, studying Ainsley's ultimatum. I realized he was not going to wait forever. I made my decision and spurred into action. I immediately approached the Permanent Secretary in the Ministry of External Affairs and told him of my plans. He supported me by arranging for my transfer to the Jamaican High Commission in London.

In a matter of three months I had to plan a wedding, to be held in New York where my mother and stepfather resided. In fact, Mum made most of the arrangements since I was far away in Jamaica. Amy made my satin wedding dress. Simple but with elegant lines, it was edged with a broad band of heavy lace along the hem, the neck, and the cuffs of the full-length sleeves. The wedding was to be fairly small. It never occurred to me to invite my natural father to the wedding. It would have been extremely awkward. My graduation was the only important occasion in my life that he attended. About a month before my departure, I said to a few of my friends, "I'll be leaving at the end of May to get married in New York City." Cries of surprise and astonishment erupted, because this had been a well-kept secret on my part. One said, "Oh, you dark horse! I had no idea that you had a fiancé and were so close to getting married. You never told us anything about him." To which I replied, "There's many a slip between the cup and the lip." Only when Ainsley arrived in New York would I believe our marriage was taking place.

This reflected my innate distrust of long-distance relationships. Even though we had known each other over a lengthy period of time, we had both changed. I wondered how well I knew him. How did I know what he was really up to when I was not around? Why was I so mistrustful? I guess because of my past experience with Ainsley. He was very popular with the girls and I figured he could change his mind at any time. My mind went through so many "what ifs." Why was I so negative? By nature the ultimate pessimist, I did not want to set myself up for a disappointment. The embarrassment of being left standing at the altar was not a happy thought. Nevertheless, I said to myself, "Nothing ventured, nothing gained." I also told myself, "It is better to have loved and lost than never to have loved at all." I figured I might as well take the plunge and go for it. I had nothing to lose.

After the wedding, we arrived in London in late July 1967. Ainsley was thrilled to be back under cool, grey skies, with temperatures of about sixty degrees Fahrenheit. It was completely the opposite for me. It had been a scorching hot summer in both New York and in Montreal, where we spent our honeymoon visiting Expo '67 and Ainsley's siblings who resided there.

Our wedding had not occurred without some drama. The best man, Ainsley's brother Lennox, got lost trying to find St. Bartholomew's Catholic Church in Queens, and was late.

Another friend, Eddie St. Hill, had to fill in until he arrived. Lech escorted me down the aisle, but then went home, refusing to attend the reception for about fifty guests. I was terribly disappointed and hurt by his absence at the reception. Lech's brother, Gounod, who also lived in New York, substituted for him and gave the obligatory speech on his behalf.

Even before the wedding Lech had behaved in an inexplicable and, to me, inexcusable manner. He had not cooperated in planning the wedding, which I suppose was to be somewhat expected. Mum, with some help from Lech's sister, Solita, made all the arrangements. Worse, he had shown extreme brusqueness toward Ainsley. Lech never explained why, even though Ainsley had written a letter to my parents beforehand. I was embarrassed and livid at Lech's lack of civility, and recalled the difficult days in my teenage years when he first entered my mother's life. While I was still angrily locking horns with Lech, Ainsley calmly said to him, "I'll go along with your wishes." "But..." I interjected. "It's okay," Ainsley said. "Lech, I'll do whatever you want."

It was that moment when I realized Ainsley had matured tremendously. His acceptance and accommodation surprised both Lech and myself, averted a crisis, saved the day, and paved the way for future reconciliation. Years later, one would never have believed that the initial relations between the two men started off so frostily, since a proud Lech later crowed about his son-in-law and his achievements.

The first couple months of our married life in London were spent at Ainsley's landlady's house. We occupied his rented room, with a bathroom that was shared with other roomers. The landlady was a Trinidadian who had known Ainsley from back home, and thus provided him special privileges of access to the living room with the telly—the television, the dining room, and the kitchen. The landlady had previously cooked his meals, but now that he had acquired a new bride, I took over this duty. Since my transfer to the Jamaican High Commission took some time to effect, I had time on my hands and spent hours preparing meals from recipes I found in my wedding-present cookbooks. Some were quite successful, while others were disastrous. My selective memory has allowed me to forget the unsuccessful ones. However, two dishes Ainsley really enjoyed were Beef Stroganoff and Chicken Kiev.

Ainsley left each morning for work in the "uniform" worn by all in the business and banking sectors of the City of London. They all looked alike, in their dark suits, starched white shirts, narrow ties, bowler hats, and carrying finely rolled brollies—umbrellas. He always was particular about his wardrobe. Very early in our marriage he stated emphatically, "Please do not hang my trousers on the rack! In fact, don't touch any of my clothes!" "Why not?" I asked, a trifle miffed. "Because you don't hang them properly and they get crushed!" He meticulously ironed the creases in his pants so they were as sharp as a razor blade, and then carefully laid them over the crossbar of the hanger, making sure not to rumple them. At the time I was offended that he did not allow me to iron his clothes; later on in the marriage I thanked my lucky stars, because the domestic chore of ironing was not a favorite activity of mine.

We had to get used to living together in close quarters. It was no longer one of his girlfriends sleeping over and then returning to her place. At times we needed our own space and became irritated with each other. At the counseling session required prior to our wedding in New York, the young priest said something about "the first blush of love." I had looked askance at this youth—who looked as if he had not even grown his first beard and who was sworn to celibacy—and wondered what he knew about "the first blush of love." Then Ainsley and I had our first tiff. I declared, "So, the first blush of love is over!" We both laughed heartily.

When my transfer to the Jamaican High Commission finally came through, we decided it was time to find our own flat. Aware of prejudicial considerations, in responding to ads for apartments in the local newspaper Ainsley would declare over the phone, "I'm a West Indian professional gentleman. Would the flat be available to me and my wife?" One prospective landlord, Mr. Mulgan, replied indignantly, "Of course it might! Why don't you come and see it?"

The tiny flat in the basement of the Mulgan home, at No. 6 Wood Lane in Highgate, had a bedroom that barely held two twin beds; a small bathroom fit with a doll-sized bath, basin, and toilet beneath the stairs; and a dining area, which was in fact the hallway at the entrance. However, we saw there were some advantages. The living room, with its bay windows, was large and comfortable, the kitchen was quite spacious, and the flat had its own entrance at the side of the house. What won me over was the fact that it was centrally heated. Plus, the price was affordable—£12 per week, the monthly equivalent of less than $200.

After viewing the flat we sat in the Mulgan's living room, where we were introduced to their two young children.

"We would like to take it," Ainsley stated. "I'm an accountant with the firm of Rooke, Lane and Company in the City, and my wife is a diplomat with the Jamaican High Commission."

"You are the very first people to view the flat," Mr. Mulgan replied. "Normally we would interview all the applicants before making a decision. However, you meet the qualifications and we have decided to look no further. You can have the flat."

We were jubilant. Although racial prejudice was not rampant in the United Kingdom in those days, we were not immune to it. I do believe that the Mulgans, who were university-trained, were stung by any suggestion they might be guilty of prejudice because of the color of our skin, and therefore offered the flat to us immediately.

One afternoon after we had moved in, while on the walkway leading to our basement flat, we heard a voice calling out to us from next door. "Hello! You must be our new neighbors. I'm Betty Kaye."

We looked up to see a tall, stately lady who looked about sixty years old but who could have been much younger. After we introduced ourselves, she went on, "You must come over for drinks one evening. You'll be hearing from me soon."

Thereafter we noticed that every day several empty bottles were piled around her garbage, which was picked up daily. "This lady must entertain a lot," Ainsley remarked. Then an invitation came for after-dinner drinks, to which a few other neighbors were invited. Betty seemed to know all the residents along Wood Lane, which included about twenty houses leading from the Highgate Underground Station to the edge of the woods. The road wound through the woods before emerging on the other side under a new name. Our lane had the feel of a quiet country road tucked away in a small hamlet, a very odd feeling since we were in fact living in the huge city of London.

We noticed that Betty was drinking scotch neat, which she poured into a whiskey glass almost to the brim. I realized she was drinking the stuff as if it were beer, or rather water. "No wonder she has so many empties by her garbage," I thought. She was drinking it mostly by herself!

Betty indicated that she wanted us to stay after the other guests departed. She then told us a lot about herself. When she learned I worked at the Jamaican High Commission, she revealed that her brother had once been the British High Commissioner to Australia, a clue that she came from an upper-class family. Divorced, she had got rid of her husband after he had callously ignored her while she was ill in the hospital. Her current boyfriend was the CEO of Dunhill, a major cigarette firm in the United Kingdom. She recalled that as a child, a busload of servants arrived at the manor house each morning and departed in the evening. She also shared that when she was a little girl, she would descend to the large wine cellar and open the taps of the casks to sample the contents. This was how she developed her taste for alcohol.

Ainsley, no mean drinker himself, had difficulty keeping up with Betty. The more she consumed, the more outrageous she grew. Betty revealed that she was acquainted with a Jamaican, a male nurse at Highgate Hospital and enquired, "Do you know him?"

"What does he look like? Can you describe him?" I asked.

"Does he have Rosemary's complexion?" Ainsley continued.

"No, no," Betty replied. "Rosemary is peach, whereas he is light grey." Betty's unusual descriptions of skin color amused us no end. We might have said "red-skinned," "brown-skinned," or "dark-skinned," never "light grey" or "peach."

Suddenly, to our great surprise, Betty reached forward and lifted my skirt. She said, "I just wanted to see if you were the same color all over." I was so stunned by Betty's brazenness that I could not react. Very quickly, Ainsley, who was getting quite inebriated, suggested we leave, and we rolled over to our little flat next door.

"Damn!" he declared. "I consider myself to be a drinker, but that woman would drink me under the table!"

With my transfer to the High Commission, I became a daily commuter on the tube—the London Underground. Londoners had the insufferable, to me, habit of climbing up or walking down escalators. The escalators were already taking us along. Why climb as well? At first I determinedly remained standing still all the way up or down, but gradually found myself being pulled into their rat race. If I could hear my train pulling into the station and knew the next would not arrive for another fifteen minutes, I soon was racing down those escalators, just like everyone else, to avoid being late. How I had changed in the space of just one year!

Although the British prided themselves on their relatively mild winters, every now and again there was an unusually harsh winter. It had happened in my final year as a student in Leeds, some two hundred miles north of London, when a blizzard occurred and hoarfrost covered the grounds of our hall of residence for days. Similarly, a snowstorm descended over London in the winter of 1967-'68, piling knee-high snow on the pathway to our little flat. London was totally unprepared for this catastrophic event. After digging our way out of the flat in an attempt to get to work in the morning, Ainsley and I found the trains had stopped running. No city bus ventured as far as Highgate in that weather so, bundled up in our greatcoats, woolen scarves, and fur-lined boots, we carefully picked our way down the hill through snow and slush for two miles to the nearest bus station, at Archway. There we caught a red double-decker bus bound for central London. Progress was excruciatingly slow. It was eleven-thirty when I finally stepped into my office. The office manager, hardy soul that he was—although he probably lived much nearer to the office than I did—enquired, "Why did you bother to come in? You may as well turn 'round and go home because nobody else is here."

My desk was in the Students' Section of the Welfare Division at No. 32 Bruton Street, immediately opposite the main office that housed the High Commissioner and the upper echelons of the staff. Reginald Philips, who, it seemed, had been in London forever, headed the Welfare Division. He had joined the staff of the former West Indies Commission, which was established during the days of the defunct Federation of the West Indies. After the federation fell apart and Jamaica achieved its independence in 1962, the High Commission took over the building. Some of the secretarial staff, which hailed from other Caribbean islands, stayed on to work for Jamaica after the demise of the West Indies Commission.

The Welfare Division handled migrant affairs as well as the affairs of students and nurses, most of whom generally occupied the lower strata of society. Reg told us tales of taking care of hordes of Jamaican migrants who had swarmed to "the mother country" in the 1950s. Times then were hard in the colony and, seeking a new and better life, thousands scraped up the fares to travel by boat to England. Many had no idea where they were going to live. Most of these immigrants were totally unprepared for life in England. They arrived without warm clothing. In winter, young girls clad only in sheer nylon dresses and sandals shivered in the cold. Reg and his fellow workers looked after these people, organizing places for them to stay and providing them with winter coats.

At the Welfare Division we definitely had the sensation of being the poor relations of the rich cousins across the street. Our ramshackle building needed a coat of paint and numerous repairs. Reg, however, kept our morale high by taking us out to eat after work on many occasions. One retirement party was held at an excellent Indian restaurant nearby. Afterward, as none of the girls on the staff drove a car, Reg piled us all into the back of his big blue Cadillac with humungous fins and dropped everyone at our homes. While he was chauffeuring us, I heard him say, "Boy, I could take a good shot of brandy now!"

I was the second to the last stop. Knowing we had large stocks of liquor at home, including Courvoisier V.S.O.P., I invited Reg and the remaining girl in for a drink. I thought it would be a good idea for Ainsley to meet Reg, who was a man after his own heart, but Ainsley was already asleep so I did not disturb him. Reg kept repeating that Ainsley had to be "a hell of a man to allow his wife to invite people in for a drink while he is in bed." When Reg finally met my husband at an official function, he repeated this statement. Needless to say, the two men hit it off.

Ainsley had a wide circle of friends. Despite the fact that he had to study hard for his next attempt at the exam, we still managed a busy social life. We dined at some of the finest restaurants in London, attended shows, and went dancing at clubs in Mayfair and other West End locations. When a Trinidadian friend threw a house party, we all had a ball. Trinidadians certainly knew how to party! Maybe it was the Carnival tradition that motivated them.

On Fridays after work we often met friends for drinks at a downtown pub. Some London pubs were very old and historic. One such, The Gate, was a favorite haunt of ours for lunch. The headwaiter called himself "Zho-sef"—Joseph pronounced with a French accent, although we believed he was British. With great panache, he cooked steak Diane, flambeau-style, at our tables. If our lunch party was particularly large, we would order a Methuselah bottle of champagne. We kept one of the empty Methuselahs, which became an original lamp that graced a corner of our living room.

To help celebrate the first Christmas of our married life, we decided to throw a party in our small flat a few days before the New Year. We invited all our friends and acquaintances, including our neighbor Betty and Mr. and Mrs. Mulgan. To accommodate the number of people and facilitate dancing, we piled all the furniture from the living room and dining area into the bedroom and shut the door. That meant it was standing room only, not a seat to be found. A crowd of sixty guests squeezed into our tiny flat.

We hung mistletoe above the doorway and Betty Kaye kept encouraging young couples to kiss beneath it. (The mistletoe certainly worked its magic for one couple. One of our friends received a proposal of marriage, and we occupied a prominent place at her wedding, since it all started at our party.) One of our English friends, whose name was Johnny Walker, had the habit of falling asleep on a chair or a sofa after a few drinks. We agreed that Johnny Walker was going to be in real trouble at the party. After a while he disappeared and we wondered where he had gone. It turned out that he found the bedroom; goodness knows how he managed to squeeze in because it was jam-packed. He managed to climb into an armchair perched atop other furniture and fell asleep.

At two a.m., the Mulgans, who had not responded to our invitation, telephoned from upstairs, asking us to wrap up the party because they could not sleep. We were embarrassed and disappointed but had to comply if we wanted to remain as tenants. At that, the festivities suddenly came to an end. Ainsley helped Betty get home. She looked stunning in a white lace pantsuit and a pearl choker, but now she was too unsteady to climb the steps by herself. He got her to her bedroom, helped her to the bed, and was trying to remove her pearl necklace when she said, "That will be quite enough, thank you." She was not so far gone that she was unaware of what was happening to her!

The only other time we threw a party was in the summer, when the Mulgans were away on vacation. On that occasion we did not have to worry about disturbing anyone.

On St. Patrick's Day our friend John Harrington, whose wife was Irish, invited us to a party at their house, which was not too far from our flat. After work, on my way to the tube station, I ran into John and a friend of his. Hours earlier, they'd gone out for a sumptuous lunch and had never returned to their office, but as John was the CEO of his advertising firm, he could do whatever he wanted. All afternoon they had been consuming "brown cows," a mixture of champagne and Tia Maria liqueur. John asked me, "How are you getting home?"

"By the tube," I replied.

John made me an offer. "We've been traveling around all afternoon by taxi. It's now waiting for us. Would you like to ride with us since you live nearby?"

I assented and the three of us climbed into the back of the black taxi. Then John decided he wanted to buy a bottle of champagne. Unfortunately, we were passing through a rough neighborhood and none of the pubs we tried had champagne. Nevertheless, John persevered until he was able to procure a bottle when we eventually reached Hampstead. Thereafter the scene was surreal for me. John popped the cork and there we were, the three of us in the back of the taxi, in turn taking swigs directly from the bottle. I tried unsuccessfully not to gulp down the bubbly liquid, since champagne is supposed to be sipped from a wide-rimmed glass. I had not eaten since lunch and soon felt the champagne going to my head. This was not good! I was relieved when we approached the corner of Wood Lane and I could alight from the taxi.

"Now Rosemary," I told myself, "make sure not to weave your way down the lane. That would surely be a giveaway." So there I was, walking slowly down Wood Lane with deliberate measured steps, one foot in front of the other, as if I were walking a tightrope. If that was not a giveaway, I don't know what is. On arriving home, I told Ainsley about my little adventure and he laughed his head off. After sleeping for an hour, I was up and ready for the Harrington's party. It is amazing how much stamina one has when one is young and strong.

By the end of summer in 1968, Ainsley had sat for and passed his final exams. It was time to head for Trinidad & Tobago. When I informed the High Commission that I was leaving, the office manager declared, "You haven't been to Buckingham Palace yet! I must arrange for you to attend a garden party there." So I acquired a turquoise outfit of a knee-length dress with a matching jacket of the same length, and a picture hat of the exact same color. Ainsley rented a pinstripe grey morning suit with tails, and a top hat, from Moss Bros., a regarded menswear purveyor that specialized in formal dress. A luxurious Austin Princess automobile with a driver rolled down Wood Lane to pick us up. We were excited about the occasion and felt like minor royalty ourselves. However, the garden party itself was no great shakes. We were served iced coffee and stale sandwiches that probably were left over from the previous garden party. Yet in the light drizzle of rain, we were among the group protected by a tent, while the commoners, even the most respected of citizens, had to open out their brollies.

The Queen and her family were not particularly outstanding in my opinion. To me, the most gracious member of the Royal Family was the Queen Mother, who at that time was in her late sixties—she remained elegant and gracious until her death in 2002, at the age of 101.

The most remarkable occurrence, for me, was the loss of my hat. Before departing for home, we decided to take a little walk around the grounds, to admire the peacocks and the gardens. It was a blustery day and a gust of wind lifted my hat, sending it skipping along the ground. Ainsley, in his morning suit, was not about to race after it. As soon as we almost reached it another gust picked it up, and off it would go again. It kept eluding our grasp. When I saw that it and we were nearing a pond, I attempted to run to capture it, but Ainsley took my arm and held me back. The hat landed in the pond. We watched silently and aghast as it floated for a while before becoming waterlogged and then sink ignominiously. Seeing that I was now the only hatless female there, we got out of Buckingham Palace as quickly as we could. I was mortified. Especially since the hat had been bought on credit and had not even been paid off yet.

Was it simply a coincidence that the Mulgans invited us to dinner prior to our departure from the United Kingdom, or had they observed the Austin Princess rolling down Wood Lane to pick up a finely dressed couple? At least they realized that we had not been fabricating our stories; they seemed anxious to part on good terms with us.

We quickly packed and bade goodbye to our many friends. Our travel arrangements took us first to North America, to visit Ainsley's siblings in Canada and my parents in New York. By this time Mum and Lech had quietly married, as Lech was at last able to get a divorce from his first wife.

It was October of 1968, after fourteen months in the United Kingdom, when we departed. Although I had shown an initial reluctance to return to Britain, the months we shared there were among the best of my life. We enjoyed a year of marital bliss before embarking on the responsibilities of raising a family. That time in London changed my opinion of life in Britain, which I will always remember with great fondness.

My gamble in responding to Ainsley's ultimatum had definitely paid off.

Photo Gallery
- I -

Frances Anderson, Rosemary's mother

MOTHERS OF INFLUENCE

Carmen Borel, Ainsley Borel's mother,
who was referred to as 'Mother'

Edna Palmer
(Aunty)

Mrs. Florette Robinson (Mother Rob)

GROWING UP
IN JAMAICA

Top right:
Rosemary Yvonne at
age eight, growing up in
Highgate, Jamaica

Bottom:
Rosemary Yvonne at
age fifteen, as a bridesmaid

Below:
Barbara (Babs) Lawson,
who also stayed with
Aunty and Uncle Bert

Majorie Smith, daughter of Mrs. Emma Smith
(Aunt Madge)

At the Odeon Guesthouse with Mr. Solomon in the middle, Lechmere Cox at left, along with visiting
family from Bermuda and Rosemary Yvonne (in back, middle).

Rosemary at age eighteen

First year students on the grounds of Lupton Hall, 1960-1961, includes the warden, Miss Worth, seated in second row fourth from the left, and the sub-warden, Miss Chester, third from the left
Rosemary Smellie first on left, middle row standing

Alva Rolston, Rodgerson Joseph, Boland Mathura (Matador), Ralph Knight, and Ainsley Borel
at the "The Trinidad Embassy," their digs

The Lupton Hall Winter Formal, 1961
From right to left, Hazel Robinson, Ram Singh, Ruth Townrow and escort,
Rosemary Smellie and Ainsley Borel

Amy Fergusson Williams (*née* Repole) on her
wedding day in Leeds

"The Sultan of Rimini" surrounded by his harem,
Rimini, Italy

Boatride on an underground river in a cave in France
Summer, 1961

SUMMER
VACATIONS

Italy and France

GRADUATIONS

Right:
Rosemary and her father, Rupert Smellie, at her graduation in 1963

Below:
Ainsley George Borel, Graduation, 1962

JAMAICAN MISSION TO THE UNITED NATIONS

New York

Counselor Silborne Clarke (fifth from the left), Third Secretary Angela King (middle), First Secretary Gordon Wells, (next to Angela King) First Secretary Lloyd Barnett (fifth from right) and Third Secretary Rosemary Smellie (right) flanked by other members of the support staff at Jamaica Mission to the United Nations, New York

The Carnegie Fellows in front of The Capitol, Washington DC, with
Program Director Reginald Barrett, (fourth from left) during the summer of 1965

CARNEGIE FELLOWSHIP TOUR

Geneva   Tunisia

Several Carnegie Fellows on a tour of Paris, France, 1965. Rosemary (with camera) center right

Carnegie Fellowship Tour

Right:
On the beach at
Hammamet, Tunisia

Center:
The women Carnegie Fellows,
1964-65: My Leung (left), from
South Vietnam, Rosemary
(middle), from Jamaica with
Njeri (right), from Kenya
in front of Jet D'eau in Geneva

Bottom:
Rosemary along with a
Carnegie Fellow on a camel
at the beach in Tunisia

Carnegie
Fellowship Tour

Rosemary at the ruins of the Roman Amphitheatre in Tunisia

Rosemary, in hat, seated center left at a luncheon at the Great Mosque of Kairouan

WEDDING

June 10, 1967

Reverend Francis
Kilcoyne with Rosemary
and Ainsley Borel at
the front entrance
of St. Bartholomew's
Catholic Church,
Elmhurst, New York

Top row: Lennox Borel, Vilma Borel, and Ainsley Borel
Bottow row: Annette Borel, Rosemary, and Gemma Borel

Lennox Borel, Gemma Borel, Rosemary and Ainsley Borel, Rosemary's
cousin Thelma Smith (Anderson), Faye Robinson, and Eddie St. Hill

Decked out for the garden party at Buckingham Palace, 1968

CHAPTER THIRTEEN | $\mathcal{A}$rrival in $\mathcal{T}$rinidad

The Pan Am flight touched down at Piarco Airport around five p.m. on an October afternoon in 1968. Ainsley and I, after a glorious fourteen months of married life in London, were in his native land. Having spent nine years in England, he was anxious to return home as soon as he passed his final professional exam.

Now I was about to face the acid test of meeting Ainsley's mother, Carmen Borel, and his sisters, Eula Williams and Roslyn Darlington. I had already met the Canadian wing of the family—Vilma, Learie, Lennox, Annette, and Gemma Alexander, who had married and moved to Britain while Ainsley and I were there. They had all attended our wedding, and we'd made two visits to Canada.

I remembered that his older sister, Vilma, had watched me very closely on those occasions. Although friendly, she appeared to be noting every detail of my appearance and manner to relay to the family in Trinidad. Ainsley's father had already passed away, but what was I to expect from his mother? He had warned me, "My mother is not soft-spoken like yours. She has a loud mouth and she isn't easy. She was the one who disciplined us as children, because Father was easygoing and left that job to her. I tell you, if it were not for Mother I would not have amounted to much, and would have ended up sweeping the streets." I felt trepidation at the thought of meeting "The Queen," as her children referred to her, or "The Dragon," if they were in a less complimentary mood. I asked Ainsley how I should address her, to which he replied, "Call her Mother just as we all do."

On emerging from Customs and Immigration, I was shocked to see the crowd of relatives gathered at the airport to greet us. Not only was his mother there, but also in attendance were his two older sisters, their spouses, and children. One sister had four children in tow. Fortunately for me, there were two familiar faces in the crowd. Cislyn and Rodger had returned home from Leeds earlier. Their presence helped to counteract the overwhelming effect of this large family gathering.

Ainsley introduced me to his relatives, and his mother embraced me in a warm greeting. The others hugged me and kissed me on the cheek. They were much more exuberant than my family, in fact more than Jamaicans as a whole, who tend to be reserved. So far so good, but I quickly became embarrassed.

Within moments of arriving on the warm, muggy afternoon, my bouffant hairstyle flopped. During the '60s, high hairdos that were "teased"—backcombed, and coated in gallons of hairspray were all the rage. By then I had graduated from using the hot-iron comb to chemical hair straighteners, which worked wonders for me in London but utterly failed in the Trinidadian heat and humidity. Just arrived from the cool climates of England and North America, and now unaccustomed to the oppressive heat, sweat poured from my skin, refusing to dry off. Ainsley had told me repeatedly that his sisters were sharp dressers, and I wondered what his mother and sisters were thinking of my bedraggled appearance. I looked and felt like a wet rat.

We climbed into one of the many cars that were lined up at the airport to meet us. My concern over my hair was replaced by the hair-raising experience of hurtling along the two-way Churchill-Roosevelt Highway from Piarco Airport to the capital city of Port of Spain. Built by the Americans during World War II, the highway was one of the island's best, but the way the Trinis drove, overtaking another vehicle seemed extremely perilous. We constantly faced headlights of automobiles traveling in the opposite direction at break-neck speeds, and our car miraculously tucked in front of the vehicle we were overtaking just in time. I was used to Jamaicans driving fast and dangerously but that evening my heart was in my mouth.

Carloads of family and friends congregated at Ainsley's mother's house at No. 9 William Terrace in Belmont, Port of Spain. Family members were all proud of the son who had been to England on a scholarship and now returned not only with a degree but also as a professionally qualified chartered accountant, with a wife, no less. The modest three-bedroom Borel house was filled with laughter, food, and drink, accompanied by the pulsating, syncopated beat of the latest calypsos. All the windows were flung wide open to catch the breeze.

Mother encouraged us all to drink and celebrate the return of her favored son, whom she had not seen for several years. She preferred the Trinidadian brand of Vat 19 rum, dubbed "The Vatican," which she tossed back from a shot glass and chased immediately with a soda, referred to by Trinidadians as a sweet drink. At one point Ainsley, who had become used to the quiet, discreet behavior of the British, became embarrassed by his mother's loud talk and laughter. He cautioned, "Not so loud, Mother, not so loud." To which she replied, "Okay son, I'll try, but you know your old mother don't know how to talk soft. I'm so happy you come back, so successful in everything you do!"

At the end of the evening my hair had completely "gone back to Africa." I asked Mother if she knew a hairdresser

I could visit the following day. She consulted with Fresh Face, one of her daughter's friends, who offered to make the arrangements for me. I asked Mother what Fresh Face's real name was. She considered a while and then said, "I really can't remember her correct name. Everyone calls her that because she doesn't sweat and her face always remains fresh, no matter how much she jumps up in the dances and Carnival parties." Much later I discovered that her real name was Glenda Solomon.

Although they were pleasant and welcoming, I knew I was under intense scrutiny by Mother and Ainsley's sisters, Rosie and Eula. Years later Rosie revealed that when they learned their brother had married a Jamaican, they wondered if he could not have found a nice Trini girl. Why did he have to marry a Jamaican?

Little was known about Jamaica, which was situated nine hundred miles to the north, near Cuba and Hispaniola. Trinidadians were much more familiar with the Eastern Caribbean islands that formed the chain of the Lesser Antilles, as the twin-island state of Trinidad & Tobago is situated in the southern Caribbean, just seven miles offshore of Venezuela in South America. Besides, Jamaica was viewed with suspicion, as it was largely blamed for breaking up the short-lived West Indian Federation in 1962. This political union of British colonies, with its capital in Trinidad and a prime minister from the island of Barbados, was very weak and lacked financial resources. There was jealousy and competition between Jamaica and Trinidad & Tobago, the two largest entities, which had contributed the most financially to the union. There was also the fear that hordes of people from the smaller, more impoverished islands would migrate to the richer islands, thus putting a strain on their resources. When Jamaica felt it was not getting enough representation in the Federal

Parliament, increasing dissatisfaction led to a referendum whereby Jamaica opted out of the Federation. Trinidad's Prime Minister, Dr. Eric Williams, said, "One from ten leaves naught," meaning that without Jamaica the Federation could not continue, and Trinidad also withdrew. Jamaica gained its independence from Britain on August 6, 1962, and less than a month later, on August 31, Trinidad & Tobago became independent.

The only West Indian organizations that allowed cooperation between the islands were the University of the West Indies—with campuses in Jamaica, Trinidad & Tobago, and Barbados—and the West Indies Cricket Board, which was responsible for the unified cricket team playing against other British Commonwealth countries. These were the only organizations that gave Caribbean people of the former British colonies an opportunity to get to know one another better.

Given this background, as a Jamaican I was viewed warily by my new in-laws. Rosie later explained that the family kept looking for faults in me but could not find any. As time went on they got to know and love me. I do not believe that Mother looked for flaws, because she was a firm believer in the institution of marriage. I never, ever heard her say anything negative about any of her sons-in-law or daughters-in-law. Rather, she tended to blame her own children whenever they had a falling out with their spouses.

I got along famously with Mother and was thrilled to be part of a large family. It was gratifying to be accepted wholeheartedly by Ainsley's seven siblings, some of whom did not always live amicably with each other. As an outsider, I never took sides, allowing me to enjoy harmonious relations with all my in-laws. I never denigrated Trinidad or Trinidadians, either to my mother-in-law or anyone else. Once I was asked by a Trinidadian acquaintance, "What do you think of

Trinidad?" I replied, "Trinidad reminds me of Jamaica ten years ago." Realizing that everyone was about to take umbrage at what I said, I hurried to explain. "I do not think that Trinidad & Tobago is more backward. In fact, Trinidad reminds me of the days when Jamaica was safer, when a person could walk the streets without fear of attack, when householders had no need to erect grill-iron defenses in front of windows and doors." When I first arrived in the twin-island state I was shocked to find that people regularly left their doors unlocked and no one entered their homes and touched anything.

Soon after our arrival, Ainsley began work at the Inland Revenue Department in Port of Spain. In return for his scholarship, he had signed a contract to remain employed with the government of Trinidad & Tobago for at least five years. Many of the experienced civil servants, having spent years working their ways up the system but lacking the certificates to qualify for promotion, were jealous of him. After a nine-year stint in Britain, Ainsley was probably a little brash and was seen as wanting to turn the inertia-prone civil service upside down. He, and indeed I, could not understand why the wheels of bureaucracy took so long to turn. Often the criterion for getting any action taken was based on who one knew, rather than what one knew. For example, our trunks and boxes traveled from England by boat and had to clear customs before we could claim them. When an acquaintance of Ainsley said he knew someone in the customs department who could assist us, my husband declined the offer, thinking we would wait our turn through the system. Our personal effects sat in the warehouse for weeks until Ainsley broke down and used our contacts to get them cleared. No money was passed but we did donate a bottle of rum to the person who helped us. "So that is how the system works," I thought.

No wonder the wheels of bureaucracy ground so slowly and so inefficiently.

I was not so fortunate as Ainsley in finding employment. I was unable to transfer from the Jamaican High Commission's London office to the office in Port of Spain. The Jamaican government had an unwritten rule that if a diplomat married a national of the country to which he or she was assigned, that person would have to resign from the diplomatic service. Although I never heard the *raison d'être* for this policy, it was assumed that breaches in national security might occur. Also, diplomats were supposed to rotate to various tours of duty, generally lasting three to six years. The thinking probably was that wives usually resided with their husbands and therefore would be reluctant to make frequent transfers. In fact, there were many exceptions to that rule. Several officers assigned to the Jamaican High Commission in London remained there for decades. One young lady, a Third Secretary who married an Englishman, was allowed to remain in London indefinitely. Therefore, it had not seemed too much for me to ask for a transfer to the Jamaican High Commission in Trinidad; still, my request was not granted. Now I had to seek a new profession. Learning that applicants to teach high school in Trinidad & Tobago needed a degree but not necessarily a diploma in education, I put in my application and waited. Without my salary Ainsley and I could not afford our own apartment, so we continued living with my mother-in-law.

This waiting period was perhaps a blessing in disguise. It allowed me time to get to know Mother, who taught me many things, including cooking in the Trinidadian style. I also learned much about the new country I was in and its culture, into which I was gradually assimilated. There was plenty of room in the house for us since Mother lived alone, her seven other children having married or gone abroad. The only downside was that Ainsley would often take off with the boys after work, since he knew I was not alone at home. In London I was always invited to after-work pub parties. It was quite the opposite in Trinidad. The mores of the society did not allow "nice" young ladies to take part in such activities.

We occupied Ainsley's boyhood bedroom at the back of Mother's house. Her home was constructed on a slope, with the front at ground level and the back elevated, thus contributing to our room being the coolest one in the house. The windows were always left open—except when it rained—to catch the breeze through the nearby avocado tree. In those days central air-conditioning was unknown in residences, and even the most well-to-do installed only window units in the bedrooms. After so many years in the cool clime of England, Ainsley felt the heat tremendously. He was always mopping his face with a large white handkerchief. "I need an air-conditioned house *and* an air-conditioned car," he kept saying. I always laughed at him. Yes, air-conditioning in the house was feasible, but I knew no one either in Trinidad or Jamaica who owned an air-conditioned car. Years later when he achieved his goal, I remembered this earlier period in our life and once again thought, "This is a man who gets what he wants."

I too found the heat and high humidity of Trinidad's climate enervating. Its position at latitude 10.5° north of the equator means that it is basically an equatorial climate, with constant temperatures of eighty to ninety degrees Fahrenheit. It also has a high annual rainfall, more rainfall than I was used to in Jamaica. One advantage of Trinidad's proximity to the equator is that the island is outside the hurricane belt and therefore not subjected to the devastating storms. During the rainy season the mornings were bright and sunny and the clouds would build up during the day. Like clockwork, around midday to early afternoon there was a cloudburst and showers poured down. Anyone caught in this inclement weather was forced to take shelter, often beneath the eaves of storefronts, until the rain abated. It was impossible to make one's way through the deluge without getting thoroughly soaked, even with rain gear and an umbrella. Then suddenly, in the late afternoon, the skies cleared and the sun re-appeared. In moments the sidewalks, roads, and gutters were dry. One would never have believed that, just a short time before, the streets had been veritable rivers rushing to the nearest canals and drains.

Ainsley and I were often sleep-deprived, owing to many interruptions during the night. The open bedroom windows, which ushered in the cool air, also allowed the noises of the night to assail our ears. We had forgotten that West Indian dogs from various homes congregated in the streets and, together with strays, ended up in tremendous fights, snarling, growling, and yelping at one another. Similarly, cats in heat howled during mating, and cocks crowed not only at daybreak but sometimes as early as three a.m. All these extraneous sounds made it difficult for us to get a good night's rest.

To make matters worse, freshly arrived from the United Kingdom, we went to bed around eleven p.m., much later than the usual bedtime of most Trinis. The maxim "Early to bed and early to rise makes a man healthy, wealthy, and wise" seemed to apply to Trinidadians. In the morning, before daybreak, the sound of the next-door neighbor performing his chores was the final straw. The swishing of a hard-bristled broom and the splashing of hose water on the concrete backyard was as loud as thunder to us. We gave up, forced to rise from our bed. In any case, Ainsley had to get ready for work. Most offices, businesses, and schools began early, usually around eight o' clock.

One of my priorities was obtaining a driver's license. I had acquired all the skills from driving school in London but, on taking the test, I got nervous and failed. In Trinidad the requirements were much simpler, which boosted my confidence. All learners were tested on a car with a standard stick-shift, and I almost laughed out loud when I saw where the examiner instructed me to do the hill start. In London a hill start was always mid-way up a huge hill. I had learned to pull up the hand brake, then slowly raise my left foot off the clutch while depressing the gas pedal with my right until the car was about to move forward. Then I quickly released the hand brake, and up the hill we would go. In Port of Spain I was asked to do a hill start on a tiny bump in the road where the car passed through a small gutter while turning into a side street. I sailed through the driving test.

Having received my license, I was astonished when Ainsley said, "Good! I believe in letting you practice by driving immediately. You can take Mother to the market on Saturday mornings." I was horrified.

William Terrace, where Mother lived, was broad enough to allow two-way traffic. However, the way out to the main road passed through a lane that must have been built in the days of horse and buggy. It could accommodate only one vehicle at a time. If another car approached from the opposite direction, one had to duck into a driveway or reverse until there was enough space for the two cars to pass each other. In addition, the neighborhood boys liked to congregate for hours at the corner of the lane, many of them refusing to budge for our car. Sometimes Ainsley sped up as he approached them, saying, "I'll just take off their toes!" There would be one mad scramble as the boys scampered out of the way.

As a new and inexperienced driver, I was not about to engage in this type of brinksmanship. With Mother comfortably ensconced in the passenger seat, I carefully negotiated the streets, avoiding taxis, bicycles, pedestrians, and sometimes animals such as dogs and chickens. As I approached the market the traffic worsened. The congested streets in the vicinity of the market at six a.m. on Saturday mornings allowed no room for errors in judgment. As the sun peeped over the trees, I slowly inched my way along, avoiding cars, big trucks, and rusty old vans. Finding a parking space was an exercise in frustration. When I eventually found one, I broke out in a sweat while trying to parallel park in a tight spot. Not wanting to hit another vehicle or dent my own, I sometimes made two or three attempts before getting it right. I give Mother credit. She sat very calmly, patiently, and quietly while I wrestled with the steering wheel. She did not know how to drive, but she showed she had faith in my abilities.

At the market we wandered from one vendor to another. Some of the stalls were inside the building. Mother preferred to patronize the vendors who set up in the open air, arranging their produce on boxes or in bags on the ground. We stopped at a stall selling calaloo bush, the Trinidad version of collard greens. The bunches had long greenish-purplish stalks and large heart-shaped leaves. Mother carefully examined a fat, healthy bunch and advised me, "Some of the farmers empty the chamber pot with urine and even more solid things on the bush. They say this is fertilizer that make the calaloo grow fat and nice. We have to see if it looks clean, and at home we have to wash it thoroughly." This information was quite an eye-opener for me.

Then we bought okra, fresh hot peppers, and bunches of herbs, including chives, thyme, celery, and parsley. Another vendor sold blue crabs with their pincers bound tightly with vines gathered from the forest. Mother selected two. I was glad their pincers were securely tied because I did not relish the idea of having a finger grabbed by creatures to which I was unaccustomed. Moving along to another stall, Mother picked out two or three long pigtails from a brine-filled pail. All these were ingredients that would be added to the calaloo dish, a staple of the traditional Trinidadian Sunday dinner. Next, she chose fresh plantains and other ground provisions, such as cassava and sweet potatoes, to provide side dishes for the meal. Mother was experienced in haggling with the vendors and never paid the original asking price.

The last stop was where a man had chickens huddled in a small coop. He caught one, which he brought close for Mother to examine. She said disparagingly, "No, I don't want that one. It is a hen." After he pulled out another chicken, which she accepted, she advised me, "You must always choose a cock because the females have too much fat on them." I had no idea how she determined the sex of the chicken and I did not think to ask. The live bird was carefully weighed and money exchanged. Finally, we carried our laden baskets to the car and wended our way home.

The entire exercise took two to three hours every Saturday morning. One advantage of these sorties to the market was that I learned my way round the city of Port of Spain. Also, I really learned to drive by gaining experience in navigating the car through the tightest of spaces.

After resting a while when we returned, Mother started preparations for the Sunday meal. First she killed the chicken. Standing in the kitchen doorway, she grabbed the chicken by the neck and swung it around and around in a circular motion, its legs splaying outwards as it made the 360 degree trajectory. The chicken reminded me of a participant sitting in a speeding amusement park ride, its seats leaning outward from the thrust of the circular orbit. When the bird's neck broke, it fluttered for a while until the life force was spent. I then assisted Mother in plucking the feathers. The fine feathers, especially on the wings, she singed off over an open flame from the gas stove's burner. Once the bird was cleaned, she cut it up and seasoned it to marinate overnight and absorb the flavor.

Mother's method of killing the chicken seemed, to me rather inhumane, but at least no blood was spilled. In Jamaica the process was much more primitive. The chicken was placed under a small metal basin in the yard, with the neck sticking out rather like a turtle under its shell. Then the head was cut off with a sharp knife or a machete. The bird, in its death throes, would shudder, often moving the basin several inches and splattering blood far and wide until it finally lay still. In Trinidad a chicken suffered a much cleaner death. When we finally rented our own place, I could not bring myself to kill a live bird, and subsequently bought my chickens already slaughtered, cleaned, and plucked.

If I thought killing a chicken was bad, killing the crabs for the calaloo was even worse. First Mother prepared the calaloo bush. After thoroughly washing the vegetable, she stripped the outer coating from the stems and chopped the leaves and stems into small pieces. These were added to a small amount of boiling water with cut up okra, chopped onions, chives, thyme, and parsley. Into the pot were dropped a few pieces of salted pigtail for flavor, and coconut milk was added. (For West Indians, coconut milk is not the clear liquid found inside the nut, which we refer to as coconut water. Rather, coconut milk is obtained by grating the white meat, adding water, then squeezing and straining the grated mixture to produce a white liquid.) Finally Mother added the crab legs and pincers to the simmering pot. But first she had to kill the crabs.

The crabs had been placed in the kitchen sink on our return from the market. Now and then she splashed water on them, as it was imperative the crabs not die prematurely. When ready for them, she inserted a large kitchen knife between their eyes. A brownish liquid oozed out—I guess that was the crab's blood. When the paroxysms of death were over and the crabs lay still, she untied the bonds holding the pincers, and quickly broke off and discarded the crab backs. I watched in amazement. Then she carefully washed the parts with water and lime juice. Finally, she scraped the hairs from the legs with a knife before adding them to the pot.

The final action, after the mixture boiled, was to swizzle the calaloo with a metal swizzle stick that had a long wooden handle. This process reduced the mixture to a green, viscous soup-like dish. It did not look pretty but tasted absolutely divine.

I watched and learned. When I had to prepare the dish I made my own adaptations. To avoid the horror of killing the crabs with a kitchen knife, I deposited them in the freezer, where they endured a slow and chilly death. It was totally heartless of me but the only way I could think of dealing with them. I also used modern technology to swizzle the calaloo by dumping the mixture into the Osterizer and setting the blender on puree.

My first Christmas in Trinidad opened my eyes to the island's culture and way of life. Apart from the food preparation—the black cake, ham, turkey, and the Christmas beverages—much energy was spent on "putting away" the house. Windows were washed, walls inside and out were painted, wooden floors polished, and new curtains sewn. (Some Trinidadians had what I found the peculiar habit of hanging curtains with the wrong side facing the interior of the room so that passersby could view the "pretty" side.)

November through Christmas was parang season, when the airwaves were inundated with Spanish Christmas carols that sounded strange to my anglophile ears. Thus I was quickly introduced to Trinidad's Spanish heritage. In fact,

Trinidad remained Spanish much longer than the other British islands in the Caribbean, and it was only in 1878 that the island became a British territory. The masses of the population were either Spanish or French-Creole, the latter speaking patois in their homes even though English had become the country's official language and was taught in the schools. Later, English became more influential as it was spoken by waves of migrants from other British islands like Barbados, Grenada, and St. Vincent. Trinidad had a small Portuguese population, although the bulk of the population was either black or Creole. Other ethnic minorities included Chinese, Lebanese, Jews, and native Caribs, making Trinidad & Tobago one of the most cosmopolitan countries in the world. To add to the melting pot, East Indians had come as indentured servants to work on the sugar estates after the freeing of the slaves who had been brought from Africa. They all brought their languages and religions with them.

The Spanish influence was evidenced by many of the place names, such as Las Cuevas, Manzanilla, Valencia, Huevos, and Santa Cruz. On one of my first trips to the beach at Maracas Bay on the north coast, Ainsley and I were approached by an old man who sang to us in Spanish as he played a guitar. He was obviously trying to make a few dollars from people whom he thought to be tourists. That incident brought home to me that many people still spoke a Spanish patois in their homes.

In the villages nestled in the valleys of the rugged Northern Range, parang groups met to play traditional Spanish carols in December. I came to appreciate this music, which at first was quite foreign to me, and learned the intricate steps of the castilian, a type of Spanish waltz. Parang groups from different villages competed, culminating with the island championship shortly before Christmas. Their instruments were typically guitars, cuatros—which are similar to the guitar but with only four strings, violins, a box-bass, tambourines, the toc-toc—basically two pieces of wood hitting against each other, and the shak-shak—a small, round dried gourd known as a calabash that is hollowed out and filled with the dried seeds of the fruit and then attached to a long wooden handle. The shak-shak makes a distinctive percussive sound from the seeds hitting inside the calabash. Usually there was a lead singer who sang in Spanish, often acquiring fame throughout the country. One noted songbird, Daisy Voisin in the town of Siparia, led her group to victory several years in a row.

One of our friends was so immersed in parang that he visited the village of Lopinot, the center of this traditional music, from a day or two before Christmas until Boxing Day, which is the day after Christmas and also a holiday. He was lost to his wife and family during this period. Sometimes a small parang group was hired as entertainment at a Christmas party. Although paid when hired for private parties, the musicians also expected to be fed and plied with constant rounds of drinks. It seemed they played better when well supplied with shots of rum. It also was the tradition of parang groups to move from house to house in the community, serenading the occupants. The madam of the house was expected to bring out a bottle of rum and the ham, quaintly referred to as "salt kinds" by Trinidadians.

On my first Christmas morning at Mother's house, we were suddenly awakened at six a.m. by the sound of singing to the accompaniment of a cuatro at the front door:

Drink a rum and a ponce crème
It's Christmas morning
Drink a rum and a ponce crème
Mama drink if you drinking ...

Mother was already up, preparing the turkey for the oven. She opened the front door and shouted, "Litvin, you ole skeffer!" It was her her nephew, Litvin Permell, whom she was calling a rascal. He and a couple of friends had been up all night playing parang, and were now passing by to greet his aunt and her family at Christmas. Of course Mother rushed to serve them ham, sweet bread, and drinks, and then they moved on.

Christmas was a grand celebration in Trinidad & Tobago. Some people installed lights around the house but the main focus was the Christmas tree. Live coniferous trees were not imported from northern climes since the cost was prohibitive. One could buy a locally grown southern pine; these were rather scraggly in appearance and without the desirable conical shape. Some creative souls decorated a live tree branch, stripped of its leaves, with tinsel, colored lights, ornaments, and cotton resting on the limbs to depict snow. Most families used an artificial tree that looked real. Those lacked the pungent pine scent, but we did not know that. Being in the tropics, we had experienced neither snow nor the scent of pine. Several households placed a nativity scene near or beneath the tree, and by doing so reminded us of the meaning of the Christmas season.

It seemed as though people concentrated more on food and parties than on gift-giving. The abundance of food prepared surpassed what I was used to. Mother usually boiled an imported ham in a large tin on a wood fire out in the back yard. This ham was referred to as a "tar ham" because it was salted and then encased in tar to preserve it. After the tar covering was removed, the ham was soaked overnight to remove some of the salt. It was boiled till tender, removed from the tin, and the water drained off. While the ham was still warm, Mother quickly took off the skin. She inserted dozens of cloves in the fatty layer beneath, causing the scent to penetrate the ham and enhance the flavor. Other dishes that went on the table included a huge baked pork leg prepared in the Spanish or Portuguese tradition. Side dishes included stewed chicken, stewed pigeon peas, rice, calaloo, and the reddish potato salad prepared with beets and carrots that Trinis referred to as "mayonnaise," which Ainsley had introduced me to during our time at Leeds. The goodies didn't stop there. There was black cake—a pound cake infused with fruits soaked in rum and wine, yellow pound cake, and various Christmas drinks like sorrel, ponce crème, and ginger beer.

The Christmas feast had many partakers. Ainsley's siblings, Vilma and Lennox, came home from Canada, with Lennox bringing his latest girlfriend. Vilma came with a huge suitcase packed with gifts for all the nieces and nephews, as well as for her siblings. The house was filled with merriment as friends and relatives dropped by continuously. Vilma's longtime friends, Vicky Carrington and Fresh Face, came practically every day to visit. The house was a hubbub of activity. In the background the radio or the stereo emitted the sounds of the latest Christmas calypsos.

The round of parties started for us on Christmas evening and continued through Boxing Day. It seemed that every day was one big party in Trinidad. Trinidadians' term for partying was "fêting" and they made a verb out of the noun "fête." No one could really fête like a Trinidadian. Family members and close friends took turns entertaining, whether it was on the Christmas and New Year's holidays or the weekend in between. House fêtes were very popular at that time, because although there were a few nightclubs in Trinidad they were nowhere as prolific as nowadays.

Immediately after Christmas the Carnival season began rising to its crescendo. In most Western societies, including

Jamaica, the festivities were over when the Christmas and New Year holidays passed. Not so in Trinidad & Tobago, where Christmas was only the onset of a season of gaiety and celebration. I later realized that it seemed Trinidadians actually held back a little at Christmas because they knew they were in for the long haul of events that culminated with Carnival on the Monday and Tuesday before Ash Wednesday. Parang music mutated to Christmas calypsos and finally to Carnival calypsos, which inundated the radio airwaves.

During my first Carnival season, the calypso tents opened in January 1969. The Borel clan, including siblings who returned home from Canada for the holidays, decided to "make a lime." "Liming" was the Trinidadian term for hanging out together, and about twelve of us, including friends, bought tickets for the New Year's night opening of Sparrow's tent. The Mighty Sparrow was a famous calypsonian known for his golden voice and driving rhythm. The tents might have started out as real tents on vacant lots, reminiscent of the revival meetings of religious evangelicals. By the time I arrived in Trinidad it was a great surprise to me that Sparrow's "tent" was actually the very solid building of the Seamen's Union Hall on Wrightson Road. We sat on rather uncomfortable wooden folding chairs in the very first row. Big mistake! When a couple in our group arrived late, the emcee stopped and pointedly cracked a joke at their expense. Cringing a little, they took their seats hurriedly.

The performance started about an hour late. A brass band and a group of backup singers came on stage, and a series of lesser-known calypsonians performed their songs in dialect. Most of the numbers were original compositions, although some were brilliant compositions created by songwriters for popular performers like Sparrow. Each year, singers worth their mettle were expected to bring out new songs. The previous year's calypsos were unacceptable to the crowd, which was not averse to booing raucously when dissatisfied. Only the most memorable calypsos such as "Hot, Hot, Hot," "Dollar Wine," or "Sugar Bum Bum" survived over the years. In fact, those songs are still popular today—outside of Trinidad.

Between songs the emcee, whose entrance was heralded by a brass fanfare, told jokes, some of them extremely risqué. The tent was definitely meant only for adult audiences, as many of the calypsos contained sexual innuendos. Double entendre spiced the lyrics of the wittiest compositions, which were well received with guffaws and raucous laughter. At first, with my unaccustomed ears, I had a hard time understanding many of the words. Songs of social commentary often threw pithy barbs—or *picong,* at important people such as politicians, and poked fun at events in the society. Some calypsos even commented on international events. For example, when in 1957 the Russians launched the Sputnik satellite with a dog inside, The Mighty Sparrow wrote a calypso on that event:

Although they trying they best
You know they making a mess
With the Russian satellite
They should all be sent to prison
For the dog that they poison
In the Russian satellite
Two Sputniks in the skies
Had everybody hypnotized
Now I'm very sorry
For the poor little puppy
In the Russian satellite ...

Other calypsos were bouncy and bright, with a strong syncopated beat intended for use as dance music at fêtes and in the streets on Carnival days.

During breaks between songs and during intermission there were onslaughts on the bars for Carib beer, rum, other hard liquor, and sweet drinks. The aromas of pelau—a mixed rice dish with pigeon peas and meat, souse—boiled pig's feet that had been washed to remove the glue and then soaked in a lime marinade, and roti—an Indian delicacy with supple flat bread enclosing delicious curried meat, were come-ons for those whose appetites opened up.

The Mighty Sparrow showed up very near the end of the program and sang six or eight songs from his latest album. His beautiful voice, accompanied by a driving rhythm and suggestive body language, had the crowd roaring. At one point Sparrow extemporized, giving *picong* to a couple sitting in the front row. He sang, "Yuh have taste, but yuh wife have none," meaning that the wife was pretty but the husband was definitely not good looking. The concert continued well into the wee hours of the morning. It had started later than anticipated and then many encores lengthened the show. After Sparrow's last triumphant number, we filed out of the hall, happily moving in time to the music from the band, which did not cease playing until the hall was empty. My first experience with the calypso tent was truly enjoyable and an education in itself.

Thereafter we visited two or three other tents, including that of Lord Kitchener, the main rival to Sparrow. Kitch, as he was affectionately called, was a born calypsonian and composed all his own lyrics and music. I never heard him speak in public—he stuttered, so he did not talk to the crowds, but he sang smoothly, with great rhythm and musicality. Kitch was frequently the Road March King since he composed primarily for the steel band and his tunes were popular on the road. The composer whose song was played most often on the road on Carnival day became the Road March King. As the

Carnival season continued, several calypso competitions took place, culminating in the Calypso Monarch competition at the Dimanche Gras show on the Sunday night before Carnival. The Mighty Sparrow was named Road March King the first year I attended, as he was seven other times during his career. But it was Lord Kitchner who won most, earning the accolade ten times before his death in 2000.

The number of fêtes thrown in January and February came as a great surprise to me. Every weekend there were at least three or four to attend, with plenty of food and drink and the latest calypsos blaring from the DJs' sound systems. If the music was good it did not take long for the party to warm up. Some were house fêtes and soon the dimmed rooms would be filled with mad figures swaying, jumping, gyrating their hips side to side, which Trinis referred to as "wining," and singing along to the popular tunes. Others were big fêtes held at huge halls or in hotel parking lots. A favored place for a big fête was the expansive ground of the Queen's Park Oval, where important cricket matches were played. Music was provided by at least two brass bands and sometimes a steel band. When a popular calypso played, the crowd exploded. The dancers went non-stop all night, pausing only to find drinks or food or to take a bathroom break. I was amazed at how people could keep going like that, sometimes fêting till daybreak. How did they do it? My own experience from Jamaica was that parties ended around one or two a.m., so it took me time to develop the stamina to continue going like Trinidadians, who really knew how to fête. However, I loved it all. Ainsley certainly expected me to attend every party with him, quite unlike some married men in Trinidadian society who attended solo and behaved as if they were bachelors, free like birds.

Some organizations threw day fêtes on Sunday, usually starting at eleven a.m. and lasting until seven or eight in the evening. These Sunday fêtes were high society parties thrown by doctors or other wealthy patrons, and often held at places like the Hilton Hotel.

With the continuous round of social events, I found myself having to buy a host of new outfits because I couldn't wear the same thing over and over again, could I, especially if we were liming with the same crowd of friends. The Carnival season was becoming really expensive! Luckily for me, Mother was a seamstress by profession and, without my asking, sewed a new party dress for me in a day. By then, Gemma, her last daughter, had returned from England with her baby son and was living at home. Mother never made a new outfit for Gemma without also making one for me. I really appreciated that she treated me the same as her own daughter.

Another new experience occurred when Litvin, of parang fame, invited us to visit a panyard. This was the home base of a steel band, a place where the panmen practiced incessantly. Trinidad & Tobago, an oil-producing country, had created the only new instrument in the twentieth century—the steel pan. During World War II many young men were out of work and would lime at street corners. They started beating rhythms on empty oil drums and found they could produce different notes according to the size of indentations on the tops of the lids, or "pans." It was marvelous to see the pans of various sizes up close, whose indentations produced different notes of the musical scale when hit with rubber-tipped sticks. Tuning of the pans was very important. The manner of tuning gave each band its distinctive sound.

A steel band, often referred to as a steel orchestra, is comprised of different sized pans that play in different registers. The big fifty-five-gallon drums are tuned to form the bass pan. Then there are different types of tenor pans, guitar pans, and cello pans. The panyard was a cacophony of sound, especially when each pannist was practicing his individual part. My friend Cislyn lived near a panyard and always complained that she could not sleep, and therefore had no use for the steel bands. As Carnival approached, the bands practiced night and day—not only to rehearse for playing social events, but also for the island-wide Panorama competitions. Winning the highly coveted Panorama trophy caused the competition to be so keen that often only fractions of a point separated the top ten bands.

My first experience at the Panorama preliminaries, at the Queen's Park Savannah, was rather hair-raising. The Savannah is a big, open park in the center of Port of Spain where horse racing took place until the 1990s, when it moved to Santa Rosa Park, outside the city. The track at the Savannah passed in front of the Grand Stand, ideal for Carnival events. Each year a stage was built in front of the Grand Stand, and the North Stand was erected directly opposite. Usually, wealthier people sat in the Grand Stand, whereas ordinary people frequented the North Stand. The preliminaries moved slowly since it took time for the panmen and their supporters to push the pans onto the stage, arrange them, settle themselves, perform, and then move off again. On average only three bands crossed the stage each hour. As approximately three hundred bands participated nationwide, the prelims often lasted an entire weekend. Groups of friends and families regarded the North Stand as a place to camp out. Baskets and coolers filled with food and drink dotted it, creating the look of a big picnic area.

On the first occasion that I attended the Panorama preliminaries, the North Stand was not yet complete, and that was where Ainsley and I found ourselves after a day fête. The upright posts were installed but there were no seats yet.

Some parts of the stand were not yet covered. The crowd got in free and stood on the risings. When a band started playing, everyone rocked from side to side, in time to the beat. As the strains of the melody filled the air, the enthusiastic rocking went up a notch. The North Stand shook precariously. The floorboards bent and creaked as the crowd stomped in time to the music. I glanced from time to time at the half-finished roof and felt fearful. "What got me into this mess?" I thought. "This structure is surely going to come crashing down, killing us all!" The authorities made several announcements through the P.A. system for everyone to vacate the dangerously unsafe North Stand, but the crowd ignored all pleas. It appeared there were not enough policemen to enforce the order, and we stayed. I tried in vain to get Ainsley to leave. I said my prayers. God must have heard because the structure held up and I lived to tell the tale.

By the week before Carnival, excitement in the entire country reached a fever pitch. People arrived at their offices but could or would not work. All they thought of was Carnival—their costumes, the calypsos, and the steel bands. Trinis living abroad, as well as tourists, poured into the country and it seemed the population tripled for the two weeks prior to Carnival. The airport was constantly congested because the facilities could not comfortably handle the hordes of passengers pouring in. With the expectation of having a good time, the crush of people still managed to keep their tempers. Some who were met at the airport drove directly to a fête, not even bothering to go home or to a hotel first to deposit their bags.

A host of competitions took place the week prior to Carnival, including the competition for the Kings and Queens of the Bands. Most masquerade bands had a King and a Queen, gorgeously arrayed in costumes depicting the theme of the band. Ingeniously created, some of the costumes towered up to ten feet and might have a horizontal span of similar dimensions. The costumes had to be light enough to be carried by the masquerader, who could not be on wheels or a float, and whose worst nightmare was the wind toppling the costume. Each contestant hoping to win the title of King or Queen of the Bands danced on stage before the judges. I was stunned by the sights, the sounds, and the sheer madness of what went on around me. I thought, "At Carnival time Trinis have gone crazy!"

Even children took part in the action, as several Kiddies Carnival competitions took place. Some of these were private events, such as the Red Cross Children's Carnival, but the main Kiddies Carnival is on the Saturday before Carnival. That event is government-sponsored and involves the participation of many of the schools. Youthful calypsonians compose and sing their own songs, vying to become Junior Calypso Monarch. Costumed bands with little bandits, pirates, Indians, and sailors paraded in the streets and then filled the Savannah stage with revelry. There was no limit to the imagination in choosing the themes of the bands. One school portrayed "Fishes of the Caribbean," with each section of the band depicting a particular type of fish: angelfish, parrotfish, stingrays, goldfish. The vitality of the masqueraders and the kaleidoscope of colors made a deep impression on me as I watched from the crowded sidewalk. But this was only a taste of what was to come.

The final competition before Carnival occurred on Sunday night with the Dimanche Gras show at the Savannah. Here the calypso contestants and the Kings and Queens of the masquerade bands vied to win in their categories. In addition, at this show the Panorama Finals climaxed the steel band competitions. Hosts of followers helped push the wheeled

pans on and off stage as each of the twelve finalists from
Trinidad & Tobago put on its best show possible. Dressed in
spiffy uniforms, the panmen showed amazing discipline while
waiting in the hushed silence for the signal to begin. Then an
explosion of sound as they struck up the chords. Their "flag
woman" danced, wining her hips while frantically waving a
flag displaying the names of the band, the arranger, and the
tune. The pannists played with verve as they jumped between
the pans, yet they also showed discipline, something I could
not imagine for Trinis who threw themselves into fêting
with gay abandon. All the effort was in hopes of bringing
home the trophy. After the last steel band passed, I could not
decide which was the winning band for me; they were all
so good. Trinis had their favorite bands, to which they gave
their undying loyalty. For me, Dimanche Gras was fantastic
because it wrapped up so many aspects of Carnival—the
calypsos, the steel bands, and the masquerades—in this single
show. Yet more was still to come.

In the wee hours of Carnival Monday morning, J'ouvert
celebrations erupt. J'ouvert signals the opening of Carnival,
and early morning revelers dressed in "Ole Mas" costumes
throng the streets of Port of Spain even before dawn. I always
thought of Ole Mas as a dirty masquerade, since many
participants covered their bodies with mud or paint of ocher,
red, black, white, or blue, to portray devils with horns, long
tails, and pitchforks. There were no restrictions on the themes
of Ole Mas bands. They could portray robbers, sailors, bats,
or Indians. There also were no limits to the ideas for the
costumes. Ainsley's cousin, Stalin, who was Litvin's brother,
had been involved in a serious accident where he lost an arm,
and only a stump remained above the elbow. The year after
the accident, at Ole Mas he played the hands of a clock, with
his full arm acting as the long hand and the stump as the

short hand. I thought that was brilliant.

On my first J'ouvert, we left Mother's house and walked a couple of miles to Woodbrook to meet the Invaders Steel Band pushing off from their panyard. This group was one of the oldest steel bands and had a large following. Our friends and we joined the band as it wended its way through the streets of Port of Spain. What a glorious experience to chip along to the music as the clear crystal notes of the pan wafted into the crisp early morning air. "Chipping" means taking small steps forward in time to the music while swaying the hips. As the skies gradually lightened, the crowd of followers thickened and members of our group had to link arms to avoid being separated. Sometimes we were close enough to help push the pans on their wheels. However, we had to be careful not to get run over by the pans when the road suddenly narrowed and became congested. We followed the pans to the bitter end, all the way downtown. By then it was eleven a.m. and the task of walking several miles home in the broiling sun was wearying. To boot, there was no longer music to enliven our return trek. Quite a letdown! The only respite was stopping at a friend's home to have a bathroom break, rest our aching feet, and quench our thirst with a cool, iced drink.

Later in the day I accompanied Mother and her grand-children to the Savannah to view the Monday masquerade. Although there were some costumes, the bands held back somewhat, as they preferred to wait until Tuesday to dress in their full glory. Mother made sure to be in the stands with baskets and coolers of food and drink, ready to share with her masquerading children and their friends.

On Carnival Tuesday, unimpeded by J'ouvert, the Parade of the Bands began early, with most pushing off about eight a.m. Masqueraders traversed the streets of Port of Spain, dancing to the music of DJs on trucks that accompanied the bands. Mother, all excited, was eager to reach the Savannah. In her young days she had "played mas"—masqueraded in a costumed band—and she enjoyed watching the bands show the spirit of Carnival with their colorful costumes. We hurried to the Savannah, parked as near as possible to our seats in the stands, and helped her carry the baskets of food to our area. A few of her young grandkids ran around. At their ages, they could not sit still too long.

As the first big bands moved across the stage, I could not believe my eyes. I had heard reports and seen pictures of Carnival. I had even seen home movies. Nothing prepared me for the spectacle that unfolded. Each big band, one or two thousand strong, depicted a theme from various categories— from history, for instance ancient Rome or the Aztec Indians; from contemporary life; or from fantasy, such as outer space with Martians and other aliens and UFOs. Each band was divided into sections of masqueraders, with each section dressed in similar costumes of the same colors. As one section after another exploded onto the stage, the effect was almost overwhelming. The colors of red, gold, vivid pink, blue, green, and silver gleamed in the sun as the masqueraders jumped high to the bright bold rhythms of the latest calypsos with a gaiety and spontaneity I had never seen before. The towering costumes of the King and Queen of the Band, as well as maybe a dozen individual characters, were interspersed in the band.

All the senses were stimulated. My own senses were so overwhelmed that I felt as if I were awash in overwhelming sounds and colors, and I am unable to recall the specifics of what I saw that first year. One band does stand out, from many years later. Wayne Berkeley was one of the most talented bandleaders and won on ten occasions. In 1975, his production was themed A La Carte, with one section depicting tastefully designed dinner plates on the headpieces of the costumes. Another section showed forks, and another knives for the place settings. One section portrayed wine goblets, and all these were part of the headpieces. Individual masqueraders depicted serving dishes and a tureen. The individual heading the next section was a teapot, surrounded by others as cream and sugar bowls and cups and saucers. The theme was ingeniously created and portrayed.

The sights, the sounds, the spirit, and gaiety of the revelers were contagious. Onlookers tapped their feet in time to the music or ran down near the stage "to take a wine." Mother and I stayed on the lookout for two of my sisters-in-law who were playing in a band, since we needed to get food and drink ready for them. On entering the Savannah the girls left the band and hurried to find Mother in the stands to get their refreshments—pelau, souse, sweet bread, and homemade drinks like mauby, ginger beer, and sorrel. It was a slow process for the bands waiting to get on stage so there was plenty of time to leave, eat, and rejoin their group. When they finally reached the limelight of the stage, we left our seats to run down to the front row and snap pictures.

I could not get over the spectacle of Trinidad & Tobago's Carnival. To me it was "the greatest show on earth." I never thought I would ever get enough of it. All I wanted to do was look at the masqueraders. What made the masquerade even more unbelievable was that nobody went to school to learn how to make the costumes. These were ordinary citizens who were extremely talented. They grew up seeing their parents making costumes and learning from them. Of course the role that the schools played in the Kiddies Carnival meant the tradition would continue forever.

The bands continued crossing the stage until eight or nine p.m. Although the last bands had a long wait to perform, they had the added advantage of the lights at night, so the glitter, gold, and silver of the costumes shimmered and shone brightly.

When it all ended, we loaded up and exited the Savannah at a snail's pace to make the long trek back to the car. What I saw next was completely unexpected. All along the streets of Port of Spain, large masquerade costumes lay in the gutters to be picked up by the garbage collectors. Citizens of humble means often saved for an entire year to pay for those beautiful and expensive costumes, which then were so easily discarded after two days. "What a waste," I thought. It was only in later years that I saw some of the best costumes displayed in the lobbies of hotels like the Hilton or Holiday Inn. Once I viewed a museum exhibit of Wayne Berkeley's costumes and, seeing them up close, realized how neat and meticulous his work was.

Then it was Ash Wednesday. All festivities ceased and everyone went back to work. The madness was over. Until the following year.

In the pre-Carnival season my first year, Ainsley's sister Vilma was home for a visit from Canada, with every intention of staying for Carnival. One evening when Ainsley and Vilma were out, I felt incredibly tired and went to our room to rest. At about eight p.m., I was awakened by Ainsley entering the room. His shirt was all dirty and torn, and there was blood on his arm. "What happened?" I asked, not fully awake but somewhat alarmed.

"It's all right," he replied. "There was an accident. I'm okay but Vilma is at the emergency room. I came to get you all." Mother started to holler and wail and he had a hard time calming her down.

Vilma and Ainsley had been driving around the Savannah

in our new Austin Cambridge, our first car in Trinidad & Tobago. She was at the wheel because Ainsley had been drinking. However, driving in Canada was totally different from driving in Trinidad. When a car coming from the opposite direction veered straight at them, Vilma swerved to avoid a head-on collision. The Austin Cambridge overturned in a ditch and was demolished, while the other vehicle escaped scot-free and did not even stop. A friend happened to pass by and took Vilma and Ainsley to the nearby Port of Spain General Hospital, then brought Ainsley home to pick up the family.

The emergency room doctor was an old schoolmate of Ainsley. He said, "Vilma injured the ligaments in her knee. I'll have to admit her and put a cast on the leg."

"You do what is necessary," Ainsley replied. "I want to see my sister properly attended to."

"How are you, man?" the doctor asked.

"I'm fine. Nothing is wrong with me," Ainsley insisted.

"Okay then. Come with me to my office."

Behind closed doors, his doctor friend gave Ainsley a drink. There was no physical examination, nor tests run, and I was too young and inexperienced to demand them. Vilma endured six weeks in a plaster of Paris cast but still was not satisfied with how she felt, so she flew back to Montreal for specialized treatment.

Not long after the accident, I discovered I was pregnant. No wonder I had been so tired and could not keep awake on that fateful evening. Otherwise I might also have been an occupant of the car with Ainsley and Vilma.

*O*n April 1969, I landed a teaching job at a government secondary school. With my income, Ainsley and I were able to move to a rented flat, at No. 14C Saddle Road. The location was ideal for accessibility and convenience, since it was not too far up the Maraval Valley and also quite near to the Savannah, the focal point of Port of Spain. The house was on a main road with a small Chinese grocery two doors away and, in the other direction, a Hilo supermarket was within walking distance. Behind the main road on either side were situated quiet residential neighborhoods. Our flat occupied the downstairs of a two-story building. The flat above ours had its own entrance by an outside staircase.

Our three-bedroom home was tiled throughout. As we had no furniture and little money to purchase any, we were glad the flat was fully furnished. With the assistance of my in-laws, we settled in quickly. Rosie, my sister-in-law, helped me pick out material for curtains and showed me how to measure, cut, and sew them. A small entrance foyer opened into a spacious living-dining area that was backed by a huge kitchen. At the kitchen counter was a small hatch, allowing us to pass dishes through to the dining table. In the dining room was a long sideboard, reaching the height of the hatch, on which Ainsley placed his stereo system. Music meant a lot to him and this piece of equipment was the first to be set up when we moved in. The back door of the kitchen opened out to a grassy lawn bordered by a low wall. Behind the house on the other side of the wall the land dropped steeply down to the Maraval River. It amazed me that the valley, which was concreted, had only a tiny, docile trickle of a stream at the bottom. This was man's effort to contain the force of nature. Later on in the rainy season I saw that concrete basin more than halfway filled with a roaring, rushing torrent. Mercifully, the Maraval River never overflowed its banks while we were there.

I was elated to at last have my husband back. Now that we were installed in our own flat and with me pregnant, he came straight home each afternoon. There was no more liming with the boys after work. He was definitely more supportive and I kept well, not even having to battle morning sickness. My acne-prone skin cleared, my nails and hair grew luxuriantly, and maybe I did have a glow about me. As I put on weight and began to show, the men on the street looked admiringly at me and offered to carry my packages while I shopped. It was almost as if they wanted to come on to me, which I found puzzling. Most of the men I had known in Jamaica or other places seemed somewhat disparaging of pregnant women, giving them the feeling that they were no longer beautiful. Maybe it was the Trinidadian propensity to equate a heavy body with beauty, a far-away memory handed down through the genes of our African ancestors.

The move to our own place would have been impossible if not for my new teaching position at Tranquillity Government Secondary School. Mother's neighbor, Mr. Donovan Palmer, was the school's principal and, learning that I was a geography major, informed us he had need of a geography teacher. He had enough clout with the Ministry of Education to get me hired. The three-term school year in the former British territories continued to be patterned after the British system, with the Christmas term from September to December, the spring term from January to April, and the summer term from April to July. I commenced my teaching career at the beginning of the summer term in 1969.

Tranquillity had been founded 150 years before as a teachers' training college. Subsequently it was divided into two schools, a boys' and a girls' school, reaching an intermediate level. With later reorganization, it coalesced into one institution offering a co-educational program at the secondary level for students from the ages of eleven to seventeen years. The grade levels were Forms I to V, with Forms I to III comprising the lower school, and IV and V the upper school. My job was to teach geography to classes in Form III. In addition, I was made form mistress of a class in that grade, with duties that included taking attendance, advising my students during the homeroom period, and organizing the social activities of the form. I was generally the go-to person when one of my students had a problem.

Although glad to finally have a job, I was more than a little fearful of entering the classroom—I had no teaching experience whatsoever. Ainsley kept encouraging me by observing, "Teaching is one of the best jobs for a married woman in Trinidad. Your hours of work coincide with your children's, you get to come home early, and you get the holidays." "Holidays" was the term used for the vacation in the British Caribbean islands.

I knew I was not a born teacher but I tried to do it to the best of my ability. Needless to say, my debut was disastrous and I only stuck with it because there was no other choice. My lack of confidence and deficiencies in teaching skills hampered my performance. (Six years later, I took advantage of a diploma of education program at the University of the West Indies that was specially designed for teachers who were already on the job. The bulk of the sessions took place during the vacations, while during the school term we had a reduced schedule to accommodate our time spent at the university. Since we were already in a classroom setting, it was easy to arrange teaching practice and evaluation. Oh, I wished that opportunity had been offered to me much earlier in my career! Life would have been much easier.)

Another difficulty in the early years was a serious communications barrier. I had a hard time understanding the Trinidadian accent and turn of phrase. Students made statements such as "It's making cold" or "It's making hot," which I realized were the literal translation of the French terms. There is a strong French-Creole heritage in Trinidad, where some people still speak French patois. Students, in turn, were puzzled by my Jamaican pronunciation, especially of Trinidadian place names, which I could not get away from with a subject like geography. In Trinidad, the town of San Juan was pronounced as "Sah Wah," a tongue-twisting sound difficult for my anglophile mouth to form. Croisee sounded like "quaysay." My poor attempts at pronouncing that name and others evoked mirth from the students. Luckily, the students were respectful of teachers, so my disciplinary problems were few. They called me "Miss," their preferred method of addressing all female teachers regardless of marital status.

At the end of the term the principal, Mr. Palmer, informed everyone during an assembly that he was no longer allowing class parties on the school premises. On a previous occasion, some teenagers had engaged in sexual encounters in the dark recesses of the classrooms and such behavior would not be tolerated. Mr. Palmer added that he had no objection to form teachers holding class parties in their homes. Students from my class begged me, "Miss, would you let us have a party at your home? We will be good, we'll do all the work, we'll clean up afterwards, and we'll behave ourselves. Miss, please, pleeease!" I told them I would consider it.

After conferring with Ainsley, who agreed to help with the chaperoning, I agreed under certain conditions. When I returned to school, I told the students, "The party has to end by nine p.m. There will be no beer or any other form of alcohol. I will make a pot of pelau but you will have to prepare the rest of the food, arrange the furniture for the party, and clean up afterwards. Also, I need written permission from your parents allowing you to come to my home." It was necessary to have parental consent for the fourteen-year-old girls.

Some of the girls arrived at my home in the morning to prepare the food. They made several platters of sandwiches and other snacks. This was the first time I saw prunes stuffed with peanut butter—they tasted really good. Some girls had made pound cake, which they sliced and piled on to platters. An East Indian girl arrived with a large pot of curried chicken and a huge tray with individual balls of dough about the size of tennis balls. She was going to make dahl pourri, a particular type of roti, an Indian flat bread. I watched with great interest as she confidently went about the involved process. First she boiled split peas until they were just soft enough to mash with a fork or a potato masher. She put about a teaspoon of the mashed peas in each ball of dough and twisted it deftly so the peas were enclosed. A rolling pin was used to flatten each ball until it was as thin as a burrito wrap. Then she baked each on a greased flat griddle, turning it over once. The pea-filled dough contained enough fat that the roti was soft and pliable, and next she filled each with the curried chicken mixture and wrapped it around the tasty contents. She made about sixty rotis, enough that each of the thirty students in the class could have two. However, these delicacies were quite filling, and many girls were satisfied with only one. Someone brought ice cream-filled cones. I remembered the large pot of pelau I had made and kept saying, "You are preparing too much food!" The teenagers ignored me.

The boys came later with their music, which Ainsley played on our stereo. They cleared the furniture from our living-dining area to make space for dancing. We all had a great time. The kids washed down the food with sweet drinks, the Trinidadian term for sodas, and by nine o' clock when the party came to a close, all the food had been devoured. I could not believe it! The boys consumed most of it, as they seemed to have voracious appetites. Up until then I had not met growing boys whose stomachs were bottomless pits. The party was a huge success and I was glad I acceded to their request. I felt that I was becoming integrated within the Trinidad & Tobago society.

At the end of the school year, Tranquillity held a ceremony for Form V graduates in a hall downtown, followed by a teachers' party at the same venue. The graduation ceremony was free, but the teachers who wished to attend the party had to pay for themselves and their escorts. Very early, I paid for Ainsley and myself, giving the money to Mrs. Elder, an older, experienced teacher who was form teacher of another class in the lower school. Miss Hughes, a teacher in the upper school, was responsible for organizing the party with Mrs. Elder's assistance.

On the night of the party when Ainsley and I presented ourselves at the door, Miss Hughes refused to admit us. "You have no tickets. I don't know you and I can't let you in."

"But," I remonstrated, "I gave the money to Mrs. Elder long ago. She never gave me tickets and I didn't know I was supposed to get any. She added my name to her list and marked me down as paid."

Miss Hughes kept us waiting by the door. Red with embarrassment because this was occurring in front of my husband, I asked, "Why don't you find Mrs. Elder inside so that she can corroborate my story?"

It took her some time to do so, as she was taking tickets. We stood awkwardly to one side of the doorway. I felt two feet tall. Eventually she got someone to bring Mrs. Elder to the entrance and the confusion was cleared up. In the meanwhile, Mr. Palmer, the principal, passed by, saw Ainsley, and took him into the inner sanctum where the male teachers were drinking behind closed doors and I did not see him for the rest of the night. I could not forgive Miss Hughes for treating me, a fellow teacher, like a liar and a cheat. I never told her how I felt, but avoided her like the plague the entire time I taught at Tranquillity, easy enough to do because we sat in separate staff rooms.

Years later after I suffered a death in my family, I found myself unavoidably in the same company with Miss Hughes. A friend and I were attending a concert at Queen's Hall and during the intermission this friend was talking with Miss Hughes. I handed my friend the drink I had bought her and was turning away when she said, "Miss Hughes offered her condolences and you did not reply." I honestly had not heard, but then I thought, "She does not even remember the incident from a long time ago. I never did tell her how I felt. I should let it go." So I thanked her and even apologized for not responding at first. A great weight seemed to lift off my shoulders. A month or two later, my Renault broke down while I was taking my children to school. The oil gasket got loose, causing all the oil to gush out and leaving us stranded. It so happened that Miss Hughes saw it all, as she was waiting to cross the road to enter her car, and was happy to assist us by dropping us at our destinations. It must have been serendipity that I had decided not to hold on to past grudges. Otherwise, I might not have been willing to receive her help when in need.

In our early years in Trinidad, the social round of house parties continued, even during my pregnancy. Family and friends also got together for beach picnics, the first held at Teteron Bay on the scenic Chaguaramas peninsula in the northwest of the island. During World War II, the United States of America had established a naval base at Chaguaramas, which was closed to the general public. After independence in 1962, Chaguaramas reverted to the government of Trinidad & Tobago and the facilities were taken over by the Defence Force. The Army and Coast Guard had headquarters there, and the family only got access to the restricted beach at Teteron because Horace Williams, Ainsley's brother-in-law, was an officer in the Coast Guard. This was one of the few occasions when all family members were present— Mother, all the siblings and their spouses, and all the children. The conviviality of the clan was heartwarming and it was a joy to bathe in the warm water after years in cold Britain. I took a walk along the beach and looked out at the stunning view of green-clad islets strung in the Gulf of Paria, separating Trinidad from Venezuela on the South American mainland. The orange-red ball of the western setting sun provided a glorious background to these islands, and a sense of peace and contentment settled over me. I felt I was going to be happy in my adopted country.

Later when I had to teach the physical geography of Trinidad & Tobago to students taking the school-leaving exam, I discovered that the island of Trinidad had once been part of South America. A number of earthquakes had cut off the land bridge connecting the northwestern peninsula to Venezuela, leaving a series of islands with deep-sea passages between them. The remaining islets were the playgrounds of wealthy Trinidadians, who built vacation homes there and accessed them by speedboats. When Trinis spoke of "going to the islands for the weekend," these were the islands they were referring to.

Our flat at No. 14C Saddle Road was situated on the main road leading through the Northern Range to the beaches on the north coast of the island, one of the most popular being Maracas Bay. We made many trips to Maracas on the winding road built by the Americans during the war. It passed through the verdant and luxuriant forest, dotted with occasional bursts of orange-red blooms of trees called "flame of the forest" by Trinidadians. The thick canopy of treetops effectively blocked the sunlight, providing shade on the route. Sometimes the road teetered on the edge of the precipice above the Caribbean Sea. We always stopped at one point to catch water from a spring emptying out from the rocks on the hillside. The water was clean and refreshing and safe to drink. We knew nothing of water pollution in those days. At one or two spots along the road we took in panoramic views of the north coast, with small curved bays lined with beaches between headlands and promontories. Eventually we reached the highest point of the climb and looked down to see Maracas Bay spread out in all its glory below us. The palm-dotted beach was arrayed with golden sand, and the breaking waves on the exposed north coast were ideal for surfing.

Sometimes the family rented a cottage at Mayaro, on the eastern Atlantic coast. As on the other beaches, we played cricket games on the long, sandy beach, using coconut boughs as bats. This beach was also known for chip-chip, a tiny clam the original native Caribs had as a staple diet. We dug in the wet sand for these tiny creatures and, when enough were gathered, washed them thoroughly and made a delicious curried dish. Mayaro, however, could be a dangerous beach, with rough seas and treacherous rip currents. Sometimes the white-crested waves towered ten to fifteen feet high. Once, Ainsley's eldest niece, Marion Williams—whom we all called Chee Chee, was in the water when she got caught in a current. Having learned to swim at the YMCA, she was able to save herself but it took all her effort. Being only a child of about thirteen years old, she could not help a nearby East Indian man who was drowning. He sank and bobbed up three times while he called for help, and then he disappeared. His body washed up on the shore the following morning. The whole incident put a pall on our vacation and we left immediately.

We explored many other areas of Trinidad & Tobago. On one occasion we joined our family friends, Elcon and Cynthia Trim, on a trip to Blue Basin, a waterfall near the head of the Diego Martin Valley in the Northern Range. Elcon was a savvy and ambitious businessman in insurance and real estate. He always drove a big American car in which he would arrive at the Borels to take the whole family out for a drive. On this trip both Cynthia and I were pregnant but we did not let our conditions stop us. We drove up the Diego Martin Valley to River Estate, which in earlier times produced sugar cane and cocoa. A big waterwheel still stood beside the river, along with aqueducts that formerly conducted water to various parts of the estate. We also saw the no longer used cocoa houses with sliding roofs for drying the cocoa beans. The roofs were opened during sunny weather and pulled back to cover the houses when the rain came down. Traditionally, workers used to dance with their bare feet on the cocoa beans to remove all traces of dried pulp and to polish the beans. This was referred to as "dancing the cocoa." The property was no longer a working estate, but with my sense of history I could see in my mind's eye how that estate must have looked.

Then we proceeded toward Blue Basin. After parking the car, we had to walk down a rocky slope to reach the river. The path was treacherous and Cynthia and I, with our big bellies, laughed and held hands while negotiating the boulders. Reaching the bottom we beheld a round pool of dark water at the base of a waterfall. Cynthia and I did not venture in, only the men. There were kids playing and diving into the cold water. They seemed to have so much fun. Years later when I returned to that place, I was amazed to find that the basin had shrunk in size. Having filled up with silt, it was a shadow of its former glory.

Another favorite jaunt was visiting Uncle Dolly and his wife, Aunty Toya, in the country. Uncle Dolly was Ainsley's father's brother and also his godfather. The first time we went, three carloads of family members drove to Cumuto, a small village in the Central Range of Trinidad. We entered through the gates of a citrus estate and ascended the long, sloping driveway to the house. The house, built on stilts, did not look like much. The citrus company had built it to accommodate the manager, which was Uncle Dolly. Ainsley's brother-in-law, Horace had telephoned the shopkeeper down the road, who then relayed the message to Uncle Dolly to expect our arrival. As we approached, he and his wife stood on the gallery—the veranda, watching for us. Tall, dark, and straight-backed, he welcomed us as we climbed up the stairs. All the family, including the children, greeted Uncle Dolly and Aunty Toya with a kiss on the cheek in the French style. When I was introduced on that first visit, I greeted them in the same manner. Aunty Toya, two years older than her husband's seventy years, was a brown-skinned lady with a bandana on her head, and her lined face showed years of experience. She broke out excitedly in French patois while talking to Mother. The old guard all spoke patois but refused to teach it to their children, thus keeping it as a secret language for expressions that were not fit for young ears. I believe she was talking about me and that she liked my looks, since I was considered by many Trinidadians to be fair in complexion. I kept hearing "Oui Papa," and "Ai yai, yai!" sprinkled throughout her remarks to Mother, which of course I could not understand.

We were invited to sit in the gallery and in the small living room, and Uncle Dolly offered us drinks. He brought out bottles of Johnny Walker Black Label, Angostura Old Oak rum, and Fernandes Vat 19 rum, the latter mainly for Mother's benefit. Coconut water from the property provided chasers for the drinks. While the adults chatted, the children went outside to play around and under the raised house. They chased chickens and rambled around the property, picking and eating their fill of oranges, tangerines, mangos, and guavas.

Aunty Toya prepared a sumptuous meal for us of stewed chicken and "wild meat," the Trinidadian term for venison. The side dishes included ground provisions, boiled plantain, calaloo, pigeon peas, and melongene au gratin, which is eggplant chopped up and mashed. Country folk consumed little rice as they ate mostly what they grew on the land. However, Aunty Toya cooked rice for us city folk. The meal was wonderful, as she was an accomplished cook. Before we left, Uncle Dolly went out to the fields to pick oranges and grapefruit, which he put in separate bags for each car. Then he cut bunches of bananas as well as several stalks of sweet sugar cane to share among us. We had a thoroughly enjoyable day with Uncle Dolly and Aunty Toya, who were superb hosts.

Dusk having fallen that Sunday evening, we raced back to Port of Spain. I mean the cars literally raced each other and it was by the grace of God that we lived to tell the tale. Ainsley drove like Jehu, especially after he imbibed "his waters," meaning he had consumed a considerable amount of alcohol.

It was not the done thing in Trinidad to have the woman behind the wheel, so I suffered the fast driving in silence. Usually, the more I complained about his speed, the faster he drove. Considering that I was then carrying his child, I was more on edge than usual. Eventually, when he drove, I sat in the backseat and closed my eyes. Mother, who was a calm and composed passenger, could sit in front. God, in His wisdom and mercy, must have been looking after us because neither then nor any other time were we ever involved in an accident.

Not long after my arrival in Trinidad, I had run into an acquaintance I worked with in Jamaica. Agnes was married to a Swiss engineer, Peter Bergen, who was posted to Jamaica to set up the Nestlé factory. With the factory in Jamaica completed, he had been transferred to Trinidad to set up one there. As fellow Jamaicans and also pregnant at the same time, Agnes and I hit it off. The Bergens often invited us to dinner at their sprawling house in Valsayn Park, with its manicured lawns and beautiful gardens. Peter prepared various sauces for the meat and cheese fondues. Our house was nowhere as grand, so we invited them to restaurants or on beach limes.

One day Agnes called me up. "We have rented a cottage in Charlotteville, Tobago, for a weekend. Would you and Ainsley like to join us?"

After checking with him I replied, "We'd love to go. I haven't yet had the opportunity to visit Tobago. But where is Charlotteville? I haven't heard of it."

"It's at the northern tip of the island, about twenty miles away from Scarborough, the capital," she replied.

Arrangements were made for the four of us to take the twenty-minute flight to Crown Point International Airport—

now named the A.N.R. Robinson International Airport—
where Peter rented a car for the drive to Charlotteville. The
trip of only about thirty-five miles took us much longer than
anticipated because the road was narrow, winding, and not
in the best condition. We followed the narrow coastal road
along the eastern side of the island, passing through numerous
small fishing villages.

The topography of Tobago reminded me of Jamaica,
since the hilly spine occupied the center of the island. Small
rural hamlets contained red-roofed houses nestled in the
valleys between the ridges. From time to time, through
spaces between the large-leaved foliage along the road, we
gained unexpectedly beautiful glimpses of the azure sea
below. At the village of Speyside we saw the outline of the
island of Little Tobago, the site of a bird sanctuary in the
Atlantic. After Speyside, the road veered inland over the
mountainous spine. The little car strained up the ascent with
the weight of us four, two big strong men and two pregnant
women. At the brow of the hill, we caught a panoramic view
of Charlotteville spread around an almost circular harbor
with a narrow entrance. The descent was even steeper than
the ascent had been. When we reached Charlotteville, what
we found was a sleepy little town. Far from the usual tourist
areas, its quiet isolation and solitude made it attractive to
honeymooners. We stayed at one of the three beachside
cottages available at that time. The beach was all right but
not the best in Tobago.

The first night Agnes called out to us, "Rose, Ainsley, come
quickly to see the crabs running!" By moonlight we could see
the entire beach covered with red crabs, even the yard. They
ran sideways and attempted to get inside the cottage but I
slammed the door shut. Agnes and Peter caught a few of the
crabs and tied them securely with string. I refused to touch

the creatures. This was a totally new experience for me, but Agnes, who hailed from Treasure Beach in Jamaica, appeared familiar and in her element with crab runs. Curried crabs became our meal the following day.

Seeking better beaches, each day we took the steep climb in the car to the gap in the hills overlooking Charlotteville, and then drove down the coastal road to the southern part of the island. Here we bathed in blue-green water fringed by white sandy beaches along the Milford Road. As this was our first visit, we knew nothing of the superb beaches at Pigeon Point and Store Bay, or the famous coral formations at Buccoo Reef. At that time, Tobago was still virtually unknown to most tourists who frequented the Caribbean, and the beaches along Milford Road were natural and unspoiled. Huge conch shells with pink apertures were strewn along the sand, and Agnes and I spent hours collecting them. Because we were flying back to the sister isle, we had to abandon most of our collection, each keeping only two of the most intact shells, which eventually became doorstops at our house. We also gathered pieces of coral from the beach. After being washed and put out in the sun in our backyard, they bleached to a pretty white.

On September 8, 1969, our daughter Denise Frances was born. It was a surprisingly easy pregnancy and nothing much had kept me back. I thought that the date of birth was well planned. The long summer vacation preceded her birth, and with three months maternity leave I only had to work twelve days in December before the three-week Christmas vacation began.

The day before she arrived was a Sunday and we entertained guests for lunch. Maybe the extra activity had something to do with it, but I went into labor at two-thirty on Monday morning, and by seven-thirty our baby was born. I cannot say that she was "delivered" because she was in such a hurry to come into this world that the doctor on call was almost too late. I was not experienced enough to know that the techniques the nurses advised me to use were meant to delay the birth so the doctor could receive his fee.

Denise arrived with a soft bump on her forehead, which turned red whenever she cried and receded when she calmed down. However, she was a pretty pink baby with not a strand of hair on her head. On return home we were greeted with several floral arrangements from well-wishers but the largest and most beautiful basket was from my husband. It was filled with large coral anthurium lilies, which traditionally signify welcome in the Trinidadian culture. He did not usually give me flowers except on special occasions—like the birth of his child.

The work for us both then began. Not having grown up around young children, I was completely inexperienced with handling a baby. Ainsley had more of an idea of what to do, since he had numerous nieces and nephews. Although I felt inadequate, whenever I held her she would calm down. I thought, "Even when I hold her awkwardly she stops crying. I could probably hold her upside down and she would not even squeak. How does she know I'm her mother? She must smell my scent or recognize my voice. I'll just have to do the best I can."

Bathing a newborn was quite another story. In the maternity home where she was born, the nursing aides had shown me what to do, but far too rapidly for me to fully understand or remember. The baby seemed so small and helpless; I wondered if I was up to the task. Rosie, my sister-in-law, who herself had five children, came to the rescue. As a primary school teacher, she gave me very clear instructions on navigating this tricky process. She said, "First, make sure you have all the equipment needed for the bath close at hand. Once you start you can't leave the baby to get anything you forgot. Remember you have to hold her all the time because she can't sit up for herself. So put everything within reach— baby soap, washcloth and towel, baby lotion, Q-tips, diapers and safety pins, and alcohol to swab the navel." She showed me how to test the bath water to ensure it was neither too cold nor too hot. I learned how to set Denise down in the baby bathtub while supporting her back and neck with one hand and washing her with the other. It was quite a feat for awkward me.

The next morning Mother came to help me with the bathing process. The third morning I waited a bit, as Mother had promised to come again. Then I saw clouds forming and knew rain would soon pour down. Rosie had advised me to get the bath done in the morning when the sun was still shining, so I began the task, holding the infant gingerly. It all went well and I realized that babies, though weak and tiny, are tougher than imagined. They were made for survival, and motherhood was going to be all right.

Three weeks after her birth, Denise was christened. Catholics in Trinidad usually christen their babies early because it was believed that if an infant died before baptism, its soul would not go to heaven and would remain forever in purgatory. Rosie and her husband were named as godparents. Even though I was not fully recovered, I went along with the plans and I could not attend the ceremony as I wanted to. Apart from the fact that I had not sufficiently recovered from childbirth, I needed to stay home to direct the preparations for the luncheon after the ceremony. The family was of tremendous help, including Rosie who gave me my first lesson in making black cake, with fruit soaked in wine and rum. Our flat was still adorned with the beautiful floral arrangements received after the birth. One good thing about anthurium lilies is that the waxy, almost artificial-looking flowers last sometimes a month to six weeks. From America, Mum sent a gorgeous christening gown and cap. She and Lech were unable to attend because they still had not sorted out their immigrant status in the United States. We had just family and a handful of good friends attending, but when the Borels got together there was a big enough crowd for a party, and party we did.

Parenthood did not prove easy. Denise turned out to be a colicky baby, crying loudly and consistently for hours. She often brought up her milk, spewing it out like a water jet. The child was obviously in pain and we were at our wits' end as to how to comfort her. Each night from seven p.m. till well past midnight she cried and screamed. One of us would be up walking and jiggling her. It was harder for Ainsley because he had to go to work in the morning. "Interrupted sleep is the worst thing," he would say. Sometimes in the evenings friends would drop by, and Ainsley held her while his stereo blasted music. She fit exactly on his forearm from the tip of his palm to the crook in his elbow, and as guests talked and joked his cradling arm would wave around a bit. These slight movements plus the sound of music lulled her to sleep for a while. The deep bass rhythms, with vibrations pounding hard enough to feel in one's heart, did not seem to bother her. If she woke up crying, he would dip his little finger in his gin and tonic, his preferred drink of that season, apply it to her lips, and she would suck up the intoxicating liquid. When I discovered that my husband was plying our three-month-old baby with liquor, I put a stop to that practice in no uncertain terms. "I have no intention of allowing you to kill the brain cells of this innocent child!"

I depended heavily on Dr. Benjamin Spock's book, *Common Sense Book of Baby and Child Care*. Looking back now, I do believe that adhering rigidly to four hours between feeding times allowed the child to become filled with gas, inflicting pain in her gastro-intestinal system. Gripe water, a liquid given to babies to soothe their stomachs, was the only remedy that seemed to help. This remedy contained bicarbonate of soda, ginger, chamomile, and a little alcohol, which we administered through a dropper. Eventually we found a pediatrician who solved the problem on a long-term basis. First he ordered us to throw away the pacifier because it caused excessive gas. He also observed that the valve leading to the esophagus was not closing properly, causing the milk to be ejected, sometimes violently. His recommendations included sitting her up for a long time after feeding and not adding cereal to her bottle, instead mixing it to a thick paste and feeding her with a spoon. The good news, he said, was that she would outgrow this problem, and she did. Despite spitting up much of her milk, the babe still thrived and put on weight. She slept very well during the day. I did not know why this was, but I was able to get the chores done— disinfecting and laundering the cloth diapers, cleaning and preparing her milk bottles, tidying the house, and cooking our meals.

Since I had to return to teaching, we needed to hire a nanny and found Josephine, a girl of about seventeen from Paramin, up in the hills of Maraval. She lived in, in fact sharing Denise's room because we did not like the dreary room in the back of the building that was supposed to be the maid's quarters. Josephine was very good with the baby and I will always be thankful for her sticking her little finger in the baby's navel to keep it in whenever she fed her. Denise had developed a hernia from so much crying, so the navel hung out one or two inches. I had visions of this child never being able to wear a bikini, but Josephine saved the day and eventually the navel remained in place.

One fine morning shortly before Christmas, we woke to Josephine's frantic knocking on our bedroom door. "A tief enter the house while we sleeping," she screamed. "Ah wake to fine the front door wide open!" Ainsley and I hurried to put on clothes and see what happened. Indeed, the front door was ajar and a side window of the living room, which was determined to be the point of entry, was unlatched. Three items were missing—our stereo, the connecting wires crudely cut by a kitchen knife that we found removed from a drawer; the Electrolux floor polisher; and a Polaroid camera, a gift from a friend in the USA that we'd carelessly left on the kitchen table. We had not even had time to read the manual or use the camera. On thinking back, we surmised that the burglar was a young man who had washed our cars a few times. As Christmas was approaching, he offered to wash our windows and, glad for the help, I had accepted. He was able to scope out the house and the electronic equipment we had. He saw that the windows had only flimsy latches that were easily forced open. In addition to paying him, I had offered him a plate of food, and from where he sat in the kitchen, he could see the floor polisher stored between the fridge and the open door connecting the kitchen to the dining room.

The police were called immediately. They came and took a report but did nothing, and we never recovered the stolen items. Josephine remarked, "Ah can't understand why none of us hear anyting. We slept sound, even the baby. The tief must have sprayed chloroform on us." Indeed Denise, who usually woke several times, had slept throughout the entire night. We could not believe that a stranger had broken in and entered the sanctuary that was our home, walked around at will—probably armed with our kitchen knife, and had taken what he wanted, and we did not know a thing about it. We felt violated. We could have been killed! Before the day was over, Ainsley got permission from the landlady to install a strong wire mesh around the windows. We could never feel safe there again without reinforcement to the windows.

Josephine did not stay too much longer with us after that incident. Maybe she was unsettled by the break-in, or maybe she found the job too demanding. Shortly after she quit, Teresa, Josephine's aunt, appeared at our door. She said, "I don't know why Josephine gave up the job but I would like to work for you." She was older, probably in her thirties, and had very good credentials. She preferred to use the little room outside instead of sleeping in Denise's room. Teresa seemed like a godsend. She knew exactly what to do without my telling her. She cared for Denise admirably and also did chores about the house. However, her shining attribute was that she was an excellent cook. Ainsley in particular enjoyed her cooking. According to Trinidadians, Teresa had "a sweet hand."

Everything went well until one Monday morning when I waited and waited for Teresa to return to work after her weekend off. I was going to be late for school. Then when I checked her room, I found that all her belongings were cleared out and our house key was on the table. No notice had been given and we were bitterly disappointed. Luckily, we could depend on Mother, who babysat Denise until we got a replacement, but Ainsley still hankered for Teresa. He kept saying, "If I were to see Teresa anywhere in the road, I would march right up to her and bring her back." My reply was, "No matter how good Teresa was, I would never want her back. I'd be afraid she would do the same thing again."

Usually after the excitement of Carnival is over, the people calm down and the country returns to normalcy. However, in 1970 this did not happen. The Black Power Movement had come to Trinidad & Tobago. In the United States, Malcolm X, Trinidadian Stokely Carmichael, and others had sown the seeds of this movement. At the 1970 Carnival a calypsonian performed a song entitled *Black is Beautiful.* Trinidadians were enthralled with the idea that descendants of Africans were beautiful, strong people who could achieve anything they wanted. After Carnival, the band followers refused to go home and remained marching in the streets. Their leader was Geddes Granger, who changed his name to Makandal Daaga and formed the National Joint Action Committee (NJAC), which later became a political party. Every day his followers congregated in Woodford Square listening to their leader. Then they marched, winding around the Savannah and ending in front of the Prime Minister's office at Whitehall. Ainsley often passed by Woodford Square after work in the afternoon, to hear what the rabble-rousers were up to. His dark complexion protected him from mob attack. He, however, expressly warned me and Selma, a Chinese friend of his from work, not to go near there, as we could be targets of mob violence because of our lighter complexions. White was a color that was frowned upon; even people in white cars had been attacked. We owned a white Vauxhall Victor and Ainsley advised me to take the longer route around the Savannah home for lunch, rather than risk meeting the marchers in front of Whitehall. The times were a bit scary, but I had the optimism of youth and never really thought I would come to a bad end. I was more exasperated at losing precious time, when I could have been spending it with my baby during my lunch hour.

In April 1970 I made a trip to Jamaica to visit my father on his deathbed. While there, all hell broke loose in Trinidad & Tobago. Two officers of the army, Raffique Shah and

Rex Lassalle, who were sympathetic to the NJAC, staged a mutiny with the intention of bringing down the government and handing power over to the people. The mutineers seized command of the army barracks at Teteron in Chaguaramas, and a motorcade of tanks and jeeps started off along the narrow coastal road to Port of Spain. However, the Coast Guard remained loyal. Horace, Ainsley's brother-in-law, was part of the contingent that left Staubles, the Coast Guard headquarters in Chaguaramas. With their boats hugging the coastline, they were able to bombard the motorcade, stop the vehicles, and capture the ringleaders. The government, saved just in the nick of time, ordered a state of emergency, with a curfew from dusk to dawn, and enlisted the Trinidad & Tobago Defence Force to assist the police in restoring order.

My return flight from Jamaica landed after dark, during curfew, and I was forced to wait at the airport till morning, when Ainsley could pick me up. Because of the state of emergency, passengers also were not allowed to remain in the lounge so we walked over to the airport hotel, which was luckily on the airport premises. I could not afford a room, having spent every cent abroad, but one of the men who reserved a room allowed a couple of us females at loose ends to join him. We sat up all night liming. Nobody slept a wink and by morning I was completely exhausted. In my mind I cursed the Black Power movement for causing me an uncomfortable, sleepless night.

Summer came and ten-month-old Denise and I made a trip to New York to introduce her to her grandparents. Ainsley, having recently started a new job as financial comptroller of the Trinidad and Tobago Port Contractors Ltd., which basically looked after stevedoring operations at the port, was unable to accompany us. We were away for one month and what joy it was to be reunited with him in August. I soon found I was pregnant with our second child.

When the school term resumed in September, the unrest, which had continued unabated during the summer, spilled over into the schools. During the lunch hour, restless teenagers liked nothing better than join the NJAC marches, as if they were Carnival bands. They listened to incendiary speeches in Woodford Square and then, after lunch, invaded the high schools. Tranquillity Government Secondary High School, because of its history of two separate schools merged into one, had two main double iron gates, one for the upper school and the other for the lower, each giving access to a quadrangle surrounded by classrooms. The principal made sure the gates were locked during school sessions but had to open them during the lunch hour for students to go home and return for the afternoon session. Guards or police were unknown in our schools at that time.

One day in late October or early November, a band of rabble-rousers and milled around in the quadrangle, shouting and making threatening noises. I was attempting to conduct a geography class in my third form classroom but, with the noise and commotion that could be seen and heard through the open door, there was no hope of teaching a lesson. The most I could hope for was to keep a semblance of order. The excited and curious students tried to leave their seats to peer through the door. I barked orders at them. "No one is leaving his or her seat to look outside! Not while I'm in this classroom!" Fortunately, the teenagers still had some respect for their teachers, and they listened. Then one fellow from the mob outside approached the classroom and called out to one of my students. "Hall, come on man. Come and join us."

Hall was a big, strapping youth with a huge Afro hairstyle resembling a bird's nest, big enough to conceal a couple of sticks of incense. He was intelligent, but of late had shown no interest in his studies. I suspected that during the lunch hour he joined the marches. Hall looked at his friend standing in the doorway and I could see he was itching to go. As he began to rise from his seat I knew this was a test for me. If Hall was allowed to leave, there was no way I could hold the dam restraining the other students.

I placed myself in front of the door and ordered him to sit down. "There is no way I'm going to let you leave this classroom, Hall! Sit down!"

Defiantly, he remained half-standing. He looked at his friend behind me, then at me.

"Sit down!" I repeated once more. We stared at one another. I was already beginning to grow big with child but held my ground. I refused to let him leave. He would have had to knock me down to exit the classroom. He was larger than I, and it seemed the thought struck him to just shove me aside. For an interminable period we faced one another. Then it seemed that he thought better of defying me, and slowly sank into his seat. The tension was broken and I took a deep breath of relief. Looking back at that incident, I realized I had taken a great chance. If Hall had decided to knock down pregnant me, there was nothing I could have done to stop him.

Gradually order was restored to the country. The curfew hours were cut back, at first from nine p.m. till six a.m., during which time we had many curfew parties that continued all night. A phenomenal number of babies were born nine months later, since husbands had to stay home with their wives. Eventually the state of emergency was lifted and life returned to normal. The NJAC ringleaders, Lassalle and Shah, were tried by a British Commonwealth tribunal but won their appeals in 1972. I recall that one of the tribunal members was a Nigerian who later led a coup in his country.

When Denise was a little over a year old, we took her on a trip to Tobago for the Divali weekend. Divali is the Hindu Festival of Lights and a holiday in Trinidad & Tobago. Because of the huge racial and religious diversity of the population, this little country celebrates probably the most holidays in the world. It celebrates national holidays, the Christian ones as well as British ones like Boxing Day, and Muslim and Hindu holidays.

Although we had enjoyed a memorable weekend in Charlotteville with the Bergens, we realized the best beaches with the most action were at the opposite end of the island. So Ainsley booked a room at the Crown Point Hotel, giving access to the famous beach at Store Bay. The twenty-minute plane hop landed us at the airport on a Friday afternoon, and we quickly checked into our nearby room. Anxious to get into the water, Ainsley determined that we should immediately don our bathing suits and go down to the beach. It was a cloudy and blustery November afternoon and I felt a little doubtful as we walked on the pathway past manicured lawns and beds of flowering shrubs. Carrying Denise, he descended the railed steps leading to the beach. I was following, but stopped. There was no beach! All I could see was a roiling sea with huge, white-crested waves breaking at the base of the steps. Cognizant of the fact that I was carrying our second child, I declared, "I am not going in!" But Ainsley was determined to enter the water. What was he thinking? That he had paid for this weekend and by God he was going to get his money's worth?

I remained at the top of the stairs. From there I watched the scene almost as if it were in slow motion. A towering wave crashed in, tumbled them both, and then they were completely submerged. When the wave receded, Ainsley, still clutching the baby, found his way unsteadily to the steps. Denise was so shocked that she was silent for several seconds before bursting out in a loud wail. That wail brought a sigh of relief to us both, because we then knew not much water had entered her lungs. I wrapped her in a huge beach towel and we beat a hasty retreat to our room. That incident gave us a tremendous scare. Ainsley admitted to me afterwards, "I was determined not to let go of the baby for dear life!"

The memory of the near drowning must have imprinted itself on her little brain; for years afterward Denise would not go near the beach, and screamed whenever she even heard waves breaking against the shore. I could only thank God that my husband and daughter escaped certain death, as they could have been swept away by the current. For years I would have nothing to do with Store Bay, one of the most treacherous of beaches, even though in good weather it is beautiful and tranquil.

Ainsley Julian was born on May 17, 1971. As with his sister, our son came the day after we had entertained at home, but unlike her he was not in any special hurry to come into this world and had to be induced. When I saw my son for the first time, I gasped with surprise. He was hirsute, with his back, shoulders, and face covered with black hair. A full head of dark hair formed a crown above his face, and his eyebrows joined together on his forehead. I thought, "I can't believe that I've made a little monkey!" I still loved him because he was mine, and a week or two later all that hair was shed.

Gaining weight rapidly, he was a handsome, quiet baby with a voracious appetite. I decided to ignore Dr. Spock's advice and not wait three or four hours before feeding him.

He was fed on demand, with us increasing the amount as needed. In five weeks he was taking six ounces, and by the time he reached two months we were adding Farex cereal to the bottle. As long as he was fed and clean he gave no trouble at all. We called him by his second name, Julian, to differentiate him from his father, Ainsley George.

Denise, at twenty months old, was naturally jealous of her new little brother and did not always treat him kindly. She was a pretty, chubby toddler, fair of face, with a cute little Afro that was tended by her father. He was the chief hairdresser, combing and patting it in place. It remained short for a long time, until her Aunt Vilma, visiting from Canada, started braiding it in cornrows. Vilma was a master of the art of combing hair. She would say, "Rose, her hair ends are all the same length. You have to keep braiding her hair so that the ends will start growing," and grow it did until it developed into a long, thick, unmanageable mane.

As was the custom, Julian's christening took place a month after his birth. Cislyn Baptiste and Rodgerson Joseph, still friends from our Leeds days, did the honors as godparents. My aunt, Edna Palmer, and a good friend of hers came from Jamaica to attend, and I was overjoyed to see them all.

It was not a long visit but Ainsley found the time to drive us around the island of Trinidad in a single day. His large Falcon, an Australian Ford modeled after its American cousin, was spacious enough to comfortably accommodate us all. First we drove on the Southern Main Road, stopping for an early lunch at Farrell House, a guesthouse near the second largest town of San Fernando. We passed the Texaco oilfields and continued south of San Fernando to the Pitch Lake at La Brea. The largest natural deposit of asphalt in the world, it was "discovered" in 1595 by Sir Walter Raleigh when Amerindians helped him use the pitch to caulk his boat. Lake

Asphalt of Trinidad and Tobago Ltd. is a government-owned company that mines, processes, and exports asphalt from the Pitch Lake all over the world to pave roads, runways, and racetracks. (In 1872, Trinidad supplied the United States with its first paved road—Pennsylvania Avenue in Washington D.C.) At the Pitch Lake, faults in the rock formation allow the heavy, viscous residue to remain after the lighter part of the oil pool has evaporated and the pitch oozes up from the depths. As the pitch is removed, more wells up to take its place. Looking at it from the road, Pitch Lake resembled a disused airfield, with solid black asphalt covering a large shallow depression, and shrubs or low bushes and puddles of water scattered here and there. Many parts of the lake are solid enough for a vehicle to drive over, but other parts are more treacherous, soft enough to suck in an object or small animal.

Next we traveled inland. On the way to the east coast we stopped to view the mud volcanoes at The Devil's Woodyard near Princes Town. Mud volcanoes are associated with petroleum deposits when cracks in the rock formation allow the release of gas, causing the mud to bubble up. We saw the small mounds of boiling mud and returned to the car as the sun was sinking low towards the horizon.

However, the car, parked on the wet grass by the roadside, could not climb the slope to the road. The wheels had no traction and skidded when Ainsley pressed the gas pedal. The more he revved the engine, the deeper the wheel ruts became. We were stuck! I had visions of spending the night with an infant, a toddler, and two elderly ladies in their seventies along the side of a lonely country road behind God's back. Then a man in his sixties appeared with a companion. They were angels sent from heaven to help us. We women and children were advised to pile out of the car and, as Ainsley gunned the engine, the two men pushed the big car out. After giving them a hefty tip we were so grateful to be on our way again.

It was dark when we reached Mayaro, on the east coast, where we stopped for supper at an English-style guesthouse. The place was half-empty and it was late, but the chef rustled up tasty club sandwiches for us. Then we hustled the fifty miles back to Port of Spain in record time. Ainsley was a fast driver. In fact, every time we were about to enter the car, Aunty remarked drily, "Okay, we're ready to take off in flight now." We were probably too ambitious and had bitten off more than we could chew, because we were all extremely exhausted by the end of the day. At least we got back safe and sound.

Barbara started working for us soon after Julian was born. While interviewing her for the job, I discovered she was the mother of two children and thought that meant she would be experienced in looking after mine. I could not have been more wrong. Barbara was a bold, brassy character who talked incessantly. I give her credit that she paid attention to what was going on in the world around her. At this time festivals imitating the one held in Woodstock, New York, were taking place in different parts of the world and Trinidad & Tobago was no exception. The flower children invaded the grounds of the Perseverance estate further up the Maraval Valley, where they listened to music, smoked marijuana, and exuded peace and love everywhere. Barbara made it her business to attend these sessions during her time off.

She liked to chat us up while cleaning but was not completely comfortable with the children. After the first time we left them in her care to see a movie, the next-door neighbor called to say the baby cried the entire time we were away. Julian was a good baby, only crying when he was hungry or dirty, so I was concerned. When questioned, Barbara admitted he was crying but that she tried to calm him down. She also tried to force-feed Denise whenever the child balked at eating. Ainsley felt we should give her a chance since it was difficult to get help, especially in the months leading up to Christmas and Carnival. Trinidadians are very independent and easily abandoned their jobs once they made a little money so that they were free for Carnival, only looking for another job when the celebrations were over.

When Aunty Palmer arrived for Julian's christening, Barbara called her "Aunty" instead of the more formal "Mrs.," as my aunt was accustomed. Barbara kept up a running conversation with my aunt, as if she considered herself a part of our family. Barbara helped me with cooking and serving at the party for the christening, but then changed into a long green gown, as if she were one of the guests. We never required our help to wear a uniform but a long green gown seemed over the limit. Nevertheless, we said nothing to her. Cislyn was highly amused and didn't stop heckling me about that for a long time.

Things took a turn for the worse when Ainsley began to miss money. He was in the habit of emptying coins from his pocket and leaving them on the dressing table, and was sure that the number of coins declined in number. Then his gold nugget tie tack went missing. I started locking away my money and my jewelry, a chore I had to remember to do. I did not like having a thief in my midst and wanted her gone. Ainsley was planning to set a trap for Barbara, by marking one of the coins, when matters came to a head.

One afternoon after I had returned to school from lunch, Ainsley received a call at work from our neighbor upstairs.

She told him that the nanny who looked after her children had reported that Barbara left our infant son lying on his back in his playpen and refused to pick him up even though he was crying non-stop for a long time. This occurred as soon as I had left the house. The nanny had asked, "Barbara, don't you hear the baby crying for so long?" To which Barbara replied, "I fed him and I burped him. I'm not being paid to be continually taking him up." It did not occur to Barbara that caring for the children was her primary job and that perhaps the baby needed to burp one more time. The neighbor's nanny was so concerned about Barbara's insouciance that she ratted on her.

We were both extremely upset that our son was mistreated and as soon as Ainsley came home he fired her. I could have kicked myself for not insisting earlier that we let her go, and was relieved when she was finally gone. Hiring her was a complete misjudgment on my part, as she had nothing to do with raising her own two kids who lived with her mother. Was I an incompetent mother? When I was home, Barbara made a big show of looking after the baby but the signs of her insufficiency were there. I had not paid enough attention and felt really awful about that.

A few months later, Ainsley told me that he was flying down the road in his car when someone flagged him down furiously, as if he were a taxi. He stopped, only to realize it was Barbara, who was bold enough to ask for a lift despite the circumstances under which she had been fired. Laughingly, he remarked that he still gave her a ride because he admired her confidence.

Shortly after that, Ainsley made plans to start his own accounting practice, as a way to get ahead and provide for our family. We had bought a lot in Haleland Park, further up the Maraval Valley, with the intention of building a house. He said to me, "Starting the practice will take every penny we've got, so we'll have to delay building the house for a while." I told him I was a little disappointed but I understood, and that I admired his ambition and drive. He submitted his resignation from Trinidad and Tobago Port Contractors Ltd., signed a lease for an office downtown, and began acquiring furniture. His sister, Rosie, started to grow a couple of large potted plants to decorate the office. Ainsley was impatient and wanted "instant" plants, so she acquired young plants, nurtured them, and when they reached an acceptable size, handed them over. Selma, one of his co-workers and also a friend, suggested he take a physical exam before leaving Port Contractors, since a free medical examination was part of the benefits. She got her cousin, a well-known orthopedic surgeon, to see him.

Then the bombshell dropped. My thirty-two-year-old husband was diagnosed with leukemia.

CHAPTER FIFTEEN | *Grapefruit Crescent*

The day we moved to our new home at No. 107 Grapefruit Crescent in Haleland Park in July of 1972 was an auspicious one. Despite the recent bad news about Ainsley's health, we still clung to hope because of the optimism of youth.

Since we possessed little furniture, we simply packed our personal effects into bags and boxes, broke down the crib and playpen, unplugged the stereo, and made several trips carting our belongings in our two cars up the two-mile stretch of the Maraval Valley to Haleland Park. Ainsley's niece, Chee Chee, was out of school for the summer and came along to help us unpack. The chief problem was that three-year-old Denise and fourteen-month-old toddler Julian got in the way. It was difficult to focus, especially since Julian repeatedly gravitated toward the edge of the rail-less, terrazzo front patio, with every intention of walking down the three steps to ground level. The entire entertainment area of the house, including the front and back patios, living room, dining room, and kitchen, was covered with twenty-four-inch terrazzo squares. The multicolored terrazzo stones, embedded in a gray base, gave off a lustrous glow when polished and shined. As the rooms flowed into one another, either through large sliding glass doors or through open archways, the pervading feature of the house was a sense of spaciousness. Julian could not negotiate the front steps of the patio without help and we were all busy. "No, Julian! You can't go there!" I cried repeatedly. "You'll tumble and fall!" Chee Chee, Ainsley, and

I all tried to discourage him from approaching the patio edge. Time and time again Julian insisted on going to the brink. How can you reason with a one-year-old? You can't, and I was not getting any unpacking done! Eventually we just left him alone and of course he tumbled, skinned his knees, and cried. No real harm was done. Bandaged, he had learned his lesson. Thereafter he crawled down the steps on hands and knees.

There was not much furniture in the house yet. Apart from the fridge and stove, we just had beds to sleep on. One snag occurred when we could not get the stove working. We pored over the instructions for an interminably long time but had no success. It was important to have the stove operating to heat up baby bottles and cook meals. Ainsley and I gave up in disgust and turned to other things. Then we heard the cry, "Aunty Rose, Uncle Ainsley, I've done it!" It was Chee Chee who had kept on tinkering and finally got the stove working. We were so grateful. "Well done, Chee Chee!" I exclaimed. It was then I realized that Chee Chee was quite a determined young lady and her indomitable will would not allow her to accept defeat. "This quality will stand her in good stead in the future," I thought.

When we stopped for a bite and a bit of rest, I mused about where we were in our life. We had not intended to move into our own home for a few more years. Circumstances dealt us a cruel blow with Ainsley's diagnosis of leukemia. He immediately aborted all plans to start his own business and withdrew his resignation from Trinidad and Tobago Port Contractors Ltd. He then observed, "Now that I'm no longer starting a practice, we can afford to build in Haleland Park after all." I felt awful for my husband because I knew he was severely disappointed by having to abandon his dream. The affliction of an incurable disease was as if a death sentence had been ruled against him. Neither of us knew how long he had to live—the doctors predicted five to ten years.

When I first got the news I was numb. I did not rant or rave but I wondered how on earth a young man in his prime could be struck down so easily by this disease. A few theories came to mind. Ainsley drank heavily at parties and, on arriving home, habitually took aspirins to prevent hangovers in the morning. Alcohol and aspirins, was that a lethal combination? Besides, he took no breakfast, just a cup of black coffee every morning. Despite my questions about the wisdom of the aspirin/alcohol combination and my pleas to eat breakfast, my dear husband did not listen. The car accident a couple of years earlier also came to mind. Ainsley had not received a proper medical examination and ever since the accident his knees hurt. He was never able to get down on them on the few occasions when he attended church for a wedding or a funeral. Wasn't the bone marrow somehow responsible for making red blood cells? Maybe an injury from the accident had something to do with the leukemia. All these were my conjectures but I never shared them with Ainsley. Privately he must have agonized about it but remained calm and matter-of-fact, and he expected me to be the same. I did not even rail against God or wonder why He had dealt us this blow. I just accepted this and went on with my life.

Very early on, Ainsley made the decision not to tell Mother about the diagnosis. "She would make my life a living hell," he said, "always crying and being sad. She'd be too solicitous, make me miserable, and try to prevent me from doing whatever I can. It's better she doesn't know, so that she is not grieving before the event, as well as after." This decision meant that he could not tell his sisters in Trinidad, because it would be hard for them to keep the information from Mother. His siblings in Canada and I were sworn to secrecy.

Ainsley had flown to Montreal to see specialists who prescribed medication, which thankfully gave him intermittent remissions. Under the supervision of a local doctor who was in contact with his Canadian counterparts, Ainsley's blood count was constantly monitored. To me, it seemed like a series of battles between the white and the red blood cells. Whenever the white seemed to be winning, only a small dose of medication was needed to initiate another remission. Throughout all this time Ainsley was able to work normally, even when he was on the medical regimen.

How did I feel about these developments? The prognosis was not good, and there was no one I could talk to about it—not my parents, none of my friends, not even Cislyn, and certainly no member of the Borel family. Ainsley and I did not talk much about it because it was a subject he refused to dwell upon. At this stage I was not going to church, so I did not even have my faith to fall back on. I had doubts about my religion, but rather than embracing atheism, I viewed myself as an agnostic. We had married in the Roman Catholic Church and, although I had not converted to that denomination, I had pledged that the children would be brought up as Catholics. Despite my doubts, it was my belief that the children should be raised in a Christian background and since Ainsley was the Catholic in our household he should be the one to take them to church. He never did.

Still, there was no doubt I was thrilled to bits to move into our very own home. As we unloaded our belongings from the car on that July day, I glanced appreciatively at the front façade of the house. So many little touches made it out of the ordinary. Instead of a plain wall backing the double carport that faced the street, decorative blocks angled out and broke up the monotony of that space, casting shadows and light in various spots. On the far side of the front patio, a wall of blue stone quarried from the north coast of Trinidad added pizzazz to that section of the house.

The use of blue stone was the signature of our renowned builder, Martin Looby, who had a high reputation for reliability, quality, and speed in getting projects done. His services were not cheap because he paid his men well and demanded good workmanship from them. When our house was under construction, Looby had discovered that an entire wall in the kitchen was misaligned. Angrily, he ordered the wall dismantled and re-done, since he did not abide shoddy work even at a financial loss to himself. Despite not sacrificing the quality of the work, Looby completed his houses in record time, five to six months instead of the one to two years that were common in the West Indies. Looby's ability to get things done was attractive to Ainsley, who was always a man in a hurry; he was now on even more of a mission to get certain things done while he had time.

When the two first met, Looby told Ainsley, "I'll show you all the houses around town I built, and if you like any of them I can build you one just like it." This was a good sign because Looby did not do business with any or everybody. He could afford to pick and choose his clients. They drove around Federation Park, an upscale neighborhood where diplomats and Trinidad's wealthy lived and that was the former haunt of officials and diplomats who had been connected with the short-lived West Indian Federation. We were attracted to the design of a U-shaped house. The entertainment section occupied the base of the U, the living quarters were on one side, and the kitchen, laundry, and maid's quarters were on the other. An open lawn between both wings formed a natural extension to the house since the back patio directly abutted it, making it ideal for the many parties we intended to throw. Looby observed, "That house was designed by an architect, but I can get you a draughtsman to draw the plans and it will cost you much less."

The finished result was beautiful yet strongly constructed, with steel girders enclosed in the outer walls. A ten-inch decorative iron grill connected the top of the walls to the roof throughout the entire building, providing extra ventilation and keeping the entire house cool. Open space between the walls and the roof would never have worked in any other part of the Caribbean, but Trinidad lies south of the hurricane belt and therefore avoids those devastating storms. The only room that boasted a window air-conditioner was the master bedroom, which Ainsley insisted on, and glass enclosed the iron grill to keep the cool air inside. We just loved our new house.

Shortly after our move, we took off on a three-week vacation to North America. With fixtures, appliances, and some furniture already installed, we needed a watchman to sleep in the house and check on it from time to time during the day. That person was Hiram John, whom we always referred to as "John the Watchman." John was employed by Martin Looby, who recommended him highly as reliable, honest, and caring about our interests. We found him to be exactly as Looby had said, and over the years John did odd jobs for us in his spare time. He related well with the children and, in fact, became a life-long friend.

While John watched over our home and interests in Trinidad, we proceeded on our trip, which turned out to be less than ideal. Three-year-old Denise gave trouble from the onset. As we left the departure gate to cross the tarmac to the plane, she refused to budge. Looking fearfully at the large mechanical bird ahead of her, she began to bawl. I was holding Julian and could not help. Even dearly beloved Daddy could not persuade his daughter to walk to the plane and he had to carry her, in addition to the hand luggage. He lifted her, kicking and screaming, up the gangway, and she literally cried throughout the four-hour flight to New York. This was not an auspicious start to our vacation.

Mum and Lech, awaiting us at Kennedy International Airport, welcomed us warmly, especially the new grandson they were meeting for the first time. We reunited with family—Lech's sisters and brother and their families, and also with old friends from my sojourn in New York in the 1960s. One evening we treated my parents to dinner and a Broadway play, *The Great White Hope,* starring James Earl Jones.

Everything went well during the day but at night Denise bawled practically the entire time. Although she was talking a little, she never said what was bothering her. She just cried and cried. Ainsley and I were supposed to sleep in the spare room, with Denise sleeping on the hide-a-bed sofa and Julian in a rented crib in the living room. However, our daughter did not adjust easily to new surroundings. Nothing we did seemed to comfort her. She was keeping her little brother awake so eventually we brought the crib to the room with me and Ainsley slept with her. Even so, she slept fitfully. The trip was becoming a nightmare.

The second week of the vacation was spent in Montreal with Ainsley's older brother Learie, his wife, Kay, and their sons Mark and Nigel, who were nine and seven years old respectively. One day Learie took our family in his big Buick about a hundred miles north of Montreal into the Laurentians. Our destination was a lake where he had made arrangements for us to rent a cottage for the weekend. On the way, he regularly topped speeds of one hundred miles per hour. Like his brother, Learie was always a fast driver. The entire time we were on the road, Kay, a nervous passenger, continually complained, "No, Learie! Slow down, Learie!" The more she complained, the faster he sped—again, just like his brother! I was in the backseat with the kids and tried not to focus on the speeds we were traveling. I knew that if I uttered any protests it would do no good; in fact he would probably go faster.

Before hopping into the car for the return journey, Learie called out to us, "Come and see something here." He showed us the bolts that kept the wheels on the axles. Each wheel was supposed to have four bolts and only had three.

We were flabbergasted. Ainsley exclaimed, "You're crazy, Learie! I can't believe that you knew this and yet exceeded a hundred miles an hour!"

Learie laughed. "It's perfectly safe. We got here safely and it's okay for going back."

The return journey was made at the same high speeds, but with what we now knew neither Ainsley nor I felt comfortable until we were on terra firma in Montreal. We felt as if we were flying and I kept thinking, "All my family is in this car, and we could all be killed," but knew it was a waste of time to voice our concerns.

The weekend in the Laurentians was a happy family reunion. Along with Learie and his family, Ainsley's sister Vilma and his brother Lennox, with his wife, Linda, joined us at the cottage. We rowed boats on the lake and drove around exploring the beautiful countryside. On our returns to the cottage, we women cooked while the men played card games of rummy and All Fours, all the time consuming Johnny Walker Black Label and Chivas Regal Scotch Whiskey. The many jokes that Lennox related had us all cracking up with laughter. We had a whale of a time.

Until one night. At bedtime Denise started crying and no one could get her to stop. We paced the room holding her, hugging and singing to her, but the child refused to be comforted. Lennox woke up and tried to reason with her. "Why are you crying?" "Wah wah!" was the reply. "Tell us what is wrong!" her uncle persevered. "Waah, waah!" several decibels higher. The more attention she received, the louder she bawled. No one got much sleep that night.

How does one get a child to calm down? She certainly did not tell us what was ailing her. A couple of years later we discovered she suffered from a hearing deficiency, but no doctor in Trinidad seemed able to put a finger on the problem. We did not know then what many modern day parents are aware of—that many small children get infections causing earaches and hearing loss. Looking back now, I wonder whether Denise then was suffering from severe earaches, an affliction her daddy was prone to from time to time.

On our return to Trinidad & Tobago, we settled down to the business of furnishing our new home. Most of our furniture was acquired locally, including our prized nine-piece mahogany dining room set, its satiny, polished wood of a rich reddish brown called "the Barclays Bank color." Barclays Bank was a regular customer of the high-end retailer Farrah's Furniture, and ordered its furniture in that color. Softer furnishings, such as drapes, bedspreads, linens, and a plush green wall-to-wall carpet for the private area of the house were acquired on our trip to the United States. A full-size table tennis board was also imported at the same time.

Our many friends visited us as soon as we got installed and kept asking, "When are you going to have the housewarming?" "As soon as the grass is grown," Ainsley replied. As was the custom then, we did not put down sod but planted individual St. Augustine plugs at six-inch intervals. Then we watered, mowed, and fertilized until the grass spread to form a thick covering. Of course the fertile soil of the former citrus estate on which Haleland Park was developed, plus the copious rainfall of the Trinidad climate, helped a lot.

Our yard was not really big because the sprawling house occupied most of the lot. Neither of us had a clue about gardening. If it were not for Ainsley's sister, Rosie, who had a green thumb, we would have been quite lost. One day Ainsley came home from work with a revelation. He was watching the Holiday Inn go up across the street from his office at the Trinidad and Tobago Port Contractors. "Rose," he said to me, "I saw huge trees transported on trucks and planted in deep holes around the hotel—Travelers Palms and the like, and in no time at all they're established. I like the idea of instant plants!" Thereafter, he had no use for tiny plants and we spent a small fortune at the agricultural center buying large ornamental shrubs, flowering plants, and several fruit trees, including a Julie mango, a navel orange, and a West Indian cherry. Rosie nurtured a number of beautiful plants, which she gave us, including a cactus and a conifer. I had no idea what kind of conifer it was, whether pine, fir or spruce, but it grew tall and straight and was trimmed by Rosie into the classic conical shape. This we decorated with colored lights as our outdoor Christmas tree during the festive season.

I planted a bed of roses along the wall of our front fence. Their large, cream heads with a touch of pink in their centers were reminiscent of the film *The Great Gatsby,* starring Robert Redford and Mia Farrow, which had just been released. I also acquired an ackee plant from the Jamaican High Commission, as a small seedling growing beneath a huge tree in front of their building.

In Trinidad when I first asked about ackee trees, the reply was, "Yes, there is a tree in St. Augustine, one in Cascade, and another in Federation Park." This amazed me because in Jamaica almost every back yard has an ackee tree. The ackee is popular there, and its fruit cooked with salted codfish is our national dish. A rough, hard, reddish bell-shaped pod encloses three soft-yellow, almost buttery pegs with large shiny black seeds the size and shape of ox eyes. The yellow pegs are trimmed and steamed after the seeds are removed. (However, one has to be careful not to harvest the fruit until the thick pod opens naturally on the tree, as it releases poisonous gases. Any attempt to force open and cook the ackee before it is fully mature will lead to food poisoning, which can be fatal.) The appearance is rather like scrambled eggs and, when cooked with salted cod, has a distinctive yet pleasant taste. Ackee and saltfish is a dish I crave when away from Jamaica, maybe because it is expensive and not easily available. Whenever I am in my home country and have had a couple of servings, then I have had my ackee fix.

Along one side of the house a row of lettuce thrived. Planted by an old Indian gardener who fertilized with cow manure, large rosettes of lettuce heads flourished. I often sent our frequent visitors home with a freshly plucked head. Subsequently, I cultivated a row of pigeon peas planted against the chain link fence, which grew tall and luxuriantly.

At first the lot next to us remained unoccupied, but later Ainsley's cousin Patricia Borel built a house. Pat's mother, her sister, Sylvestrina Gonzales, and Syl's children lived next door while Pat lived abroad. Syl's two girls, Helen and Françoise, were around the same ages as Denise and Julian, and the children played through the chain link fence. I don't know how they did it because space was limited by the pigeon peas shrubs, but I guess their small sizes allowed them to fit into the tight spaces. Barbie dolls and Action Man toys passed through the fence during play.

I loved to sit on the back porch at dawn on weekends and view the scene in front of me. In the empty lot behind the back chain link fence, wild cane proudly raised their heads, their gossamer cream tassels waving gaily in the light breeze. As the sun slowly rose over the horizon, birds raised their early morning songs of praise. A bright corn-colored bird, attracted by velvety, deep mauve flowers, alit on the splendid passion fruit vine that had taken over the fence. Another bird, sky-colored, flew past and perched on the fence post. I did not know their names but I loved watching these birds adorned with feathers of vibrant hues. I felt that if I had the talent to write poetry, I could create an ode to nature. The serenity of my surroundings soothed my soul and was one of the reasons I adored this home of ours. It felt like country living, yet we were only three miles away from Port of Spain.

The passion fruit vine bore, in abundance, fruit the size of oranges but with a rather hard shell, green at first and then turning yellow, that enclosed small dark seeds in a bed of a watery, almost jelly-like substance. This liquid was swizzled, strained, diluted with water, and sweetened with condensed milk or sugar to produce a unique drink reminiscent of guava juice. I loved the passion fruit for its beauty and because it supplied us with an exotic drink. So you can imagine my consternation when one day I returned from school to find the passion fruit vine gone. Cut down and uprooted. When I accosted the gardener, he replied, "De Massa ordered me to do it. He say dat the passion fruit stunting the growth of the hibiscus hedge." It was true that the variegated green-and-white leafed hedge was not growing well, but there had been no consultation with me and I was fuming. In my opinion, that was almost grounds for divorce. Eventually I got over my anger. The hibiscus survived but only as an all-green hedge since the hybrid green-and-white leafed variety was rather delicate and did not grow well.

One Sunday afternoon Cislyn was visiting us, as she often did. Ainsley was not around. Probably he was on one of his job-related trips, to Mexico or France or Singapore. As we sat on the front porch, to our horror we saw quiet Grapefruit Crescent becoming clogged with cars. Cars mounted and parked on the verges beside the road, which, although designated as right-of-way for pedestrians, had been planted with grass interspersed with clumps of ginger lily bushes. Some of these bushes were run over by the cars, and some drivers even attempted to park in front of our driveway. They might have succeeded had Cislyn and I not stood guard. If they had, Cislyn would not have been able to get out when ready to go home. These were the hippies who had gathered to attend the Woodstock Festival at the Perseverance property up the road. Perseverance was a former citrus estate at the head of the Maraval Valley; its great house with a huge hall was often the venue of Carnival dances. Woodstock was an even larger event and was held on the extensive grounds. However, even this vast property could not accommodate all the vehicles, and many spilled over into the quiet neighboring streets to park. We had little tolerance for the hippies with their slogans of peace and love when their "peace and love" infringed on our right of access to our home. What irked us most was their lack of consideration.

Eventually our grass grew and the long-awaited house-warming took place around Christmas time, almost six months after we moved in. We invited all our friends and family, and about two hundred guests attended. Rented tables and chairs were set up on the front and back lawns and even in the limited spaces along the sides of the house. The party occupied what I called the public area of the house—the front patio through double sliding glass doors to the living room and dining room which lay side by side, then through double sliding glass doors from each room to the long back patio, and onto the back lawn in the center of the house's U-shape. On the back patio stood the focal point of the party, a custom-built movable bar sandwiched between the two sets of sliding doors. Dropping down by a chain from the ceiling, a colored-glass lantern provided sufficient light over the bar for mixing drinks. Ainsley hired two barmen—John the Watchman and Paul, a chauffeur at Trinidad and Tobago Port Contractors Ltd.— who moved among the guests at the start of the evening, serving drinks. Later they manned the bar, as guests made their orders. Liquor flowed freely, as we had ordered cases of Johnny Walker Black Label, Vat 19 and Angostura Old Oak rums, brandy, gin, and the local Carib beer. Gallons of potent homemade rum punch contributed to the beverages. The traditional Christmas drinks of sorrel, ginger beer, and ponce crème were also provided. A favorite plaque of ours hung in a prominent place above the bar, with the inscription:

The four saddest words that were ever
Composed are these dismal sounds
THE BAR IS CLOSED

Our household helpers and I did the catering for our two hundred guests. We prepared baked chicken, mounds of sliced roast pork, sliced ham, macaroni pie, pigeon peas and rice, fried rice, tossed salad, and the dish Trinis referred to as "mayonnaise"—potato salad with beets. We also ordered rotis, another dish popular with the Trini crowd at parties. Our large dining table was laden with these dishes and guests helped themselves buffet style. Our helper, as well as our laundress, very much enjoyed when we threw a party and the housewarming was no exception. Even though these occasions involved a tremendous amount of work, with the food preparation, serving, and washing and cleaning up (in those days we did not do paper or plastic plates, cups or cutlery), both women were amply remunerated. Besides, they enjoyed the music and often moved in time to the lilting beat of the calypsos while doing their work in the kitchen.

For the housewarming we hired a DJ who played popular dance music on LP platters and on big reel-to-reel tapes as well as on eight-track tapes. In addition, Ainsley hired a steel band, about twenty-five to thirty pans, from a band sponsored by the Trinidad and Tobago Port Contractors Ltd. They were arranged on the back lawn near the fence, where they could still be seen and heard. At the foot of the hibiscus hedge along the chain link fence a string of colored lights glittered, giving a fairyland effect to the background. The steel band played for quite a while. After they packed up and left, the DJ remained and then he really got the party rocking. The guests got louder and more raucous, all inhibitions gone. They jumped high to the tunes of the popular calypsos, pausing only to replenish drinks, eat, or take bathroom breaks. The pulsating rhythms reverberated in the valley, but in Trinidad neighbors did not complain. In fact, we took the precaution of inviting our closest neighbors.

Come five a.m. I made pots of coffee for the inebriated guests who needed to sober up so they could negotiate the winding Saddle Road back to their homes in Port of Spain. As we were seeing the last people off, I realized that the sun had started to peep over the horizon. With horror I glanced at my watch. It was six a.m.—the party had lasted all night! I could not believe it. As a couple of early church-goers were slowly driving along Grapefruit Crescent, there was I in my long green dress, leaning with Ainsley against the last car at the curb while saying our goodbyes. Weird!

After our move to Grapefruit Crescent, we employed a succession of women as nannies for the children. They also did general housework but these helpers did not stay long in our employ, for various reasons. One girl would stay out all night and then jump the fence in the early morning to return to her room. We padlocked the gate late at night before retiring and probably might have tolerated her sneaking out because she had her needs, but our next-door neighbor reported that the girl was also leaving our children alone for long periods during the day, and that would not do.

On one occasion when we were without help, a young girl who looked about sixteen years of age appeared at my gate enquiring about a job. I introduced myself and asked, "What's your name?"

"Christine Gibbs," she replied.

"How did you know that I needed help?" I asked.

"I know the maid who works across the street from you and she told me," she responded.

I thought to myself, "The grapevine really works very well because I didn't ask any of my neighbors to look out for anyone needing work."

I invited her in but when she reached the front patio, my heart sank. I did not think she could manage the work. She was a slip of a girl barely five foot, two-inches in height, of mixed African and Indian descent (dougla was the name given in Trinidad to this racial combination). She had a center part in her hair and two long, fat, glossy black plaits reaching below her waist, Indian style. She looked so young and small, I really did not think she could handle the work.

"How old are you?" I asked.

"Nineteen," she replied.

"I did not think you were more than sixteen. We have two young children. Denise is aged three, and Julian is two. Have you any experience with children?"

"I got married at sixteen and I have two girls. The older is the same age as your daughter."

"Who is caring for them now?"

"My mother."

"What about your husband? This is a live-in job and you would only get two weekends per month."

"That's all right," she said.

I decided to tell her all the requirements of the job ahead of time so if she decided not to accept, my time would not be wasted. "My children are in school half-days, until midday. Apart from looking after the children in the afternoon, we'll need you to babysit at night whenever we go out. Also, this is a big house and I do need it to be kept tidy—the floors swept daily, mopped as needed and polished once a month, furniture dusted and carpets vacuumed once a week, fridge and stove cleaned once a month. I insist that the washbasins, baths, and toilets be scrubbed daily. It is a lot of work but can be done if you have a method. We have a laundress who comes in once a week so you won't have to worry about washing and ironing. I will cook but will need help sometimes."

Because I was so dubious about her ability, and knowing she would need to be trained, I offered her a lower starting wage than the previous helper received. "When can you start?" I asked, thinking she would have to go home to gather her belongings.

"Well, if it's all right with you," she said, "I can start right now. I have all my things with me."

"Okay," I said and led her to her room.

Christine turned out to be the best helper we ever had. A quick learner, she listened carefully to my instructions and I never had to tell her the same thing twice. Easily stung by criticism, she never repeated a mistake. She soon became familiar with our ways. She worked very hard and efficiently. By the end of only one week Ainsley and I agreed to increase her pay.

Christine loved the children. She looked after them, played with them, took them on afternoon walks, and read to them. My mother had sent, from New York, twelve volumes of fairy tales published by Reader's Digest, and Christine read every single one to the children. Although I had not expressly given her permission to spank them, I turned a blind eye whenever she meted out discipline, as I realized she was treating them like her own. She came from a decent family; we met her mother, who visited soon after Christine began working with us, presumably to see how her daughter was being treated. Unlike her predecessors, Christine did not stick to her room when her work was done. She sat with us to watch television or listen to music and she felt like a part of the family. If visitors dropped in, she discreetly disappeared with the children to their bedrooms. Normally I was the one to get them to bed but she would quietly take over if I was entertaining. When Mother's Day came around, Ainsley not only got me a gift on behalf of the children but also gave Christine one. "She is every bit a mother to our children," he remarked to me. "In fact, she spends more time with them than you do." I agreed wholeheartedly and was indeed thankful to have Christine with us.

After her first month, I noticed Christine had begun to put on weight and remarked on that. She replied, "This is my usual size. I had got small when I came because I was seeing hard times." It turned out she had not been treated well by her husband; she had made the sacrifice of leaving him, and asked her mother to care for her small children so she could work to support them.

One evening Ainsley brought home a puppy, a black Doberman-Weimaraner mix that was a gift from a Chinese friend. Plato, as we named him, was a scrawny pup and was cared for by Christine and myself. We were the ones to feed him, add whipped eggs to his milk, dose him with cod liver oil capsules, and bathe and groom him. A wooden kennel was built for him in the back yard. Plato grew rapidly and became a loving guard dog. He did not bark much. Whenever I went outside to care for my plants, he startled me by silently padding up to me. I quickly learned to expect him whenever I opened the sliding doors, and it was comforting to have his companionship. He was also very good and gentle with the children. Soon we acquired another dog that needed a home. Because of his white coat we called him Winter, but this dog was by no means as intelligent as Plato. Worst of all, he was not easily trained and would not obey. However, he was a companion for Plato and the two animals frolicked all day long.

Our other pet was a male tabby cat. Since we never came up with a name, he was simply referred to as Kitty. Ainsley did not dislike animals but cats gave him the creeps, especially when they extended and retracted their claws. Ainsley was a night eater and habitually raided the pantry or the fridge before retiring. Kitty would appear, meowing pitifully as if he had not seen food for days, and Ainsley would butter a slice of bread, cut it into squares, and leave it on a napkin on the floor for Kitty to devour. Then the cat would express his thanks by rubbing his head against Ainsley's ankles, purring loudly and happily. My dear husband could not stand the purring sound or the foot rubbing, so he would provide another slice, hoping the cat's behavior would stop. He could not understand when I told him he was only encouraging Kitty and all he had to do was to stop feeding the cat. The ritual continued every night.

The table tennis board acquired in the United States became a center of activity in our home because few of our friends had one. We had sessions twice a week—on Wednesday evenings and Sunday mornings, and our main playing partners were a couple of friends who lived in our subdivision of Haleland Park. At first the sessions were manageable but soon escalated. Other friends started coming. With drinks and snacks offered on each occasion, people of course stayed longer and longer. The Wednesday night sessions went on so late that I started leaving the players and going to bed, since I had to rise early for work the following day. On Sundays I always cooked a big meal and inevitably those who were in the house partook. People stayed, we had to eat, so we just invited them to share with us. More and more people turned up at our house on Sundays, ostensibly to play table tennis but it seemed more and more like a day fête. Often people whom I did not even know were in our house. They tagged along with friends and nobody objected. The entertainment became extremely one-sided and expensive and I was getting tired of being the hostess every Sunday.

The last straw happened one Sunday morning when one of our acquaintances appeared with his three-year-old daughter. He was in a custody battle with his English wife, who had run off with the child to the United Kingdom. He, in turn, had gone to England and snatched the child, returning with her to Trinidad. However, as a man he was unable to care for his daughter properly by himself. When he saw that I was about to bathe my two children, he begged me to bathe his daughter at the same time. I did it but was angry with him, not with the poor innocent child. "What nerve!" I thought, "Why did he have to snatch the child if he knew he couldn't take care of her himself?" Later, I let my husband know what I thought. Ainsley then stopped the Wednesday sessions and changed the Sunday ones to Saturdays. That ended the madness because people had their chores on Saturdays and did not show up. I breathed a sigh of relief. Finally we got the peace and quiet of our home back, after months of continuous entertaining.

A couple of years after we moved into the house at Grapefruit Crescent, Ainsley's brother Learie and his family returned to Trinidad from Montreal. They stayed with us for a few months until they got settled. Our children loved having their older cousins around. Mark, the older son, often played with four-year-old Julian, tossing him in the air and also teaching him the rudiments of boxing, and thus became my young son's hero. While this rough play made Julian fearless and impervious to hard knocks, which was probably a good thing, it was rather frustrating to me as the chief disciplinarian in the family.

Ainsley was reluctant to exercise the parental right to mete out discipline. I had to take on that role, as I had no intention of letting the children grow up without restraint. West Indian parents are not averse to issuing corporal punishment and I was no exception. Denise was not a problem because she was afraid of "licks," that is, a flogging. Julian was so tough that my using a belt on him had no effect whatsoever. He just laughed at me, which was infuriating. I had to find other means of punishment, such as banishment to his room. That really hurt him, since Julian was a gregarious soul. Denise was sneaky, usually instigating her little brother to get into trouble, and then they both received punishment. Daddy would become the peacemaker by getting them to tell Mummy they were sorry.

Life was good for us and I lived in a bubble. Foolishly, I had no thought for the future and believed the good times would go on forever. Ainsley was able to function quite normally and it was easy for me to forget that he was suffering from an incurable disease. I was sometimes annoyed that he spent so much time listening to music. The strains of James Last's

"Romance," the songs of Neil Diamond, Bob Marley, Stevie Wonder, and other beautiful sounds pouring from the Bose speakers filled the house as he lay on the couch, when I would have appreciated help with the children or the housework. Looking back now, I wonder if he was feeling a bit weak and tired and did not tell me.

Ainsley always had his illness at the back of his mind. Whenever we had a spat he would say to me, "Where in the world would you ever find another man like me? Don't you know I don't have long to live?" He was very good at promoting himself but I had to admit to myself the truth of his assertions. Nevertheless, I would end up with, "One never knows who will go first. It could be me."

Maybe he used those down times to think and plan long-term for the family. There was no doubt about it, Ainsley spent considerable time planning and he was always a man in a hurry, wanting everything immediately, like the "instant plants" he installed in the garden. He also purchased a nearby three-bedroom condominium, as a source of rental income but also as a place for us to live in case anything happened to him. In addition, he invested in stocks and shares, and ensured that my name was on everything we owned.

Ainsley started talking about moving to a bigger, more valuable house on a larger lot of land. I was quite satisfied with our home and did not want to move. Besides, I had started the diploma of education course at the University of the West Indies and could not devote the time to packing up and moving. However, he bought a lot round the corner. Martin Looby was asked to build a house similar to the one we had, but on a much grander scale. Ainsley got me to agree by offering to do the packing. But, in fact, Christine did much of it and some of our good friends helped. In the summer of 1975 we moved to No. 27 Perseverance Road.

Our years in our first house, at Grapefruit Crescent, were idyllic. I wanted to stand still and remain in the home I loved. What did life at No. 27 Perseverance Road hold in store for us? I had no sense of foreboding, but was my reluctance to the move intuitive and indicative of what was to come? We could not foretell the future and I did not know that life was about to change drastically.

Chapter Sixteen

Perseverance Road and Afterwards

The new U-shaped house at No. 27 Perseverance Road was magnificent but too big. There was too much walking from one wing to the other. We had added a library and a half-bath next to the music room, plus an office near the front entrance. We chose not to face the two-car garage toward the road but set it sideways, with the wall shielding the cars from view. In the garage, a door provided access to the kitchen. Behind the garage a two-chamber kennel, constructed of brick and stucco similar to the rest of the house, accommodated the two dogs. John the Watchman remarked, "De dogs live in a better house than some people. Dey would love to live in yuh doghouse." I kept thinking that only midgets could live there, though. The expansive lawn was planted, with beds of tropical plants installed and fruit trees dotting the property. A luxuriant croton hedge with variegated leaves of yellow, red, and green lined the long driveway and separated our property from the vacant lot beside us. Two stately Royal Palms towered in magnificent splendor at the end of the front driveway. Unfortunately the rose bushes I planted did not thrive—large red ants attacked them and nothing I tried kept them away. Was this a sign of what was to come?

The housewarming was not on the same scale as that for our first house. For one, we had incurred enormous debt in building and furnishing it, so we decided on two things—to limit the number of invitees, and to host a Sunday morning brunch instead of an evening party. By "limit," we meant less than one hundred people. I was rather dubious about the duration of this celebration. I reminded Ainsley, "When our friends the Winchesters invited friends for breakfast, the fête went on all day! Nobody would go home once the drinks were flowing and the music playing. Remember? They ended up cooking lunch, and when evening came, the whole party moved over to another friend who had big pots of food already cooked."

"That's right," he replied, "but I can't think of an alternative."

"Well," I stated emphatically, "we're only going to prepare breakfast, so when they're ready for lunch they'll just have to go home."

With Christine's help, I prepared several large pans of a homemade bread called "bake." We made several loaves of coconut sweet bread. We made large quantities of buljol, a dish made from salted codfish that is soaked, shredded, and garnished with chopped onion, chopped peppers, tomatoes, black pepper, and olive oil. The hot Trinidad pepper sauce added piquancy to the dish. Saltfish cakes called akras were prepared, as well as soused pig feet. We baked a ham and bought Charley's famous black pudding—blood pudding, which went well with hot crispy hops bread. (Hops bread is rather like Chicago hard rolls, but perhaps a bit larger and a bit lighter, of the consistency of French bread.) We also bought a few dozen flaky Jamaican patties, and to round off the meal there were fried plantains and avocado slices. The breakfast was highly appreciated and the guests stayed, enjoying the conviviality, the music, and the drinks.

At lunchtime we served the same food; it was a good thing we had made a lot. And still the crowd stayed. Evening came. As the shadows lengthened, the guests would not go home. I refused to make anything else and those who got hungry ate the same food again. I could not believe it!

Not too long after our move, Christine left to set up house with her new boyfriend and start a family with him. We realized she was a young woman who had much of her life ahead of her and we could not keep her forever. We were sorry to see her go, and were never able to find another nanny of Christine's caliber. After she left we kept in touch and I was honored to be asked to be the godmother of her next baby daughter.

We lived at Perseverance Road for about three years, and at first life was good. Having received my Diploma of Education at the University of the West Indies, I went back to teaching full-time at Tranquillity Government Secondary School. Both Ainsley and I had decent jobs but we were deeply in debt, even after selling the Grapefruit Crescent house. Denise and Julian grew like proverbial weeds and were doing well in school.

In 1977, the bubble burst.

Trinidad and Tobago Port Contractors Ltd., where Ainsley had the position of financial comptroller, was a quasi-government organization. It existed side by side with the Trinidad and Tobago Port Authority, which was wholly government controlled. Port Contractors took over the privately owned Shipping Association, which managed the stevedores and longshoremen, while the Port Authority took care of the facilities. The employees of the Shipping Association who came across to Port Contractors were allowed to keep their seniority and their pensions, and new employees, including Ainsley, were also hired. Looking back, I now realize that the government never intended Port Contractors to last forever. Establishing a new organization was just a ruse to take over the privately owned Shipping Association. When the government was ready to cut Port Contractors loose, it decided to discredit the two top executives: the general manager and the financial comptroller, my husband.

Government subsidies required to run the organization stopped. Ainsley sent a letter to the Prime Minister's office informing him of this development, but it was ignored. Lack of sufficient funds meant that Port Contractors could not submit the tax withholdings to the Inland Revenue Department, even though these had been deducted from employee paychecks. Ainsley sent another letter to the Prime Minister's office. Again, no response.

Then the Inland Revenue Department pounced. Ainsley and his boss were accused of fraud, and the news was splashed across the headlines of the daily newspapers. The scandal newspapers alleged we had stolen money and that was how we could afford a big house in Haleland Park. This rotten affair had a deleterious effect on Ainsley, who valued his good name more than anything else. As a chartered accountant from England and as a former president of the Trinidad and Tobago Association of Chartered Accountants, he was in danger of losing his hard-earned certification. I only learned from his friends and the news media how the subsequent trial proceeded because, to protect me, he refused to let me attend. Luckily, Ainsley had copies of the letters he had sent to the Prime Minister, who was subpoenaed as a witness. As the Prime Minister had no intention of testifying, the case was quietly dropped. Ainsley and his boss were off the hook. Nevertheless, neither of us felt adequately satisfied. Whereas the initial allegations were splashed across the headlines and the front pages, the withdrawal of the case received only a tiny notice buried near the back of the papers. Ainsley resigned from Port Contractors and started his own practice, but the damage to his reputation and his health was already done.

The leukemia that had been kept at bay for seven years reared its ugly head again. The medication no longer worked. A trip to Montreal in August 1977 revealed that his options were practically zero. No other medications had been developed, and bone marrow transplants were still in the experimental stage. If Ainsley had tried this, it would have meant remaining in Canada, away from his family, for a long period of time and still there would be no guarantee of success. He was given six months to live.

My husband came home. Bravely, he started his practice and continued working but this was an up and down period. As his health deteriorated, there were days when blood transfusions were needed to keep him going. There were a couple of crises but each time he bounced back. There were no hysterics. I had to keep strong for him, as he could not bear to see me cry. I could not let him see my tears and what made the situation worse was the fact that I could not confide in anyone. During this period it was really difficult keeping his illness secret from his mother and the rest of the family in Trinidad.

Ainsley kept going as long as he could. On February 4, 1978, he attended the funeral of an aunt, the mother of his cousins who had lived next door to us on Grapefruit Crescent. I could not attend because it was Carnival time and five-year-old Julian was participating in the Kiddies Carnival. As a member of his school band portraying Treasures of the Sea, our small "goldfish" paraded all day on the streets of Port of Spain under the hot sun and I, as parent, had to accompany the band on the sidelines. Three days later, on Carnival

Tuesday, I drove Ainsley to the starting point of the Edmund Hart Band, in which he had played mas' several years in a row. While he could no longer participate, he wanted to see his friends before the band pushed off. None of them had an inkling of what was going on with him.

After yet another blood transfusion, Ainsley remained in bed for about five days, too weak to do anything. I was in a quandary because of my promise not to tell a soul. Although he was sleeping a lot, his mind was still working and he still had an appetite. He had reached the brink a couple of times before and then had made a comeback. Was this going to happen again? I do not remember praying for guidance but circumstances miraculously provided a way out.

I had harvested some pigeon peas to give to Mother, and had not been able to deliver them. I phoned, and spoke to Kay, Ainsley's sister-in-law. She and her two boys, Mark and Nigel, were staying temporarily with Mother. "Girl," I said, "I have some pigeon peas for you, but haven't had the time to bring them." "It's all right, Rose," she said. "We're all going to church this evening and if we feel up to it, we might just take a drive to you afterward."

On arrival at our house Kay said, "After church, it was as if the car turned automatically towards Haleland Park and so here we are." I wondered if she had detected something in my voice. Was there a hint of panic or worry in my words when I had called? Anyway, when Mother saw her son's condition, how he lay so weakly on the bed, she decided not to go home. I always thanked my lucky stars that she stayed because, in twenty-four hours, on February 12, 1978, Ainsley was dead. Mother was by his side and I do not believe she would have forgiven me if she had not been there at the last.

Earlier that evening he had asked me to call the doctor. I bent my ear close so I could hear his words. "Tell him I can't go on." The doctor came, reluctantly. As he was leaving the house, I asked, "How much time do you think he has left, Doctor, because I need to call his siblings abroad." The doctor, looking uncomfortable, mumbled, "About one week," and beat a hasty retreat. I was on the phone on the other side of the house trying to get the brothers and sister in Canada when I heard Mother let out a loud shout. By the time I rushed back to the bedroom, Ainsley was gone. Mother wept and wailed. I felt numb.

Kay rounded up the sisters in Trinidad and they all arrived. All I could say to them was, "You're too late. He's gone." Their shock and pain was excruciating because they had no idea he had been so ill.

Mother had her moments of grief but it surprised me that she still had the presence of mind to advise, "Before you call the undertakers, wake the children so they can see their father. Otherwise they'll never believe that he is dead." Eight-year-old Denise refused to enter the room to look at him, but Julian did. Not yet six years old, he did not fully understand the meaning of death. He did not cry but wrote a little poem on a scrap of paper in his childish scrawl. Full of spelling errors, the gist of the poem was that he wished his daddy had not died. Then Julian pronounced that he wanted to be called by his first name, Ainsley.

The other piece of advice Mother gave me was to put away anything of value. She said, "Your house will be full of people, some of them strangers, and you don't want to lose anything that's precious to you."

The next few days were hazy. I did not cry, nor did I break down at the funeral. I had the advantage of being mentally and emotionally prepared for the worst, and my tears had already been shed in secret. There was so much to be done. The children had to be cared for. As Mother had predicted, our house was filled with people every day until after the funeral. It fell to me to try to comfort those who took the news hard. Various family members in turn broke down, and I felt I had to be the strong one. However, I received support. The neighboring Borel cousins helped out tremendously. Having recently lost their mother, they were familiar with the steps to be taken in arranging a funeral, and one brother slept in our house with us until my parents arrived from the United States. Cislyn came early on the day of the funeral and dressed with us. Her presence every step of the way was comforting.

Picking up the pieces after a devastating loss was something I went about stoically. I had no choice. Having two young children meant that I had to be everything for them. They were my life and I felt my priorities belonged to them. Then my sister-in-law, Rosie, said to me, "Your first priority is to yourself. You need to look after yourself because if you cannot function, you can't care for your children." "You know, you're right," I acknowledged. Rosie's advice contained essential wisdom. Perhaps there was some inner strength and resilience I had not known I possessed. I put on a brave face in front of my children and the world, while at night in the privacy of my lonely bed I cried my eyes out. This is when I found God. He was always there but I had neglected Him. Perhaps my faithful mother was praying for us unceasingly.

Friends and family were heartbroken but supportive. One of my colleagues at school introduced me to the Daily Word booklet, a source of comfort and inspiration to me. It turned out that my sisters-in-law, Gemma and Kay, also subscribed to that publication without giving up their Catholicism, and every month I obtained a booklet through them.

The principal of my school, Mr. Wilfred Phillips, a widower himself, gave me all the time I needed to settle legal matters.

After my return to work, he allowed me to leave during my free periods to handle business at the various offices downtown as long as I was present to teach my classes. As the wheels of government, with all its red tape, moved ever so slowly, Mr. Phillips' understanding was invaluable to me. Of course the time I would have spent during school preparing lessons and correcting assignments had to be made up at home in the evenings, but this concession was worth it since I did not have to use up all my annual leave.

I still tried to carry on as normally as possible, especially during the holiday season that year. My attempts to have family members get together, like before, often fell flat. With Ainsley missing, their hearts were not in it. It was then I realized that Ainsley was the glue that had kept the family together—a family whose members were passionate and loving, but very strong-willed.

People whom I always viewed as Ainsley's friends proved to be very loyal, and became my friends too. This was the time when I discovered who was truly supportive. Some people—the partiers, no longer invited me to fêtes, since I was without an escort. Henry Jeffers, one of Ainsley's oldest and dearest friends, continued to ask me to his parties, and it was up to me to decide whether I could make it or wanted to ask one of my girlfriends to accompany me. The Leeds crowd, including Rodgerson and Ralph, visited often, and Cislyn was always there for me. She and her sister, Corinne, embraced me into their group of friends who attended concerts, plays, recitals, whatever was being performed in Port of Spain. Corinne never even bothered to ask if I wanted to go. She purchased tickets for everyone and got reimbursed later. A couple of times I asked her to purchase two extra tickets for my children to attend the opera, when their music teachers were performing in the productions.

Three of Ainsley's friends were helpful in sorting out his business affairs. I had pretty much left those in Ainsley's hands, saying, "You're the accountant. You know what you are doing. Go right ahead." He never made an investment without including my name as co-owner, but I was largely ignorant of our business arrangements. Investments Ainsley made in real estate and on the Trinidad and Tobago Stock Exchange were known to his friend and co-worker, Selma Lee Ghin. They often invested in the same companies and he confided in her. Together with Zabar Baksh, Ainsley's assistant at the Trinidad and Tobago Port Contractors Ltd., she sorted out his papers. Another friend, John Hunt, a chartered accountant who had a professional practice, offered his assistance. The three worked very hard to clear the debts, including the mortgage on the new house. John Hunt, as a member of the board of directors of The Workers Bank, which was the mortgagor, was particularly instrumental in working out a payment plan. John declared that he was only doing what Ainsley would have done, had the tables been turned. If anything had happened to him, John believed Ainsley would have assisted his widow in a similar manner. I will never forget how these three friends gave me invaluable help at that crucial time.

They made the decision that my children and I should vacate the house at Perseverance Road and lease it to a foreign company doing business in Trinidad. The size of the house and garden, as well as the extensive entertainment area, made it ideal as the residence of a chief executive officer or other senior staff member. My children and I would move into our condo at Catalina Court, about half a mile down the road. Both Ainsley and Selma had invested at Catalina Court, and Selma was already residing in her condo there. The immediate snag was that our unit was occupied, and the tenant's lease was not due to expire for six months. Another friend, Winston Padmore, stepped up to the plate and offered to let us stay at no charge in his condo at Alldec Gardens in Petit Valley. His kindness was shown in a tangible way. However, at the end of our time there, knowing that he had mortgage payments, I made a contribution, which I am sure was not enough.

At Alldec Gardens we lived right next door to our friends, Rae and Judy Stewart. Their son, Renny, was my godson and about the same age as Julian. The boys played together constantly. Renny's four-year-old sister, Jillian, tried valiantly to keep up with the boys, while Denise, who was older, pretty much kept to herself in a little world of her own. I had to show more vigilance with Julian, who was bright and did well in school, but had started to slip in his homework because of his hurry to go off and play with Renny. His teacher, knowing that he has recently lost his father, was far too lenient. I had to tell her not to cut him any slack, to treat him just like the other boys in class.

As we grew closer to the Stewarts, often Judy would step over the low dividing wall between our condos, calling out "Neighbor, neighbor," to get my attention. Judy was incredibly patient with me, listening to my incessant talk about Ainsley—what he used to do, what he liked, the jokes he gave. I guess she knew this was my way of grieving, of dealing with the pain. Our two families engaged in many activities together. Sometimes when Judy or I needed to go out alone, the other would babysit all four kids. I really valued the deep friendship we had with the Stewarts.

Eventually we moved to Catalina Court, which at the onset had two buildings separated by a driveway connecting the front and back parking lots. Each building had four units, two upstairs and two below. Selma's unit was upstairs in one building, while we occupied a ground floor unit in the other building. Tiny in comparison to the Perseverance home we had vacated, the condo had a master bedroom, a mid-size bedroom and a wee room at the rear, and a bathroom with just enough space for a shower stall, a washbasin, and a toilet. In the small kitchen I was able to squeeze in a stacked washer-dryer unit. The good-sized living-dining area gave access to a tiny porch through sliding glass doors. Having lived in limited spaces during my early years, it was not difficult for me to adjust to a smaller area. It was much harder for my children, who had lived in a big house ever since they could remember. Julian always had visions of living in a big house again. I told him he needed to study hard, do well at school, and eventually get a good job so that he could acquire all the things he wished for, and that he was not going to steal or swindle anyone in order to get what he wanted.

To me the best part of our condo was the porch, which faced an open grassy area interspersed with tall coconut palms. Whenever I got the chance I loved to sit out there in the morning, sipping my coffee and observing the beauty of nature—the green, dew-filled grass, the shadows cast through the fronds of the majestic coconut palms, the birds singing. This little piece of God's country was a sanctuary allowing me privacy. One can imagine my sense of loss when the decision was made to cut down the palm trees in order to expand the complex. Another building, with six units, was constructed and there was nothing I could do about it. The decision had already been made when we bought the condo. Of some compensation, for me, was the addition of a swimming pool at the rear of the buildings. This we all enjoyed immensely, especially the children. We often invited family and friends to visit and swim, as the poolside was an ideal venue for parties.

The grounds of Catalina Court were fairly extensive and a safe place for the children to play. Although there were other children, Julian's favorite playmate became Perry, who lived in the opposite building and was about the same age. They played wildly, chasing each other along the walkways. A neighbor, Richard Butcher, a loud and cheerful man, used to refer to Julian as "Gairy" because he was so wild. Eric Gairy, the Prime Minister of Grenada for a number of years, ruled his country with an iron hand. Although duly elected with overwhelming majorities, Gairy operated like a little dictator. There were no term limits written into the constitution. Rumor had it that Gairy controlled personal retainers reminiscent of the ton ton macoutes of Haiti, with allegiance only to him.

The most influential of the residents was Mr. Laughlin, who occupied one of the newly added units. Retired, he had been part owner of Laughlin and De Gannes, an automotive parts company in Port of Spain. Accustomed to having his own way, he quickly dominated the homeowners' meetings. Even though the units were not restricted to seniors, he introduced rules and regulations limiting the children's activities. They were banned from using the pool in the afternoons between one and four p.m., so he and his wife could have their afternoon siesta free of noise from the pool area. Kids under the age of ten had to be supervised by an adult, and I had no objection to that. My son was particularly irked by Mr. Laughlin's rules, but since the latter had influenced the homeowners in setting them, we had to abide by them.

Denise stayed indoors most of the time, playing with her dolls or doing arts and crafts. Julian, however, liked to spend time outside playing, so I had to make a few strictly enforced rules. I needed to know whenever he went outside, and by no means was he allowed to enter another condo without my permission. I or another adult also had to be present whenever either he or his sister entered the pool. They had learned to swim at the YMCA but still I kept tabs on them.

Maybe my experience as a teacher at Tranquillity influenced my decisions, and I had seen so many children go astray because they were left too much to their own devices. I knew the time to keep them in check was in the pre-teen and early teenage years. After then, the task would be much harder. With Ainsley gone, I was the sole arbiter of our children's lives. I was always the chief disciplinarian in the family, since their father had left that role to me. Not wanting the children to grow up without boundaries to their behavior, I was the big bad wolf. Then their father would be the great conciliator, bringing the transgressor to apologize to Mummy. After he was gone, there was no one around to perform that role. After some time elapsed, I would find myself having to give the cue, "Now what are you supposed to say?" "Sorry, Mummy." Then peace would be restored.

During school vacations, my children usually spent a week with their Aunty Rosie, who was also Denise's godmother. Rosie adored children, having five of her own. Her love of children was reflected in her choice of profession—she was a teacher for many years and eventually rose to the position of school principal. Denise and Julian enjoyed spending time with their cousins but after Ainsley passed away, I could not bear to let them go. Selfishly, I needed to have them with me all the time. Sometimes Giselle, Rosie's youngest and about the same age as Denise, spent a week with us during the vacations.

Giselle was with us when Kay, who lived near our house at Perseverance Road, got word to us that a flood had just flowed through the entire property. There had been several hours of heavy showers but nothing extraordinary enough to cause flooding. The children and I dashed to the house to survey the damage. What we found was enough to make my heart sink. A canal beside the property had become blocked with debris from construction further up the hillside. The water, having nowhere to go, flooded the front and back lawns. Worse yet, the tenant, an expatriate who was alone in the house because his wife was then in the United States, had left the double sliding glass doors open. A sheet of water raced through the entire house, covering the floors with about six inches of mud. I believe the tenant had been in a drunken stupor at the time, and as soon as we arrived he left.

The children, armed with brooms, mops, and a wet vacuum, worked tirelessly with me to clean up. Denise and Giselle were about eleven at the time and Julian almost ten, and I felt badly that at that tender age they had to toil so hard. Everything was a mess. The plush wine-colored wall-to-wall carpets were completely ruined, and had to be ripped out and discarded. All the electrical appliances were destroyed—the stove, refrigerator, washer, dryer, and water heater. It was a terrible day for all of us.

It took forever to replace the appliances and furnishings, especially since I had to fight with the insurance company. Meanwhile the tenant terminated the lease, citing that I was unable to make the house livable in a reasonable time. We survived this ordeal but up to this day I have a fear of residing in any low-lying area prone to flooding. I have no desire to ever go through such a situation again.

Luckily for me, Charles Hull had entered my life. Charles had grown up in the same neighborhood as Ainsley, and they had attended the same high school, St. Mary's College. Having joined the Trinidad and Tobago Defence Force, Charles received his military training from Sandhurst in England and obtained a civil engineering degree from RMCS Shrivenham, which was affiliated with the University of London. Charles retired from the military as a captain, after which he held jobs with Trinidad and Tobago Port Authority and the Point Lisas Industrial Development Corporation. At the time of the flooding incident Charles was managing his own construction firm and was able to advise me on how to solve the problem. He got the remedial work done by building a retaining wall along the rear of the property and along the canal to stave off any future floods.

I had first met Charles in London in 1968, when he and his wife attended a mutual friend's wedding. On our return to Trinidad, Ainsley and I saw them from time to time. I always thought of him as my husband's friend, and we had little to say to each other. He seemed quiet and a bit standoffish.

One evening Charles knocked on my door at Catalina Court. He had business with a neighbor living in the condo above us, and subsequently paid me a visit to see how I was getting along after the loss of Ainsley. He dropped in a couple more times after visits to the neighbor. By then Charles had moved out of his marital home and was living in and running his business from San Fernando, the second largest town in Trinidad.

One evening he invited the children and me to dinner at a Chinese restaurant. After dinner he brought us home and stayed after the kids were in bed. He proceeded to ask me some uncomfortable and leading questions: "What are your plans for the future?" and "Where do you see yourself in the next ten years?" My replies were all about my children, and that eventually we would migrate to the United States where my parents resided. He kept insisting, "But what are your plans for yourself?"

It was then I realized that I did not have a long-range plan for myself. With his military training, Charles was used to planning ahead, whether it was for five years or ten. Ainsley had been good at that too, but not me. Perhaps it is a gender difference that men tend to look way down the road, whereas women are generally better at day-to-day planning. With his continual probing, Charles wore me down and I dissolved into tears. Next thing I knew we were kissing.

Before we got further involved in a relationship, I asked about his wife—after all, I knew her. "Let's put it this way," he said. "I moved out and I have no intention of moving back." So I took the plunge, for better or for worse. I am not proud that I was having an affair with a man whose wife I knew and had entertained at my house. It hurt her deeply, as well as their children.

At the time I was too selfish, thinking only of my situation and myself. It seemed to me that if he had already left, then it was all right for me to step in. I had become scared of being alone with the children at night after a neighbor knocked at my door one evening and informed me a man was snooping outside the bedroom window. The drapes were closed but he was trying to peep through the sides. This news was particularly traumatizing because other condos in the complex had been burglarized recently, including Mr. Laughlin's, which had been hit twice. It seemed a good idea to have a man around on some nights.

Charles visited whenever he came from San Fernando to Port of Spain. One night I picked him up from the airport when he returned to Trinidad from a business trip. As it was late, he stayed over at my place, and after that never went back to his house. That was the beginning of a mad affair. I was surprised that I could have feelings again for a man, but I certainly was not contemplating marriage at that time. Marriage was a step I took very seriously. I needed to know him—or anyone else, very well before committing to the state of matrimony, and I needed to see how that person related to my children. Besides, Charles was not free to marry, and that was fine with me.

After Charles moved in, we lived together for about three years. At first the children were not particularly happy, especially my son. I had not sat down and talked with them about Charles moving in. Julian was not enamored with a man joining our household and competing for his mother's attention. How history repeats itself! I remembered the rocky relationship I had with Lech when he entered my mother's life. Like my mother before me, I was pulled in different directions. On my suggestion, Charles starting paying more attention to Julian, on one occasion taking him on a trip to San Fernando. Gradually the tense relationship within the household improved.

When I had first arrived in Trinidad, I never thought I would ever want to "play mas'," that is, dress in a costume and dance with a band for two days in the streets of Port of Spain. Ainsley had played mas' every year with a group of friends, and once when we lived on Grapefruit Crescent I had participated. The band portrayed various countries around the world and we were in the section depicting Mexico. Ainsley and I sported huge sombreros that thankfully provided ample shade from the broiling sun. Although it was an enjoyable experience I never took part again while Ainsley was alive. We always had visitors, and someone had to be home to prepare meals and transport our guests to the stands at the Queen's Park Savannah to view the masquerading bands.

After losing Ainsley, I played mas' every year with my sisters-in-law—Vilma, who came from Canada every year for Carnival; Kay, Learie's wife; and Rosie. Playing mas' was a completely different side of Carnival. Jumping up in a band during the hot sun was all right, and it was obligatory for us to parade at two competition sites, downtown and at the

Savannah, but my favorite time was when the sun started to go down around five o' clock in the evening. It was pure pleasure then to chip down the road to the strains of the popular road marches. The entire experience was so enjoyable I never thought I could go back to sitting in the stands to watch the bands.

While we were at Catalina Court, a schoolmate from Jamaica, Claire Tavares, asked if I could accommodate her for Carnival. Claire was far junior to me at school and I was closer to her older sisters, Shirley and Norma. In fact, Shirley had visited us at a previous Carnival when we lived on Grapefruit Crescent. I agreed that Claire and her friend Yvonne Senior could stay with us, but could not guarantee transporting them around as I was playing mas'. Their friend George Campbell was staying at the Holiday Inn, and joined them in all the Carnival activities. With a rented car, he was able to take them to the fêtes, to the shows, including the steel band Panorama, J'ouvert, and the Parade of the Bands. Claire, Yvonne, and George then came every year, sometimes with other friends who found accommodations elsewhere. Our house became the hub of activity as Claire and Yvonne kept abreast of all the events and planned the movements of the group, which became known as "The Jamaican Posse." I made sure to have a huge pot of food prepared each day, giving a lifeline to some of the Jamaican visitors who did not always receive meals where they were staying. Some crashed at our place after excessive partying. One guy earnestly begged us to accommodate him, declaring he would even sleep on the floor. We let him sleep on the hide-a-bed in the living room, which at the time was without drapes. He was exposed to passersby but did not seem to mind.

Each year it became a foregone conclusion that the Jamaican Posse would arrive. It was not a matter of if they were coming, but rather when, and also how many. I made my Toyota Corolla station wagon available to George so he could transport the group. All I needed was for him to drop the children and me at school in the mornings and pick us up in the afternoons. The rest of the time the car was theirs, since I could move around with Charles in the evenings when he got home.

When we played mas', we pretty much had to organize where we would stop to eat and use the restrooms. Luckily, Mother lived in Woodbrook, a central location where the bands paraded through the streets, so it was easy enough to make a detour to drop in on her for a few minutes and later rejoin the band. One place where our band always stopped to eat and rest was at the Holiday Inn downtown. Each year the hotel provided an excellent buffet not only for guests but also for outsiders, and we looked forward to having a meal there. However, each year drunken masqueraders made a mess, several jumping into the pool fully clothed, and then, dripping wet, sloshing through the halls and corridors of the hotel.

One year Rosie, Kay, and I were with the band on Carnival Day when it found its way as usual to the Holiday Inn, only to discover a tall and solid gate barring entrance to the establishment. Seeing a nearby bus, Rosie said, "You know what, I'm going home. I'm tired anyway and have had enough." She hopped on the bus, leaving Kay and me standing on the far side of the road from the hotel. We watched with bated breath to see what would happen. The crowd of masqueraders in our band, enraged at the barricade, moved forward like mad bulls to attack the gate. They shook it repeatedly until, like the walls of Jericho, it fell dramatically. Then, like an invading army, the horde swarmed inside. Kay and I looked at each other in disbelief and shock. There was only a deafening silence. No response, no police guards, nothing. Moments later, Kay and I crept in to use the restrooms and quickly left. Not wanting to be associated with the unruly, badly behaved crowd, we did not partake of the buffet. In subsequent years, our band was prohibited from parading downtown since the bandleader was unable to control his masqueraders.

When Charles and I first got together, I was already a seasoned masquerader. He had never played mas', and that I found strange. "You're the Trini," I remarked. "How come you never played mas'?" He replied, "I always walked around and took pictures of the masqueraders and the bands." On Carnival Tuesday evening towards the end of the festivities, Charles found me with the band on the way back to its headquarters. Night was falling rapidly and he chipped beside me as we were returning. He must have really enjoyed it because the following year, in 1982, he decided to play mas' for the very first time. The band we were in, entitled "The Sting" and produced by Raoul Garib, won Band of the Year. Rosie and I were in the section of killer bees. Aggressive Africanized bees had reached the Americas and swarms had killed animals and even people, instilling fear in some communities. Our gold and black-banded body suits fit our frames tightly, and cotton mops, dyed black to depict antennae, formed our head-dresses. It was a simple but effective costume. Charles, on the other hand, portrayed a scorpion fish in a different section. The costume was so tall, reaching over seven feet, that he could not enter a regular doorway without removing the headpiece. I was therefore the one designated to enter the parlors to buy the cold drinks we needed to prevent dehydration. The fact that I, like a handmaiden, had to dance attendance on him was not a source of amusement to me, but he thoroughly enjoyed the attention.

It was now approaching the time for our family to emigrate to the United States. Mum and Lech, who had legalized their status and had become citizens, filed for us. On receiving our green cards, we made semi-annual trips to Tampa, where my parents had moved from New York. We spent the entire summer with them each year, and the kids enjoyed trips to Disney, Busch Gardens, and other theme parks. I always knew we would move to the United States, but it was important to choose the right time.

An opportunity presented itself to test the waters when Julian was almost eleven years old. Denise was already in high school. Julian had just sat the Common Entrance Exam for entry to secondary school and was awaiting his results. During that three-month period, from March to June, he went to live with his grandparents in Tampa, during which time he attended elementary school. I found he was not challenged enough by the curriculum in the sixth grade and was growing bored. He aced every subject and would have been promoted to the seventh grade. On my arrival in Tampa that summer, I decided to have him return to Trinidad and start at St Mary's College, his father's alma mater. My feeling was that the children were getting a good groundwork in the Trinidadian educational system, and that it would stand them in good stead when they eventually entered high school in Tampa.

In 1984, the decision finally was made to sell the home at Perseverance Road and for our family to leave for good. If I had sold six months earlier, I would have got the peak price for it. By the time I placed the house for sale, the market was turning in favor of the buyer, yet I still did rather well before the steeper slide in real estate prices. Of the three of us, Julian was the one most eager to leave. He did not realize that vacationing in Florida was totally different from living there year round. Denise was extremely reluctant to move. She did not do well with change. For my own part, it was heart wrenching to leave Trinidad, my friends and family, and especially my mother-in-law.

Mother had been nothing but good to me, welcoming me warmly into the family. Her house in Woodbrook was the meeting place for the grandchildren after school. They could walk there easily after classes or extra-curricular activities and were always welcomed with a plate of good Trini food. Knowing they were in a safe place until I could pick them up gave me peace of mind. After the loss of her son, I tried to assist Mother to the best of my ability. I helped her with transportation to doctors' appointments, to the grocery, and to pick up her survivor benefit. The benefit was small because it had to be divided between her and my children, but she felt she was still getting some help from her deceased son. As he was not around anymore, I tried to do what I could.

I had spent six years in Trinidad after Ainsley's passing, but now it was time to go. Mother had other daughters in Trinidad to give her support and my parents in Tampa were alone in their declining years. They ran a small upholstery business, but needed family close to them. It was also important to get the children enrolled in high school in Florida, from which they could more easily gain entrance to a Florida university. There was no way could I have afforded the overseas student rate, and I was determined that they should attend college. It was a promise I had made their father, that both Denise and Julian would get college degrees and professional qualifications.

Leaving Charles was particularly difficult. We had grown close and he had many endearing qualities. As the time to leave approached, it seemed he was pushing me away, urging me to leave. I knew it had to be done.

In July of 1984 our family left for the United States permanently. I had reached the end of an era. Trinidad & Tobago had been my adopted home for sixteen years. They were years when I had enjoyed immeasurable happiness and also the deepest sorrow. Now I set my face toward a new country, moving toward the future with some trepidation mingled with hope.

Epilogue

After arriving in Tampa, we spent six months living with my parents. Then, using the proceeds from the sale of my property in Trinidad, I bought a home on Brucie Place in Citrus Park, where I resided for nineteen years.

Denise and Julian graduated with honors from Leto High School, Tampa, then both proceeded to the University of Florida. Denise earned her bachelor's degree in graphic design. Julian's course of study followed in his father's footsteps, as he qualified as a Certified Professional Accountant and then as a Certified Financial Analyst. They are both married, with two children each, and live in the Chicago area.

I was fortunate enough to find employment with the United States Postal Service, with a salary that enabled me to pay for the children's college education. I retired in 2006 after twenty years' service.

I kept in touch with Charles Hull, who later became widowed. We married in 1996. It seems nothing short of a miracle that after a devastating loss I found it possible to love again. We are living our lives happily, one day at a time.

Photo Gallery
- II -

AT THE BEACH

Family gathering at Teteron Beach, Chaguaramas, in Trinidad

Back row (from left to right):
Rodgerson Joseph (sitting on car), Ainsley, Roslyn (Ainsley's sister), Rosemary,
Carmen (Ainsley's mother), Horace (Ainsley's brother-in-law), Eula (Ainsley's sister),
and Cislyn Baptiste (Rosemary's best friend)

Middle:
Marion (Horace and Eula's eldest daughter), holding baby Nicole (Roslyn's daughter)

Front row:
Gerard at left, Maurice, Elizabeth Fay (children of Roslyn),
and Beverly (Horace and Eula's 2nd daughter) at right

Denise Frances

Rosemary with young
daughter, Denise, Mrs.
Hannah Pigott (middle),
and Aunty (Edna Palmer)

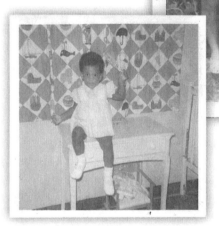

Above:
Denise at two years old

Denise at
Las Cuevas Beach,
Trinidad

LIFE AS A MOTHER

Ainsley Julian

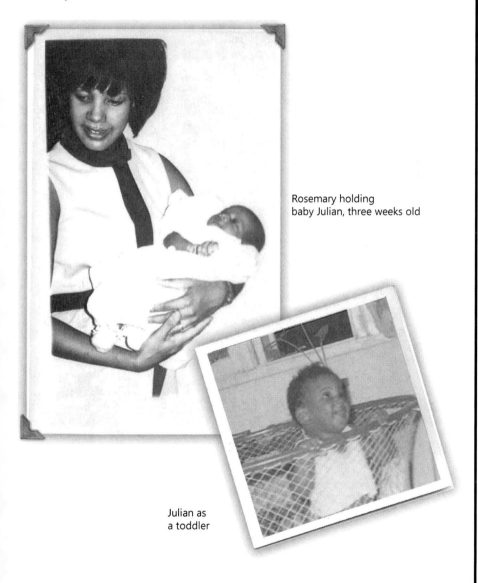

Rosemary holding
baby Julian, three weeks old

Julian as
a toddler

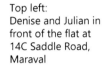

Top left:
Denise and Julian in
front of the flat at
14C Saddle Road,
Maraval

Below:
Rosemary dancing
with daughter, Denise

Above:
Denise and Julian
playing in the kiddie pool
at Grapefruit Crescent

Right:
Ainsley and Rosemary's
last New Year's Eve cele-
bration together
at a home party,
December 31, 1977

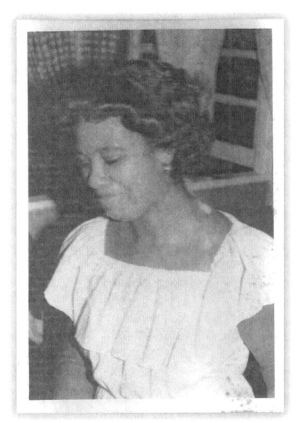

Christine, who cared for Denise and Julian as children

Top:
Rosemary, with sisters-in-law, Vilma Borel (middle) and Kay Borel in Edmund Hart's presentation of "U.S. Sailors."

Right:
Sister-in-law Roslyn Darlington with Rosemary as killers bees in Raoul Garib's masquerade band, "The Sting."

Julian playing mas' as a goldfish with his school's band, February, 1978

Denise playing mas' as an African princess February 1978

It's Carnival

Charles in his scorpion fish costume,
designed by Raoul Garib for "The Sting" masquerade band.

Rosemary's sisters, Avrill Crawford, at left, and Barbara MacMillan, at right

Rosemary with her mother-in-law (Mother), Carmen Borel

ᴼ𝓃dex

Page numbers set in bold indicate photos

CPSIA information can be obtained at www.ICGtesting.com
Printed in the USA
BVOW02s0822030916

461066BV00002B/88/P